Publications on Asia of the
Institute for Comparative and Foreign Area Studies
Number 22

This book is sponsored by the Modern Chinese History Project of the Institute for Comparative and Foreign Area Studies (formerly Far Eastern and Russian Institute).

Liang Ch'i-ch'ao and Modern Chinese Liberalism

By PHILIP C. HUANG

Seattle and London
UNIVERSITY OF WASHINGTON PRESS

Library of Congress Cataloging in Publication Data
Huang, Philip C   1940–
    Liang Ch'i-ch'ao and modern Chinese liberalism.
    (Publications on Asia of the Institute for Comparative and Foreign
Area Studies, no. 22)
    Bibliography: p.
    1. Liang, Ch'i-ch'ao, 1873-1929.   2. China
—Politics and government—1900-   I. Title.
II. Series: Washington (State). University.
Institute for Comparative and Foreign Area Studies.
Publications on Asia, no. 22.
DS763.L67H8   320.5'1'0924   71-178703
ISBN 0-295-95175-3

Publications on Asia of the Institute for Comparative and Foreign
Area Studies is a continuation of the series formerly entitled Far
Eastern and Russian Institute Publications on Asia.

To Professor K. C. Hsiao

Preface

This study of an early Chinese liberal, Liang Ch'i-ch'ao, is concerned with his ideas and their origins, with his intellectual tensions, with the challenges he encountered in action, and with his attempt to reconcile the differences between his Confucian and his liberal precepts.

Three principal bodies of materials form the backbone of this study: the forty-book *Yin-ping-shih ho-chi*—the most complete collection of Liang's writings—the three-volume *nien-p'u* of Liang edited by Ting Wen-chiang, which contains thousands of Liang's letters, and the hitherto unexplored Japanese materials on Liang, including the unpublished Japanese police reports on Liang's activities in Japan.

My debts to the large body of existing scholarship on Liang are discussed in the bibliographic essay and acknowledged in appropriate places in the text and footnotes.

Professor K. C. Hsiao, to whom this study is dedicated, first set me on the trail of Liang as a dissertation project in 1963. Dr. Hsiao's teaching and scholarship have remained for me a model to emulate and a constant source of inspiration. He, together with my other mentors at the University of Washington, Professors Donald Treadgold and Hellmut Wilhelm, saw the dissertation through its successive drafts and gave me invaluable guidance throughout its preparation from 1963 to 1966. Subsequently, at a moment when I doubted if this work should ever be set in print, Professors Hsiao, Treadgold, and Wilhelm gave me once more the encouragement and help that were necessary for me to complete what often seemed to be the interminable task of revising a dissertation.

Professor Ichiko Chūzō introduced me to Japanese scholarship on modern China and set me on a search for documents that led to the discovery of the thousands of pages of Japanese police reports on Liang. Mr. Yü-chün, a student of K'ang Yu-wei, opened my eyes to Chinese classical scholarship and the Kung-yang school. Professor Frederick Mote read the entire dissertation and gave me valuable criticisms. Marty Wolfson and Richard Louie provided me with helpful editorial suggestions even before the task of revision began. David Farquhar helped me to appreciate the usefulness of loan-words as an index to cultural influence. Through conversations with Ed Friedman, I was saved from some serious misconceptions of the political scene in early republican China. Arif Dirlik, David Farquhar, Larry Kincaid, and Peter Reill gave me helpful suggestions on various aspects of the manuscript.

My wife Kate shared with me and knows better than I all the trials and joys of this first effort in serious scholarship.

Contents

1. Introduction   *3*

2. From New Text Confucianism to "Democratic"
   Reform, 1890–1898   *11*

3. The Idea of the New Citizen and the Influence of
   Meiji Japan   *36*

4. Liberalism and Nationalism in Liang Ch'i-ch'ao's
   Thought   *68*

5. Reformer or Revolutionary?   *84*

6. National Politics   *112*

7. Syncretism and Liberalism   *141*

8. Modern Chinese Liberalism   *160*

   Notes   *167*

   Glossary   *195*

   Bibliography   *203*

   Index   *223*

Liang Ch'i-ch'ao and Modern Chinese Liberalism

CHAPTER 1

Introduction

Liang Ch'i-ch'ao's life spanned the last four decades of imperial China and the first two decades of republican China. When he was born in 1873, China was still attempting to meet the challenge of the modern West merely by adopting Western technology. Confucianism, whether as imperial order or as an ethical system, was not questioned. When Liang died in 1929, the assumptions of thinking Chinese had undergone a metamorphosis—Confucianism had come under total attack and many Chinese intellectuals now took for granted that China must change root and branch in order to modernize. The political revolution of 1911–12 had brought an end to the two-thousand-year-old imperial system; the intellectual revolution of 1917–21 had launched an all-out attack on Chinese tradition. These were decades of violent and radical change, and Liang, for nearly three decades, from the 1890s to the 1920s, was a leading actor in this drama of modern China's political and intellectual transformation.

He embarked upon his career as reformer and publicist in 1895, in the wake of China's disastrous defeat in the Sino-Japanese War of 1894–95—a defeat that exposed the inadequacy of the reforms of the preceding generation. His persuasive and often impassioned arguments, and his clear and simple prose made him a national figure almost overnight. But the coup

of 1898, engineered by the conservative forces around the Empress Dowager, put an abrupt end to the reform movement,
and Liang fled to Japan. There, for the next fourteen years, he
edited and wrote for a score of journals, introducing to his contemporaries such novel ideas as nationalism, imperialism, social
Darwinism, and liberalism. During these years he, with his
erstwhile teacher K'ang Yu-wei (1858–1927), organized a party
dedicated to constitutional reform and competed with the revolutionary party of Sun Yat-sen (1866–1925) for control of
China's destiny.

Never firmly committed to the Manchu dynasty, Liang was
easily reconciled to the republic when the revolution came in
1911–12. In the setting of early republican China, he led in the
formation of the Chin-pu Tang, a moderate political party that
became the principal contender with the revolutionary Kuomintang in China's infant parliament, and he served twice as a
cabinet minister. He hoped to "do as much as possible within
existing circumstances,"[1] but his efforts were always frustrated
by military men who held the real power and who had no use
for liberal reforms.

After 1917, he took to teaching and scholarly writings, focusing his attention once more on what he saw as the necessary
foundations for liberal-democratic government—education to
create a new kind of Chinese citizen. In his historical writings,
he sought to define the broad outlines of a new culture, one that
would be neither East nor West, yet containing elements of both,
and capable of providing the basis for China's modernization.

Throughout these years, Liang wrote prolifically on a variety
of subjects. In all, his published writings total more than forty
volumes,[2] including monographs, lectures, speeches, and essays
that appeared in the nine journals[3] he edited between 1895 and
1916. These writings range over literature, law, finance, and
politics; they deal with Western, Chinese, and Japanese history,

and explore Western, Chinese, and Japanese thought; and they contain continual commentaries on current issues and problems.

In the broad perspective of the history of modern Chinese thought, Liang and others of his generation (especially the translator Yen Fu, 1853–1921) stand out as the ones who were pivotal between nineteenth- and twentieth-century Chinese thought. They grew up under, but were not bound by the ideology of the self-strengthening movement, an ideology represented by Tseng Kuo-fan (1811–72) and Li Hung-chang (1823–1901) and given its final formulation in 1898 by Chang Chih-tung's (1837–1909) famous formula: "The old [Chinese] learning is to be the substance; the new [Western] learning is for application."[4] They greatly influenced, but were then overshadowed by the generation of young intellectual revolutionaries of the May Fourth period. They were the last generation to grow to maturity under the traditional educational system, and the first to confront the full impact of modern ideas. Theirs was the generation that truly straddled the traditional and the modern, Chinese and Western civilizations.

Liang was the outstanding member of this pivotal generation, not so much on account of the originality or profundity of his ideas, but chiefly because of his great influence as a popularizer of new ideas. His writings helped pave the way for the political revolution of 1911–12.[5] Although he was identified with K'ang Yu-wei's party, and hence with the opposition to the revolutionary party, he in fact wavered between revolution and reform, and his writings often argued as much for one as for the other. During the years from 1898 to 1903, especially, his essays were infused with revolutionary sentiments. This was also the period when Liang was at the height of his popularity and influence. His *Journal of the New Citizen* enjoyed in 1903 a circulation of nearly 10,000.[6] Through this journal, Liang's scathing criticisms of despotism and the Manchu government, his introduction of nationalistic and liberal-democratic ideas, and his impassioned calls for *p'o-huai*, for doing away with old habits and values, helped prepare the minds of many for the program of the revolutionary party.

The influence of his writings also went beyond the revolution of 1911–12. Liang was an advocate of colloquial writing as early as 1896,[7] two decades before the literary revolution that marked the replacement of classical *wen-yen* by colloquial *pai-hua* as the standard medium in writing. Between 1902 and 1905 he published a journal entitled *The New Fiction*, to which he himself contributed a colloquial novel.[8] Even when he wrote in classical Chinese, as he did in the bulk of his essays, his prose was "simple and clear," often "mixed with colloquial expressions, irregular verse, and foreign expressions."[9] And it "carried an intensity of feeling that made the reader follow him."[10] The eminent literary historian Cheng Chen-to credited Liang's prose with having "toppled the drab and lifeless old style" and "enabled the youth to express themselves freely."[11]

His historical writings began a new trend in Chinese historiography. He called in 1902 for a "new history," not of courts or individual personalities, but of the people.[12] His own "General Trends in the Development and Changes of Chinese Thought"[13] of the same year was the first modern Chinese study of intellectual history. Hu Shih (1891–1962), a leading figure in the intellectual revolution, recalled that this essay of Liang "opened up a new world" for him, and he decided at the time that he would carry on Liang's plans for a comprehensive history of Chinese thought.[14] Ku Chieh-kang (1893–   ), another distinguished twentieth-century Chinese historian, similarly recalled that during the years before the revolution of 1911–12, "Mr. Liang's writings swept the country"; Ku himself "was carried along by this current."[15]

Indeed, Liang's writings of the early 1900s, more than those of anyone else of the time, helped shape the minds of a new

Liang Ch'i-ch'ao circa 1900

Liang Ch'i-ch'ao circa 1920

generation of intellectuals in China. This was the generation
that would be the first to grow up under the new educational
system established after the abolition of the old examination
system in 1905, the first to study abroad (mostly in Japan) in
substantial numbers, and the leaders of the May Fourth intellectual revolution. Ch'en Tu-hsiu (1880–1942), the editor of the
most influential journal of the May Fourth period, the *New
Youth* (*Hsin ch'ing-nien*) and the founder of the Chinese Communist Party, acknowledged his debt to Liang in the following
terms:

> . . . when we were young, we studied the eight-legged essay and
> the orthodox old learning. Often we disdained those scholars and
> officials who studied European languages and talked about the
> new learning. . . . Only later when we read K'ang Yu-wei and
> his student Liang Ch'i-ch'ao's writings, did we suddenly realize
> that foreign political principles, religions, and learning had much
> to offer. . . . The fact that we today have some knowledge of the
> world is entirely the gift of Mr. K'ang and Mr. Liang. . . . Sub-
> sequently Mr. Liang taught while he learned, and contributed
> much to our people. . . .[16]

Mao Tse-tung similarly recalled for Edgar Snow that at sixteen he "worshipped K'ang Yu-wei and Liang Ch'i-ch'ao,"
and that he "read and reread" Liang's essays in the *Hsin-min
ts'ung-pao* until he "knew them by heart."[17] To express his admiration for Liang, Mao adopted the alias Tzu-jen, or "Follower of Liang," who was known as Jen-kung.[18] As Hu Shih
observed, among those who read Liang's impassioned writings
of this period, "there was none who was not shaken and moved
by him."[19]

The fact of Liang's influence on such thinkers as Ch'en, Mao,
and Hu raises the question: what was Liang's legacy to subsequent Chinese thought? Ch'en was of course correct when he
credited Liang with having introduced him to new ideas and

making him realize that "foreign political principles, religions, and learning had much to offer." Liang himself in 1920 assessed his contribution to modern Chinese intellectual history as that of having "exerted much destructive influence," thus "opening up new ground," rather than of providing constructive direction. But the intellectual historian, with the aid of hindsight, can say more: Liang's writings from 1898 to 1903, I suggest, defined some of the fundamental assumptions of much of twentieth-century Chinese thought, and they were assumptions that cut across the later divisions between liberals and Marxists. In the May Fourth period and after, these assumptions, because they were already taken for granted, were obscured by more fashionable isms that came to occupy the foreground of intellectual dispute. But they were crystal clear in Liang's writings of the early 1900s, because they were new and controversial at the time.

Influence, of course, is only one aspect of the significance of Liang's life and thought. Liang's inconsistencies, no less than his more influential ideas, tell a larger story. The tug-of-war between his classical-liberal inclination to emphasize individual liberty and his nationalistic call for a strong state reveals a basic dilemma of modern Chinese liberals. And the continual frustrations Liang encountered in the face of a widening gap between his ideals and the realities of China tell of the difficulties that beset most modern Chinese intellectuals.

The last phase of Liang's intellectual career, after he had receded from the limelight of the Chinese intellectual scene, tells another, larger story. Liang had received an orthodox classical education as a child. In the 1890s, following the lead of K'ang Yu-wei, he had turned against the orthodox tradition on the basis of the heterodox, but nevertheless Confucian, New Text school. After 1898, he had criticized the Confucian tradition as a whole and had embraced in its stead his newly acquired values. The break had not been total; his Confucian ideas had continued to influence and interact with his new ideas. In the May Fourth period and after, alarmed by the radical cries for "wholesale Westernization," Liang turned to emphasize the abiding values of his Confucian heritage. But the Confucianism to which he turned was very different from that which had held his allegiance in the 1890s—it had been stripped of its institutional and social encumbrances. Liang's emphasis was now on a way of thinking and a general attitude of altruism. For the intellectual historian, Liang's intellectual life represents a microcosmic case of the recession of the lines of defense of Confucianism in a Westernizing China. And the content of Liang's thought in the final phase of his life helps to distinguish the more basic and tenacious aspects of Confucianism from the more easily dispensable.

Finally, the very nature of the process of change in Liang's thinking is indicative of how Chinese and Western ideas interacted in modern China. In Liang's case, this process of interaction centered around two particular clusters of ideas—classical political liberalism and Confucianism. It also involved an added complication, and one common to many of Liang's contemporaries: Liang never learned a European language; Japanese was the only foreign language he could read. The profound changes in his thinking during the years after 1898 came largely as a result of reading Japanese books and coming into contact with Japanese intellectuals. In some instances, his new ideas were a result of the influence of indigenous Japanese ideas. More frequently, they were the result of an interaction between his Confucian ideas and Western ideas that had been filtered through Japanese selection and interpretation. This process of interaction did not involve simply the replacement of one set of ideas by the other. Instead, as in a chemical reaction, each element influenced the other, and the product was neither simply one nor the other, but something new, with unique qualities

of its own. Such was the process of change in Liang's thinking,
as it was in modern Chinese thought.

CHAPTER 2

From New Text Confucianism to "Democratic" Reform, 1890–1898

Liang Ch'i-ch'ao was born in 1873, into a family and a village that had not been touched by the changes occurring in the treaty ports. The family had lived for "several hundred years" on an island village named Ch'a-k'eng, in the district of Neng-tzu, a part of Hsin-hui county, southwest of Canton. The grandfather, Liang Wei-ch'ing (1815–92), had earned the lowest examination degree of *sheng-yüan* and had made his way into the status of "lower gentry." But he got no further, and the family remained of modest means. The father, Liang Pao-ying (1849–1916), also a scholar, did no better—he made a living out of teaching in the village. When young Ch'i-ch'ao proved to be a precocious child, it was small wonder that the family should have pinned all its hopes on him, for the Liang family well understood that, for a boy of modest station, success in the Confucian world meant one thing—climbing the ladder of the examination system. Ch'i-ch'ao would go through the rigorous preparation required.

He did it well and more quickly than most. He studied the four books and the Book of Poetry under his grandfather and his mother at the ages of three and four. At five, he came under the tutelage of his father, and soon completed the study of the five classics. At eight, he was already able to compose thousand-word long essays, and soon acquired a reputation as a child

11

prodigy. Three years later, he passed the first level of examinations and became a *sheng-yüan*.

His attention had now to be concentrated on preparing for
further examinations. For one year he took up *t'ieh-k'uo*, the not
very stimulating practice of memorizing rhymes made up of
difficult passages in the classics. Then came the introduction to
hsün-ku, the prevalent discipline of textual criticism. In 1887
Liang enrolled in the Hsüeh-hai t'ang, a nearby school known
for classical studies. Two years later he passed the provincial
examinations. Only sixteen years old, he was now a *chü-jen*, a
member of the "upper gentry," and eligible for official appointment. And his performance had so impressed the chief examiner
Li Tuan-fen that the latter betrothed his younger sister to
Liang. The young couple was married a year later. Little else
stood in Liang's way to a brilliant official career—he had the
degree and the other important qualification: good connection.

Somehow the young man's intellect survived the stultifica-
tion of years of stale memorization. As early as eleven (the year
he concentrated on memorizing rhymes made out of difficult
passages from the classics), he rebelled against his formal education and took refuge in the few other books he could find in his
family's meager collection— T'ang poetry, the *Historical Records*, and the *Han History*. In 1890 he came across Hsü
Chi-yü's *A Brief Description of the World (Ying-huan chih-lüeh)*,
published in 1848. It was an eyeopener—for the first time he
came "to know of the five continents and the various nations."[1]
He would soon turn against all that he had memorized.

He heard about K'ang Yu-wei (1858–1927) from Ch'en
T'ung-fu, a fellow student at the Hsüeh-hai T'ang, and decided
to go with Ch'en to call on K'ang. The meeting proved to be a
momentous encounter. By Liang's own account, K'ang, "as
though with the thunderous sound of the surf, and the roar of a
lion," dispelled point by point the "useless old learning," and
caused the young man to feel "as though cold water had been

poured over his back," as though "he had been hit over the head." After a sleepless night, Liang went once more to see K'ang, and learned about "the broad outlines of history and 'Western learning.' " For Liang, this was "the first time in [his] life [he] knew there was such a thing as learning." He decided to withdraw from the Hsüeh-hai t'ang to take leave of the "old learning," and urged K'ang to establish a new school in Canton. This school, the Wan-mu ts'ao-t'ang, opened the following year, and Liang became its outstanding pupil.[2]

For three years thence Liang studied K'ang's radical New Text reinterpretations of the classical heritage. He helped K'ang in the writing of *A Study of the Forged Classics of the Hsin Dynasty* (8 A.D.–23 A.D.) (*Hsin-hsüeh wei-ching k'ao*), which charged that all the orthodox Old Text classics were forgeries of Liu Hsin (?–23 A.D.) and the products of the dynasty founded by the usurper Wang Mang (45 B.C.–23 A.D.). Liang was also among the few students who were acquainted with the even more radical ideas that K'ang would later set forth in *The Great Community (Ta-t'ung shu)*.[3] The New Text doctrines that he learned at K'ang's school would become the springboard for his subsequent thought.

*The New Text Legacy**

The terms "New Text" and "Old Text" originally referred only to the style of the script of the classics. In the early period of the Former Han dynasty, all classics preserved by memory after the burning of books in Ch'in, were written in the con-

---

* The brief discussion of the history of the New Text school that follows is drawn from the existing studies of the subject. Some of the points are based on my studies in Taiwan with Yü-chün, a student of K'ang Yu-wei. A full treatment of this complex story would require of course years of ground-breaking research and hundreds of pages.

temporary *li* script. There was not yet the later distinction between Old and New Texts. During the reign of Ching Ti (156 B.C.–140 B.C.), however, texts written in the pre-Ch'in styles of *ta-chuan* (Old Texts) ostensibly were discovered in Confucius' old residence. Still, the New Texts—those written in the contemporary *li* script—retained their preeminence for a time. The Confucianism that, under the sponsorship of Wu Ti (140 B.C.– 86 B.C.), came to preside over official and intellectual life, was entirely of the New Text school.[4] The Old Text school began to come into its own only under the sponsorship of Liu Hsin and Wang Mang during the last years of the Former Han.[5] Thereafter, though the New Texts were restored under Kuang-wu Ti (25 A.D.–57 A.D.) to their earlier position of preeminence at the court, the old Text school continued to grow in influence. By the time of Ho Hsiu (129 A.D.–182 A.D.), the New Text school was placed on the defensive.[6] After the Han dynasty, it receded into the background of Chinese intellectual history until the second half of the eighteenth century.

The nineteenth-century New Texters called especially upon the legacy of Tung Chung-shu (176 ? B.C.–104 ? B.C.) and Ho Hsiu. What were the elements of the thought of Tung and Ho that were relevant to such nineteenth-century reformers as Wei Yüan (1794–1856), Kung Tzu-chen (1792–1841), and K'ang Yu-wei?

Tung's political thought centered around his interpretation of the *Spring and Autumn Annals.*[7] For Tung, this terse chronicle was not just a historical record of the events of the Spring and Autumn period, but contained "hidden and subtle meanings" (*wei-yen ta-i*). If properly read, this classic would reveal the political ideas that Confucius intended for a "new king" (*hsin-wang*). For, according to Tung, Confucius was the *su-wang*, or "uncrowned king"—even though he had not the position of ruler, he had the necessary virtuous qualities of a king and created the principles of rule for the "new king." These principles could be uncovered in the hidden and subtle meanings of the *Annals*, and the commentary that best guided one to these meanings was the *Kung-yang Commentary*.[8]

Tung's idea that Confucius was the creator of a new system of rule was particularly relevant to nineteenth-century reformers who sought in the classical heritage a rationale for reform. His theory of *san-t'ung*—that there were three institutional patterns, each corresponding to the three dynasties Hsia, Yin, and Chou, and each symbolized by the colors black, white, and red, respectively, that a new dynasty adopted a new institutional pattern[9]—could also be used to buttress arguments for change. Moreover, the emphasis on the subtle meanings of the classics lent a wide degree of flexibility to the interpretation of the classics. All of these ideas would be dramatically applied by K'ang Yu-wei to argue for radical reforms.

Another aspect of Tung's ideas added to the pertinence of the Han New Text school for the nineteenth-century Kung-yang reformers. Tung's political ideas centered around the original ideal of humane government (*jen-cheng*) of pristine Confucianism: the ruler was also the moral teacher; politics was fundamentally moral education.[10] But in his elaboration upon the hidden meanings concerning the ways of Heaven, Tung went far beyond pristine Confucianism. Confucius spoke little of the "ways of Heaven." Hsün-tzu explicitly rejected any speculations about Heaven. Mencius, admittedly, evidenced an element of mysticism.[11] But for Tung, with the fusing of Yin-yang and Confucian thought,[12] the assumption that there was constant interaction between Heaven and man was the very cornerstone of his political thought. Heaven, in Tung's view, not only conferred the mandate to rule, but continued to watch over the ruler and indicated its approval in portents (*tsai-i*). The ruler's duty was to serve as an intermediary between Heaven and the people (and here Tung went into elaborate discourses on patterning rule after the Yin-yang, the five elements, and so forth).

In following the example of Heaven, the ruler would set an example for his people. If he failed in his duty, he would be warned by portents, and, ultimately, might lose the mandate itself.[13]

This argument could be and later was used to render the ruler's person virtually supernatural and inviolable. But Tung's intention, as Professor Hsiao points out, was to limit the despotic power of the emperor by calling upon the greater heavenly power. He spoke little of good omens but primarily of the opposite.[14] This ambiguity in the New Text tradition would facilitate K'ang Yu-wei's use of it to assail despotism.

Ho Hsiu, the outstanding successor in the Latter Han to the New Text line of classical learning, contributed yet another aspect that made the Han New Text legacy especially relevant to the late nineteenth-century Kung-yang reformers. Tung's view of history was a cyclical one, but Ho Hsiu, in equating the "grandfather's generation" (*ch'uan-wen chih shih*) with "disorder" (*shuai-luan*), the "father's generation" (*suo-wen chih shih*) with "approaching peace" (*sheng-p'ing*), and the "current generation" (*suo-chien chih shih*) with "great peace" (*t'ai-p'ing*), set forth a view of lineal progress.[15]

Ch'ing New Texters

The revival of the Han New Text school that came in the second half of the eighteenth century was both an outgrowth of and a reaction against the prevailing school of Han learning (*Han-hsüeh* or *k'ao-cheng*). Under the oppressive controls of the Manchu government, especially those called the "literary inquisition" of the Ch'ien-lung period, the literati had come to restrict themselves to narrowly academic pursuits of textual scholarship. The New Text revival that began with Chuang Ts'un-yü (1719–88) was an outgrowth of mid-Ch'ing "empirical scholarship" because the latter's revival of Han learning quite naturally led back to the New Text learning of the Former Han.[16] But it was much more than a mere outgrowth, for a scholar such as Chuang Ts'un-yü was consciously reacting against the prevailing narrow preoccupation with textual studies.[17]

In Chuang, the *Kung-yang Commentary* was once more singled out as the most important of the three commentaries on the *Spring and Autumn Annals*. Chuang also upheld the authority of Tung Chung-shu's *Deep Significance of the Spring and Autumn Annals*.[18] Though Chuang was not completely aligned on the side of the Han New Text school (he acknowledged, for example, the authenticity of the Old Text version of the *Classic of History*),[19] he is nonetheless properly considered the first to revive the New Text school. With him began a line of thinkers for whom the classics were once again to be read for their "hidden and subtle meanings."[20]

The outstanding successor to Chuang's studies was his grandson Liu Feng-lu (1776–1829). For Liu, as for Chuang, the *Spring and Autumn Annals* was the key to the Confucian classics.[21] Liu wrote more than ten studies of this classic. He reexamined the disputes in the Latter Han between Cheng Hsüan and Ho Hsiu,[22] and stressed that it was Tung and Ho who preserved the "hidden meanings."[23] In a study that was epoch-making in the history of classical learning, Liu sought to demonstrate that the *Tso Commentary* was originally a history, the *Tso-shih ch'un-ch'iu,* only later misused and rearranged by Liu Hsin to form a commentary of the *Spring and Autumn Annals*.[24] This study broke the ground for K'ang Yu-wei's later challenging of all Old Text classics.

Chuang, the grandfather, had lived during the heyday of the orthodox school of Han learning and had had to restrict the teaching of his views to the immediate members of his family and a few students.[25] By Liu's time, however, there had been a shift in the climate of opinion. Liu openly applied the principles he derived from his classical studies to practical affairs.[26] Indeed, this very application was a logical outgrowth of the revival of the New Text school and its reaction to the academic concerns of Han learning. Liu set the tone for the use of Kung-yang ideas as a theoretical basis for reform by the next generation of New Texters.

Wei Yüan and Kung Tzu-chen[27] witnessed growing commercial relations between the Chinese empire and the West. They saw the expansion of the opium trade and the eruption of the Opium War, a war that marked the beginning of the full challenge of superior Western power to the decaying empire. Wei Yüan lived to see the disastrous T'ai-p'ing Rebellion. For both men, practical reforms were the central concern.[28]

Kung had an extremely frustrating career, never being able to rise above petty positions. But he remained preoccupied with the larger practical problems of his day. He blamed the Ch'ing government for the social, political, and economic decadence of the time. He stressed the importance of cultivating talent, and of the "people's hearts." He criticized absolutist government, and even went so far as to propose a modification of the ceremony whereby one knelt before the emperor.[29]

Wei Yüan showed a similar preoccupation with "applying classical learning to practical affairs" (*t'ung-ching chih-yung*). His thought evidenced a degree of political realism that set him off sharply from the thinkers of the preceding century. His *An Illustrated Gazetteer of the Maritime Countries* was the first serious study of foreign geography, and it called for "knowing the enemy in order to control him." He criticized blind adherence to past principles and stressed action in accordance with current realities.[30]

K'ang Yu-wei

The use of Kung-yang doctrines as a theoretical basis for

reform reached its final formulation in K'ang Yu-wei.

K'ang first turned to Kung-yang learning in 1888.[31] As a youth he had been schooled in and had accepted the orthodox tradition, first Sung Neo-Confucianism and then the school of Han learning.[32] But in the 1880s, through his studies of "Western learning" and Mahāyāna Buddhism, he was already coming to some of the radical ideas later expressed in his *Ta-t'ung shu*.[33] By 1888, the Kung-yang doctrines seemed to him strikingly pertinent. Two years later, he completed *A Study of the Forged Classics of the Hsin Dynasty (Hsin-hsüeh wei-ching k'ao)*, his first major study in the New Text tradition. All Old Text classics, according to him, were the forgeries of Liu Hsin.[34] K'ang's intention was to clear away all Old Texts, and hence the entire orthodox tradition of Confucianism. The next task was to reinterpret the New Texts.

In 1896, he completed *Confucius as a Reformer (K'ung-tzu kai-chih k'ao)*. Here he underscored the Kung-yang precepts that Confucius, the "uncrowned king," was the creator, not the transmitter, of the classics; that the Master was actually a reformer who had set forth a system of rule for a "new king." Drawing on the doctrine of *san-t'ung*, K'ang added ammunition to his argument for the necessity and the legitimacy of reform. To the criticism of despotism implicit in the New Text legacy, K'ang added the borrowed ideal of a "constitutional monarchy" that would ultimately evolve into "people's rule."[35]

K'ang would give final formulation to this line of thought in 1901–2 in his famous *Ta-t'ung shu*. There he wedded the "three ages" theory to the "Li yün" chapter of the *Book of Rites* by equating the age of approaching peace with *hsiao-k'ang* or minor peace, and the age of great peace with *ta-t'ung*, the "great community."[36] The "great community," in K'ang's vision, was one wherein all suffering had been brought to an end by erasing boundaries—national and familial. Government in this utopian society would be entirely representative. In addition to the "Li

yün," K'ang used the *Mencius* to legitimize and elaborate upon
the "democratic" aspects of his utopian vision.[37]

K'ang had already formulated the outlines of these ideas by
the time Liang came to study at the Wan-mu ts'ao-t'ang in
1890. It was with this corpus of ideas that K'ang "cleared
away" the "old learning" for Liang and brought him "the beginning of [his] awareness that there was such a thing as learning."

Liang Ch'i-ch'ao and Kung-yang Thought

Liang did not accept all of K'ang's teachings uncritically.
K'ang sought persistently to apotheosize Confucius, to make
Confucianism a religion.[38] Liang did not share this concern.
Years later, he recalled that he had at this time disapproved of
K'ang's tendency to draw on Han apocryphal texts and to
mystify Confucius.[39] After 1898, Liang would reject outright
any effort to "preserve the Confucian religion." As for the
radical social ideas contained in K'ang's *Ta-t'ung shu*, Liang
left them alone—he never advanced the idea of doing away with
the family as a social unit.

Liang, however, did accept the general Kung-yang precepts.
He came to hold that Confucius was a reformer, that Confucius' political ideals were contained in the *Spring and Autumn
Annals* and passed down in the *Kung-yang Commentary*, and
that the entire tradition of orthodox Confucianism represented
a perversion of Confucius' original teachings.[40] In addition,
Liang was taught that Confucius' ideal political system was
"democratic," and that this ideal was contained in the "Li
Yün" and the *Mencius*.

The "democratic" element within the Confucian tradition
Liang singled out for special emphasis. He harped on the theme
that Confucius's thought had been divided into two schools,
separately represented by Mencius and Hsün-tzu. Mencius had

succeeded to the highest political ideals of Confucius, while Hsün-tzu had been heir only to the teachings intended for the intermediate stage of partial peace. But it was Hsün-tzu's school that had dominated subsequent Confucianism. Liang wanted to reestablish the "democratic" lineage represented by Mencius.[41]

In K'ang's thought, and hence Liang's, Chinese ideas were entwined with ideas borrowed from the West. Like K'ang, Liang identified Mencius' political ideals with "democracy," and would continue until 1898 to speak of one in terms of the other. It is necessary to ascertain first the actual content of the Mencian legacy before attempting to determine the precise meaning that Liang associated with "democracy."

A key element of Mencian political thought is the idea of *min-pen*, or "primacy of the people," which has occupied much attention in recent research.[42] In Japan it has been a political issue since the 1910s, and in the postwar period has become linked to the emotion-laden assessment of the failure of "democracy" in prewar Japan. There have been sharply divergent interpretations, extending from those who have argued the modern and "democratic" aspects of the Mencian legacy[43] to those who insist that it was essentially despotic.[44]

Critics of the Mencian ideal of "primacy of the people" point to the fact that Mencius took for granted the absolute power of the ruler, that he never raised the issue of sovereignty, and that he paid no attention to institutions for limiting the ruler's power or for assuring benevolent rule. Thus, some critics have seen in *min-pen* thought similarities to "enlightened despotism"—to government under a Frederick the Great, who exercised despotic powers while calling himself "the first servant of the state." The analogy between pristine Confucianism and the European Enlightenment is of course misleading. But the point is well taken—Mencius suggested no other means than the benevolent exercise of despotic power for the realization of his ideal of "primacy of the people."

On the other hand, some of the ideas contained in the *Mencius* unmistakably point in the direction of liberal thought. There is the passage that implicitly recognizes that a ruler's mandate is contingent on his being accepted by the people:

> The Emperor cannot give the empire to another . . . of old, Yao recommended Shun to Heaven and Heaven accepted him. He presented him to the people and the people accepted him. . . . He [Shun] was appointed to preside over the sacrifices, and all the spirits were pleased with him; that indicated his acceptance by Heaven. He was placed in charge of public affairs, and they were well administered and the people were at peace; that indicated his acceptance by the people. Heaven thus gave him the empire; the people thus gave him the empire.[45]

When the ruler abuses his powers, as in the case of Chou, the last emperor of the Shang dynasty, then the people might rebel against him. There is also the passage stressing the ideal that the ruler governs in the interests of the people: "the people come first, the spirits of the land and grain come next, and the ruler counts least."[46] The *Mencius*, we might say, calls for a government "of the people" and "for the people." It even counsels the ruler always to consult public opinion:

> When all those about you say, "This is a man of talents and worth," you may not therefore believe it. When your great officers all say, "This is a man of talents and virtue," neither may you for that believe it. When all the people say, "This is a man of talent and virtue," then examine into the case, and when you find that the man is such, employ him. When all those about you say, "This man won't do," don't listen to them. When all your great officers say, "This man won't do," don't believe them. When the people all say, "This man won't do," then examine into the case, and when you find that the man won't do, send him away.
> When all those about you say, "This man deserves death," don't listen to them. When all your great officers say, "This man deserves death," don't listen to them. When all the people say,

"This man deserves death," then inquire into the case, and when you see that the man deserves death, put him to death. . . .[47]

But its message is intended for the ruler; its method for realizing the ideal of "primacy of the people" consists of no more than trusting in the benevolence of the ruler. It does not approach the idea of government "by the people."[48]

However, Huang Tsung-hsi, the early Ch'ing spokesman *par excellence* of the *min-pen* tradition, hovered on the brink of the idea of limiting autocratic power by the establishment of "representative" institutions. Huang called for a system of "academies" (*hsüeh-hsiao*)—institutions of learning that would serve not only the purpose of training scholar-officials but would also be a sort of forum for monitoring the ruler.

What the Emperor considers right is not necessarily so; what the Emperor considers wrong is not necessarily wrong. Thus will the Emperor not dare arbitrarily decide upon right and wrong and will make public his views in the *hsüeh-hsiao*.[49]

Huang would have the emperor and his ministers attend lecture sessions at the Imperial Academy (*t'ai-hsüeh*) twice each month. The head of the academy (*chi-chiu*) would "make criticisms without reservation should there be failings in the government." In the prefectures, Huang went even further. He provided for a similar arrangement between the prefectural official and the local "Official of Learning." This "Official of Learning" would not be appointed but must be selected by literati opinion. Furthermore, he could be recalled by literati opinion should he fail to live up to the standards of "scholarly criticism."[50]

It is easy to see how such ideas would readily blur any line that might be drawn between the Mencius–Huang Tsung-hsi ideal of "primacy of the people" and the democratic one of a government "of the people, by the people, for the people." It

was no doubt for this reason that K'ang Yu-wei fused the ideas
gleaned from Mencius and Huang with the new ones of "constitutional monarchy" and "people's rule."

As for the seventeen-year old Ch'i-ch'ao, he studied K'ang's
teachings as matters of faith. A case can be made that Kung-
yang ideas for K'ang were merely convenient arguments for
reform; after all, K'ang came to them only after he had studied
"Western learning." But for the young Liang these doctrines
were not merely relevant; they were true—that is to say, he
believed they were true representations of the ideals of Confucius. It was therefore perfectly natural for Liang to identify
Mencian ideas with what little he understood at the time of
Western democracy.

Armed with K'ang's Kung-yang doctrines and still rather
vague notions of "democracy" (the precise content of which
will be discussed shortly), the young Ch'i-ch'ao was ready to
take an active role in the reform movement.

Liang Becomes a Reformer

When the news of the humiliating peace treaty (of Shimonoseki) came in April, 1895, Liang hastened to organize a petition, and obtained the support of one hundred and ninety *chü-
jen* from his home province, Kwangtung. Soon afterwards, he
helped K'ang lead a national petition to call for reforms and a
strong stand against Japan. It was signed by more than twelve
hundred *chü-jen*.[51]

In August, K'ang established in Peking the Ch'iang-hsüeh
Hui, literally "Society for the Propagation of Learning." The
society had a library as well as a showroom of modern maps and
instruments. Its aim was to spread knowledge about the West
and to push for reforms. Liang became the Chief Secretary of
the society, as well as the editor and principal contributor to the
society's organ, the *Chung-wai kung-pao*, or "International

Gazette." This gazette was a daily, comprising only a single sheet, generally an editorial of several hundred words written by Liang. It came to have a circulation of about three thousand within a month after its inception. Although the gazette, together with the society, was banned a short three months later, Liang had acquired through it a reputation as a publicist.[52]

In the spring of the following year, the diplomat-poet-reformer Huang Tsun-hsien (1848–1905) invited Liang to help him start a new journal in Shanghai. This was the *Current Affairs (Shih-wu pao)*, which appeared thrice a month from August 9, 1895, until August 8, 1898. It reached in its second year an unprecedented circulation of twelve thousand. Liang, as editor-in-chief and the principal contributor to the journal, was now the nation's leading publicist.[53]

His writings earned him the recognition of some of the prominent officials of the time. When Huang was appointed Minister to Germany, he asked Liang to go with him;[54] but Huang's own appointment failed to materialize.[55] Then Wu T'ing-fang, who had been Minister to the United States and to Japan, and Chang Chih-tung, who was Governor-General of Hupei and Hunan at the time, tried in turn to enlist Liang's services.[56] He chose to remain in Shanghai, to give his attention to the *Current Affairs*, and to a host of other projects, including the establishment of an anti-footbinding society, a translation bureau, and a school for girls.[57]

These were intellectually exciting years for Liang. His close friends included the brilliant young reformer T'an Ssu-t'ung (1865–98),[58] the New Text classicist Hsia Tseng-yu (1868–1924),[59] and, of course, Huang Tsun-hsien.[60] He also came to know Yen Fu (1853–1921), and read the draft of Yen's translation of Thomas H. Huxley's *Evolution and Ethics* in 1896.[61]

Toward the end of 1897, Liang joined his close friends in a small-scale reform program in Hunan. The effort was under the direction of Governor Ch'en Pao-chen and his son San-li and aimed to make Hunan the spearhead and model of modernization in South China. It gathered together some of the leading reformers of the time; Huang Tsun-hsien became the Acting Judicial Commissioner of the province in July, 1897, and introduced a modern police bureau. In addition, Huang helped to organize the Academy of Current Affairs (Shih-wu Hsüeh-t'ang), the Reform Association of South China (Nan-hsüeh Hui), and the *New Hunan Gazette* (*Hsiang-hsüeh hsin-pao*), the first gazette of the province. Tan Ssu-t'ung, who was a native Hunanese, became the editor of the gazette, the Chairman of the Reform Association, and a lecturer at the academy. T'ang Ts'ai-ch'ang (1867–1900), later the leader of the abortive revolt in 1900 known by his name, was an assistant lecturer at the academy. And Ts'ai O (1883–1916), the central figure in the antimonarchical movement of 1915–16, was one of the forty-odd pupils at the academy. Liang was the Chief Lecturer.[62]

In the generally progressive atmosphere of the academy, Liang was able to give vent to some of his most radical ideas. He spoke to his students and his colleagues about "the political authority of the people," and about "representative assemblies." He and others secretly reprinted and distributed Huang Tsung-hsi's *A Plan for a Prince* to propagate "democratic" ideas. They even gave vent to their anti-Manchu sentiments by circulating the *Ten Days' Sacking of Yang Chou* (*Yang-chou shih-jih chi*)—a record of Manchu brutalities in the sacking of the city in 1645.[63]

Liang's activities in Hunan were terminated by a serious illness in the spring of 1898. As soon as he recovered, he hurried to Peking to join K'ang in the reform movement that was fast gathering momentum. On June 16, K'ang was given a formal audience by the Kuang-hsü Emperor, now twenty-six years old and trying to move out of the shadows of the Dowager Empress's domination. K'ang succeeded in gaining the complete confidence of the young emperor. What followed in the next "hundred days" was a series of almost frantic imperial decrees for reform, including the abolition of the eight-legged essay, the weeding out of numerous high-ranking sinecures, and the placing of four of K'ang's trusted followers—including T'an Ssu-t'ung—in key positions, all intended as first steps toward sweeping administrative and educational changes.[64] Liang, for his part, was appointed to head a newly established translation bureau, and received imperial approval to found a school for training translators. On July 3, he was given a personal audience by the Emperor, a great honor for a man without official rank.[65]

But behind the excitement and the expectations of the reformers loomed the uncertainty over the position and power of the Emperor. The conservative forces around the Empress Dowager were strongly entrenched and the Emperor's position during the "hundred days" was at best precarious. On September 21, the worst that the reformers feared came—six of the group were arrested, soon to be executed, the Emperor was placed under house arrest, and K'ang and Liang barely managed to escape with their lives.

All the reforms were rescinded by the Dowager Empress after the coup. And a wave of reaction followed, to climax in the Boxer catastrophe of 1900. Still, the reforms had set a precedent. Many of the changes would be effected in the aftermath of the Boxer War when the court finally promulgated a series of reforms.

Liang's role in the "hundred days" was of course only secondary. Nevertheless he emerged from the coup of 1898 a national figure—his name came to be associated invariably with K'ang's as one of the two key figures in the episode. This was no doubt due in part to his success as a publicist. His influence was in fact far greater in the spreading of new ideas than in policy making within the reform movement.

"Democratic" Ideas

The new ideas he helped to publicize centered around three terms—*min-ch'üan, min-chu,* and *i-yüan.* The crucial term here is *min-ch'üan,* literally "people's authority" or "people's rights." The following quotation, taken from a proposal that Liang submitted to Governor Ch'en Pao-chen of Hunan, gives some idea of how he understood the concept *ch'üan*:

> If we wish now to reform thoroughly, we must begin by establishing communication between the sentiments of those above and those below. If we wish to establish communication between the sentiments of those above and those below, then we must revive the intentions of the ancients, adopt Western institutions, and stress the authority (*ch'üan*) of the local districts (*hsiang*). . . . [Toward these ends] we must develop the knowledge of the literati . . . and fix the limits of authority (*ch'üan*). What do I mean by delineating authority? The Westerners separate discussion and legislation (*i-shih*) from execution (*hsing-shih*). The legislators (*i-shih chih jen*) have the authority to decide upon general procedures (*ting-chang*) but do not have the power to carry out such. The executors have the authority of implementation but do not have the authority of deciding upon general procedures. When something is about to be done, the assemblymen get together and deliberate over its advisability. If they approve, then they will discuss its procedures. After the procedures have been drafted, they are given to the administrator (*yu-ssu*) to carry out. The administrator may not arbitrarily change them. If, in carrying them out, obstacles and difficulties are encountered, then he will inform the assemblymen who will in turn discuss and change them. The Westerners' laws for this reason are constantly changing and are refined with each change, becoming ever better adapted to the people's interests. This is because the assemblymen are elected by the people.[66]

It is clear from the above passage that Liang understood

ch'üan to mean primarily political authority. Elsewhere he used the term *min-ch'üan* in contradistinction to *chün-ch'üan*, or authority of the ruler. After the three dynasties, Liang wrote, "the authority of the people daily dwindled while that of the ruler increased."[67] In other words, *min-ch'üan* meant to him "political rights," the "right" of the people to a voice in government, to exercise political authority. Nowhere in his writings before 1898 can be found any mention of "rights" in the sense of the doctrines of the rights of man as set forth in the American and French revolutions, of the inalienable rights of "life, liberty, and the pursuit of happiness." Nor did the inviolability of property, so central to the concerns of classical liberalism, occupy any place in his conception of "rights" at this time.

This "political authority of the people" was to find expression in the institutions of *i-yüan*, or representative assemblies. As the quotation above shows, Liang envisioned a separation of the legislative and executive powers of government.

The goal of the development of the "political authority of the people" was *min-chu*, which was associated in K'ang Yu-wei's thought with the ideal "great community." Liang's ideas at this time were similar. He felt that the age of "minor peace" would be that of monarchy, while that of the "great community" would be *min-chu*, or *min wei cheng chih shih* (the age of people's rule). The latter stage may in turn be divided into two: rule by a president and rule without a president.[68] In other words, *min-chu* stood for the end of the imperial institution and the full authority of the people. In fact, Liang tended to use *min-ch'üan* and *min-chu* interchangeably, both in contrast to "authority of the ruler." In a letter to Yen Fu in 1897, he wrote,

. . . today the principles concerning *min-chu* are not yet prevalent. Therefore, it is better to use the power of the monarch (*chün-ch'üan*) to change the situation.[69]

Together the three terms—*min-ch'üan, min-chu,* and *i-yüan*—sum up Liang's political aims in the years before 1898: the establishment of representative institutions (*i-yüan*) to exercise legislative power or "political authority of the people" (*min-ch'üan*), and the eventual abolition of the imperial institutions under full-fledged "people's rule" (*min-chu*).

How would China prepare for such democratic institutional reforms? The key, according to Liang, was education. In "On Reform," his fullest statement on the subject at this time, Liang wrote:

> . . . the basis of reform lies in the cultivation and development of talent; the flourishing of talent depends on the setting-up of schools; the establishment and success of schools depend on changing the examination system; and the substance and success of all this lie in reforming the official system.[70]

Of the official system, Liang criticized the current corruption, the fact that there were no clearly defined spheres of responsibility, and that officials were not trained for the functions they were to perform. But the focus was on reforming the educational and examination system.[71] "If the nation wishes to strengthen itself," Liang wrote, "then this matter [the setting up of modern schools] is the most important."[72] China must establish modern schools after the pattern of the West and of Japan.[73] The examination system must be adjusted to accord with the new educational system. Traditional degrees must be altered to conform with graduations from elementary and secondary schools and universities.[74]

Toward the aim of spreading knowledge and education among the people, Liang proposed a measure that was truly radical for the time.

> The written language of the ancients corresponded to their spoken language. But the written language today is different from the

spoken language. . . . If we only use the colloquial language of today . . . then there will necessarily be many who can understand, and the number of literate people will accordingly increase. . . . We should use only the colloquial language today and write plenty of books.[75]

The emphasis of Liang's ideas on reform, then, was on the spread of education to prepare for the establishment of democratic institutions.

The stress on democratic institutions is easy to explain— Liang thought they accounted for the secret of superior Western power. In the preface to his *A Catalogue of Books on Western Learning*, Liang pointedly addressed himself against those who "thought that China was better in all respects than the West, that she was only inferior in her military power." It was Western institutions, Liang stressed, that constituted the real source of Western power. The decline of the "people's political authority," he asserted, accounted for China's current weakness.[76] "Parliaments," he wrote, "were the basis of a strong country."[77] "In the last hundred years, the democratic spirit (*min-ch'i*) has spread in the Western countries. If only China will do the same, then she will be as strong as the Western countries in a few decades." Because, he continued, "people's rule" (*min-chu*) was "the very source of a country's strength."[78] There was the example of America—"If we look at the wealth of America, then we will understand that the political authority of the people should be revived."[79] There was also the example of Japan. Japan, he argued, had attained power through institutional reform.[80] "Political institutions are the foundations for the establishment of a state. Japan has worked on the foundations but China has only worked on the periphery," hence the current discrepancy between Chinese and Japanese power.[81]

The preoccupation with national power shows Liang to be very much a product of late nineteenth-century China. The impact of the West on China was above all the impact of superior power. It was the discrepancy of power that made the Western challenge (as opposed to, for example, the earlier challenge of Indian Buddhism) dangerous and urgent, that made reform necessary. From midcentury on, the most immediate question for Chinese reformers was simply: how is China to close the gap between Chinese and Western power? Beginning in the 1860s, China tried first to close the power gap by adopting Western arms and technology; then in the 1870s a few men took the lead to establish modern industrial enterprises, thought to be the source of Western wealth. But the disastrous defeat in 1894–95 exposed the inadequacies of these efforts. Why had China failed? The power of the West, many thought, must have to do not only with her firearms and industries but also with her political institutions. After all, Japan had adopted a constitution and she had grown strong. It was in such a context that Liang advocated democratic institutional reform as an answer to the challenge of superior Western power.

Liang's response must be understood also in the context of the sources of inspiration for his ideas and of his Kung-yang background. He had first begun his "Western studies" at the Wan-mu ts'ao-t'ang under K'ang.[82] Later, as secretary of the Society for the Propagation of Learning (Ch'iang-hsüeh Hui) he went through a period of intensive reading of "Western books."[83] He of course could not read any foreign language at this time and translated books constituted his principal access to knowledge about the West. The scope and content of the translated "Western books" available to Liang can be surmised by examining the two catalogues of books on "Western learning" that Liang compiled in 1896 and 1897.

The "Western learning" Liang and his contemporaries had in mind was limited in scope. *A Catalogue of Books on Western Learning*, which Liang compiled specifically for the purpose of instructing the Chinese youth on what to read for "Western learning,"[84] contains mainly titles concerned with military and applied sciences. The second section, which covers "Western government," includes only a small number of administrative treatises. There is not a single book on Western political philosophy or theory.[85] As Liang himself observed in the preface, Chinese official translations had been largely in the field of military science; the missionaries' work had been largely in medicine.[86]

A Catalogue of Books on Western Government, compiled the following year, evidences similar limitations. It includes such subjects as histories, administrative systems, education, commerce, industry, and so on, but once again, there is the conspicuous lack of Western political theory.[87] Such notions as Liang was able to gain about Western political theory were probably derived from Timothy Richard's translation of Robert Mackenzie's *The 19th Century: a History*,[88] a crude glorification of progress in the nineteenth century and hardly a source for serious political philosophy.

Outside of these translated titles Liang's only other substantial source of information about the modern West was the reformist writings of the missionaries and contacts with the missionaries themselves. In 1875, Young J. Allen had set the tone for subsequent missionary writings on reform by calling for changes in China's educational system. Until the Sino-Japanese war the focus of the missionaries' proposals remained on the reform of China's educational and examination systems.[89] Liang was certainly familiar with these essays. Moreover, during the latter part of 1895 and the first two months of 1896, at about the time he was writing the essay "On Reform," he maintained very close contacts with Timothy Richard. He might even have served briefly as the latter's "secretary."[90] Some of the inspiration for his proposals to modernize China's education system must have come from missionary writings and from Richard. In "On Reform" he specifically called upon the authority of Richard to argue for educational reform.[91]

Finally, the fact that Liang particularly adopted Western concepts on democratic institutions must also be understood against his intellectual background. The Mencian ideal of "primacy of the people" approximated the democratic ideas of government "of the people." This was precisely the area in which Liang turned to borrow from the West. Representative institutions were to be established to exercise legislative authority on behalf of the people. The ideas of *min-ch'üan, i-yüan,* and *min-chu* were meant to augment the political principles derived from the Kung-yang school and from Mencius. Liang assumed the two—the Western ideas and what he had learned at K'ang's school—were compatible. This explains why Liang frequently spoke of one in terms of the other. He cited, for example, the passage in the *Mencius* that advised the ruler to follow the wishes of the people to argue for representative institutions.[92] Years later, he recalled that he had applied Mencian ideas to elaborate upon the concept of "political authority of the people."[93]

One might speculate that Liang was apologizing for his tradition when he identified elements of Mencian thought with modern democratic thinking; one might even agree with Joseph Levenson that Liang was already "intellectually alienated from his tradition, but still emotionally tied to it," and that he was trying to "smother the conflict between history and value."[94] I have suggested that Liang was both emotionally and intellectually tied to his tradition, especially to the Kung-yang reinterpretation of it that he learned from K'ang Yu-wei. When he identified elements of that tradition with his newly acquired Western concepts, it was because he thought they were identifiable.

In short, Liang's thought until 1898 was a combination of ideas culled from New Text Confucianism and notions drawn from a limited contact with Western thought. He particularly emphasized the Mencian ideal of "primacy of the people" and augmented this ideal with the borrowed notion of establishing representative institutions to exercise the "political authority of the people." Like most other reformers of the time, his emphasis was on institutional reform to strengthen China. But now the coup of 1898 changed everything—it shattered the hopes for reform from above. It also forced Liang into exile and to a new setting—Meiji Japan.

CHAPTER 3

The Idea of the New Citizen and the Influence of Meiji Japan

The Setting

Figure 1 shows the numbers of Chinese students in Japan between the years 1896 and 1937,[1] and figure 2 the numbers of Chinese translations of Japanese books between these same years.[2] Together the two graphs point to the two major periods of intensive Japanese influence on China. The first wave of this transmission reached its peak in the years 1902 to 1907. After 1907 both the numbers of Chinese students in Japan and Chinese translations from Japanese declined. After 1912, the trend was again upward, but this ceased abruptly in 1915, no doubt because of the Twenty-one Demands. From 1926 on, the numbers rose again, signifying a new period of Chinese receptivity to Japan.

Figures 3[3] and 4[4] show the shift in the areas of influence. In the first period the books translated were predominantly in politics and law, and history and geography. This was the time when Chinese reformers looked to the example of Meiji Japan in constitution-making and institutional reform, and the more radical thinkers learned the new ideas of nationalism, republicanism, and modernization. From the mid-1920s to the mid-1930s, on the other hand, the bulk of the translated books was in the areas of literature, economics, and sociology. Nearly one-

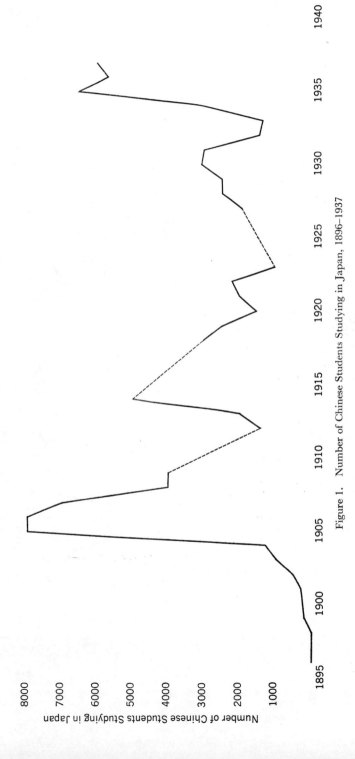

Figure 1. Number of Chinese Students Studying in Japan, 1896–1937

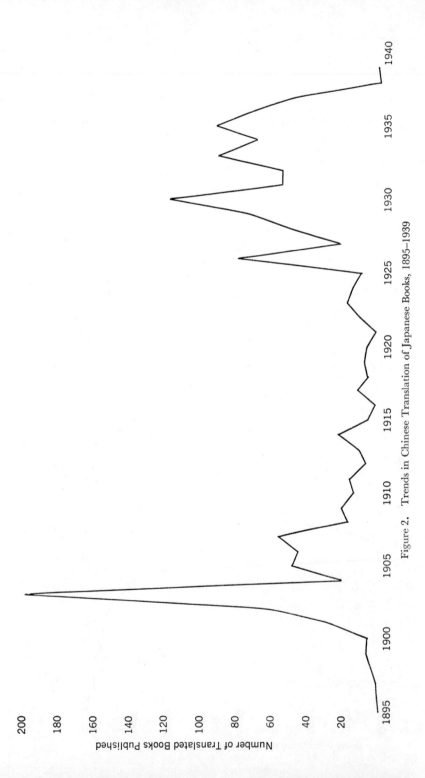

Figure 2.   Trends in Chinese Translation of Japanese Books, 1895–1939

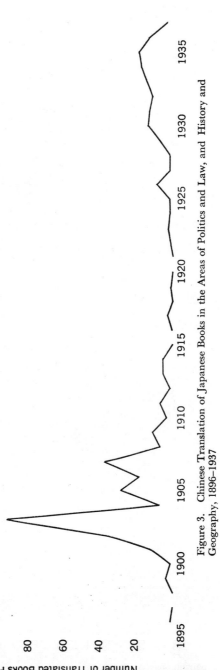

Figure 3. Chinese Translation of Japanese Books in the Areas of Politics and Law, and History and Geography, 1896–1937

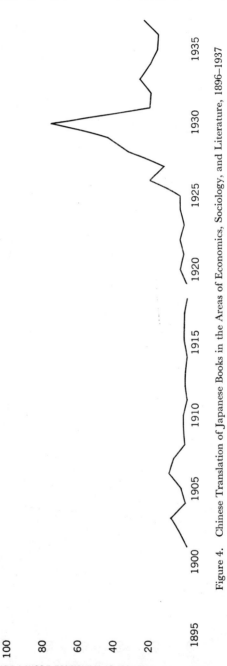

Figure 4. Chinese Translation of Japanese Books in the Areas of Economics, Sociology, and Literature, 1896–1937

half of the books on economics and sociology were Marxist works, the most translated author being Kawakami Hajime (1879–1946).[5] In this decade Chinese leftists were turning to Japanese Marxist writings for guidance.

The year of China's shattering defeat by Japan was 1895. The defeat dramatically exposed the weakness of China's program of reform in the preceding generation—a program of "self-strengthening" by adopting Western technology and industries. Clearly, more basic reforms were needed. And the war brought an abrupt change in the attitude of Chinese intellectuals and officials toward Japan.[6] The little neighbor to the east proved that she had been far more successful than China in modernizing herself. China, many thought, must learn the secret of Japan's success. In the reform movement that gathered momentum after the war, leading advocates of change, such as K'ang Yu-wei,[7] Chang Chih-tung,[8] and Huang Tsun-hsien[9] repeatedly urged the emulation of Meiji Japan.

The desire of many Chinese to learn from Japan was reflected in the increasing numbers of students going to Japan to study. In 1896, closely following the defeat, the first group of students was sent, giving momentum to what had been, since 1872, no more than a sporadically implemented program.[10] The number of Chinese students in Japan quickly increased after 1896, reaching an all-time high by 1905 and 1906, with a conservatively estimated total of 8,000 students.[11]

Eight thousand was an enormous figure, especially by comparison with the numbers of students going to countries other than Japan. In 1905, for example, there were only 130 Chinese students in the United States.[12] In 1909 and 1910, the number of Chinese students in Japan was between four and seven times the combined total of those studying in the United States and in Europe.[13] The importance of Japan as the center for overseas study by Chinese students continued until after the first World

War, when the balance finally began to change—the United
States attracted a growing number of students[14] and France, for
a few years after 1919, drew a large number of students and
student-laborers.[15]

The impetus for the massive movement of students to Japan
in 1905 and 1906 came from two developments—Japan's victory in the Russo-Japanese War, a victory that established her
as a world power, and the end of the examination system in
China, which meant that study abroad became the principal
means of climbing "the ladder of success" in China.

There were also more basic reasons for the overwhelming
preference for Japan in this period. Some of these were summed
up neatly by Chang Chih-tung in his "Exhortation to Learn"
of 1898:

> First, Japan is closer and involves less expense. . . . Second [the
> students sent] are close to China and easy to supervise. Third, the
> Japanese language is close to Chinese and easy to master. Fourth,
> . . . the Japanese have already expunged the parts [of Western
> books] not essential to Western learning and modified these
> [books]. Since Chinese and Japanese conditions and customs are
> similar, it is easy to imitate Japan, reaping twice the results for
> half the effort.[16]

We might add to Chang's list the consideration that learning
from a country with which many Chinese thinkers of the time
felt a cultural and racial affinity took away the psychological
sting of learning from the completely alien West.

One outgrowth of this turn to Japan was the predominance
of the Japanese-educated among the first generation of leaders
in twentieth-century China. Y. C. Wang has tabulated the
"Who's Who" section of *The China Yearbook* according to the
educational backgrounds of the men listed. His figures show that
for 1916 and 1923, the "returned students" constituted about
one-half of those listed.[17] In 1916, more than two-thirds of the

group came from those who had studied in Japan.[18] In 1923, the Japan group still constituted 56 percent of all the "returned students" who appeared in the "Who's Who."[19] The preponderance of the Japanese trained was replaced by that of the American trained only after the mid-1920s.[20]

That Japan, at least in the two decades after 1895, was the predominant source from which forward-looking Chinese sought training in modern skills and answers to their questions about the modern world is further evidenced in the translations of the time. Translation of Japanese books reached a peak from 1902 to 1907—the all-time high was 1903, when 200 titles were published; in 1902 and 1905–7, an average of more than fifty titles appeared each year. As Liang Ch'i-ch'ao observed, "there were dozens of regular journals [for publishing translations from the Japanese]. Every time a new book appeared in Japan, there were several translators. The infusion of new thought was like a spreading fire."[21]

The statistics of translations reflect not only Japanese influence but also its relative weight, as opposed to Western influence. The majority of the books translated during this period were in fact Japanese books—that is, not Japanese translations of books in other languages. One scholar has tabulated 551 titles of books on the "new learning" that were listed in seven well-known catalogues spanning 1896 to 1905. His figures show that while translations from British books totaled a meager 55 titles, those from Japanese originals, not counting translations of Japanese translations of books in other languages, totaled 321 or 60 percent.[22] In other words, translations from the Japanese in this period outnumbered the combined total of translations from all other languages.

These early translations from the Japanese (as well as the later translations of Japanese Marxist works) have left their imprint on the modern Chinese language. The translators frequently had to invent a new vocabulary to convey new ideas.

In most instances, they turned to Japanese. Sometimes they borrowed purely Japanese words, such as *baai—ch'ang-ho, tetsuzuki—shou-hsü, kokufuku—k'e-fu, mibun—shen-fen, shihai—chihp'ei*, etc.[23] More often they borrowed Chinese words that had been given a new meaning in Japanese—for example: *bunka— wen-hua, kakumei—ke-ming, shakai—she-hui, jiyū—tzu-yu, bungaku —wen-hsüeh*, etc.,[24] or Japanese loan-translations of European models, such as *chūshō—ch'ou-hsiang, handō—fan-tung, jichi—tzuchih, kakkan—k'e-kuan, kagaku—k'e-hsüeh, shugi—chu-i*, etc.[25] Because of the affinities between the two languages, these graphic loans from Japanese tended to be assimilated more readily into modern Chinese than the phonemic loans from the European languages.[26] The result is that loans from Japanese predominate among modern Chinese loan words in such areas as law, politics, philosophy, economics, and sociology,[27] precisely the areas in which Chinese translations from the Japanese were the most vigorous.

In short, the three indices of cultural influence discussed above—the records of overseas study by Chinese students, Chinese translations of Japanese books, and foreign loan-words in the modern Chinese language—converge to point to this conclusion: in the two decades after 1895 Japan was the principal source of inspiration for new Chinese ideas. Not only was Japan the major center of Chinese students abroad, it also became, after 1898, and with the coming of the political exiles, the principal base of operations for both the reform and revolutionary movements. Under these conditions, as Liang Ch'ich'ao noted, Tokyo became in fact "the center of the new thought movement,"[28] for the students and political exiles in Japan were the ones who led the intellectual transformation of China during the two crucial decades between 1895 and the beginning of the May Fourth movement. And they were the recipients and transmitters of Japanese influence—some of them translated Japanese books; others wrote or talked about their newly acquired ideas. The influence of Meiji Japan on Liang must be seen against this general background of vigorous Chinese reception of Japanese influence.

Liang Ch'i-ch'ao and Meiji Japan

Liang Ch'i-ch'ao arrived in Japan on October 16, 1898, having narrowly escaped the clasp of the reactionary coup. With the exception of a trip to Hawaii in 1899, a trip to Australia in 1900, and one to the United States in 1903, he remained in Japan for the next fourteen years, until 1912.[29] He was 25 years old when he arrived; he was 39 when he finally left Japan to return to China.

These were exciting years in Liang's life; they were years during which Liang changed from an essentially Confucian intellectual orientation[30] to that of a modern liberal-nationalist. Fortunately for the historian, the documents on Liang's life during this period are extraordinarily full. Many of his letters have been preserved in the *Chronological Biography*.[31] In addition, Liang's development as a writer and thinker contributed to the richness of the documentation—he seldom kept his thoughts to himself; rather, he was in a habit of spilling out new notions almost as soon as he came upon them. The "Tsu-yu shu," or "Notes on Freedom,"[32] for example, was something like a collection of random study notes, and they record Liang's initial reactions to the great variety of new books and thinkers with whom he came into contact during his first years in Japan. Finally, Liang was under constant police observation during these years, thanks to the Japanese government's interests in Chinese domestic affairs. These police reports have survived in the archives of the Japanese Foreign Ministry, and they provide an almost day-to-day record of Liang's activities.[33] Together these sources afford the opportunity to trace in some detail the influence on Liang of Meiji Japanese thinkers and the course of Liang's intellectual transformation.

Even prior to his arrival in Japan, Liang had been influenced by K'ang Yu-wei and Huang Tsun-hsien and had proposed Japan as a model for China.[34] Once in Japan, he learned to read Japanese and plunged himself into the intellectual world of late Meiji Japan. He adopted the name Yoshida Shin, after Yoshida Shōin (1830–59) and Takasugi Shinsaku (1839–67),[35] two of the heroes of the restoration movement. In the journal he kept of his travel to Hawaii in 1899, he reviewed his own intellectual debt to Japan:

Since coming to Tokyo . . . I have lived in Tokyo for four hundred and forty days. . . . In these four hundred and forty days . . . I have made several Japanese friends who are as close to me as my own brothers. There are dozens of other acquaintances. . . . Also, since coming to Japan, I have widely collected Japanese books and read them. . . . My mind has as a result changed, my thinking and words have become so different from before as to appear to be those of another person. I have read Japanese newspapers daily, becoming so involved in Japanese political affairs that they seem to be those of my own country. My relationship with Japan can indeed be called intimate. Many habits have become so deeply ingrained in my mind that I cannot forget them even if I wanted to.[36]

Liang's thinking would still continue along the main lines set before 1898—a special interest in liberal-democracy and an assumption that the establishment of liberal-democratic government would somehow contribute to the cause of national "wealth and power." But beyond these main directions, Liang came to Japan with little intellectual baggage; the more dogmatic aspects of K'ang Yu-wei's Kung-yang Confucian ideas were not to limit Liang's receptivity to a host of new ideas.

Japanese Pan-Asianism

His first contact was with Japanese Pan-Asianism. It was
with the help of the Japanese Pan-Asianists Hirayama Shū and
Yamada Ryōsei, who were acting under the orders of the ruling
Okuma (Shigenobu) government, that Liang escaped to
Japan.[37] Okuma and his supporters also subsidized Liang's
housing and maintenance after his arrival.[38] Under such conditions, Liang's first Japanese friends were for the most part
those supporters of Okuma who had a Pan-Asian interest—
members of the Tōa Dōbun Kai.

There was Kashiwabara Buntarō (1869–1936), Okuma's
principal liaison man with Liang.[39] Kashiwabara had founded
the Tōa Kai, and had been instrumental in joining his organization with Konoe Atsumaro's Dōbun Kai to form the Tōa Dōbun Kai in November, 1898. He was at the time secretary of
the newly merged society, and a renowned educator.[40] Only
four years Liang's senior, he soon became Liang's closest friend
in Japan; the two men even became sworn brothers.[41]

Inugai Tsuyoshi (1855–1932), who served as Okuma's education minister in 1898 and was the chief representative of
Okuma's Asian concerns, also became one of Liang's close
friends.[42] Konoe Atsumaro, president of the Tōa Dōbun Kai,
was another one of Liang's acquaintances.[43] Others with whom
Liang maintained close contacts included Hirayama Shū and
Miyazaki Torazō,[44] whose associations with Sun Yat-sen have
been studied by Marius Jansen.

Pan-Asianism in men such as Okuma, Inugai, and Kashiwabara consisted of a romantic vision of an East Asia united on the
basis of a common race (*dōshu*) and a shared cultural heritage
(*dōbun*), and freed from Western encroachment. It was infused
also with such Western-inspired values as "liberty" and
"equality."

For a time Liang came to share with his hosts in Japan this Pan-Asian vision. As early as 1896, he had spoken of a "united Asia of the yellow races," and an inevitable struggle between the "white and yellow races" in the future.[45] In 1899 he wrote,

> Japan and we are brother countries. Only if we put an end to the boundaries between us and help each other can we maintain the independence of the yellow race and stop the spread of the power of Europe. In the future China and Japan will become one country, and the fact that our languages are understandable to each other will be of great importance. Therefore, the patriots of Japan should consider learning spoken and written Chinese as their foremost task, and the patriots of China must consider learning spoken and written Japanese as their foremost task.[46]

In the first issue of his journal, *Upright Discussions (Ch'ing-i pao)*, he stated two of the four avowed aims of the journal as: "To establish communication between China and Japan; to establish friendship and affection between the two. To clarify and develop the learning of East Asia in order to maintain the essence of Asia."[47]

He agreed with his Japanese friends' view of the West as the common enemy of China and Japan. In the setting of the 1890s he was understandably outraged by Western imperialism, which he dubbed a wickedly "debasing, barbarizing, enslaving, and animalizing" encroachment upon China.[48] This anti-Western sentiment underlay his frequently racial statements between 1896 and 1899, as when he called for "the elimination of all boundaries among the yellow race," "so as to war against the white race in a battlefield of a circumference of 90,000 *li*."[49]

But he also espoused the Western-inspired values of his friends. He began to translate one of their favorite novels, Shiba Shirō's *Kajin no kigu* (Strange Encounters of Elegant Females).[50] This was one of the three most popular political novels of the Meiji period,[51] and abounded in such slogans as "liberty" and "equality." Liang shared, in other words, with the Japanese Pan-Asianists an ambivalent attitude toward the West—although he harbored strong anti-Western sentiments, he was coming to accept certain Western-inspired values.

Liang's espousal of Pan-Asianism illustrates the great appeal that Meiji Japan held for many Chinese thinkers at the turn of the century, but it was a tenuous alliance. The supranationalistic ideals of Pan-Asianism called upon "culture" and "race" to supersede "nation" as objects of loyalty. Liang could accept such an ideal, partly because of his own Confucian inclination to place greater emphasis on the cultural heritage than on the political entity, and partly because he saw no threat to the national integrity of China in this utopian vision. But he would soon learn that liberal Japanese Pan-Asianism could easily be used to rationalize Japanese military expansion, and he would show that such a Pan-Asianism was not acceptable to him. In fact, his brief espousal of the vision of an East Asia united on the basis of a "common cultural heritage" and "race" against Western imperialism should be seen as a way station between his earlier tradition-oriented culturalism and his later full-fledged nationalism.

A full record of his courtship with Japanese Pan-Asianism is provided in his translation of Shiba Shirō's novel.[52] He was first given the novel to read on board the *S. S. Oshima*,[53] by which he escaped to Japan. He immediately began to translate it.[54] This translation is of special interest, for Liang did not read the novel in its entirety and only then proceed to translate. Instead, he probably translated while he read with the help of a tutor.[55] The modifications, deletions, and additions he made in the translation's course actually record his changing reactions to Japanese Pan-Asianism from late 1898 to early 1900.

Shiba's novel centers around a certain Tōkai Sanshi (Wanderer of the Eastern Seas) and two beautiful European girls, Yūran and Kōren, whom the Wanderer first encounters before

the Liberty Bell in Independence Hall in Philadelphia. Yūran
turns out to be a Spanish patriot, and Kōren, the daughter of an
Irish patriot who had died a victim of tyranny. Soon the
Wanderer also meets the old servant of the two girls—Han Kei,
actually a Ming loyalist. It is not a romance, but a series of
separate episodes unified by the theme of revolutionary movements throughout the world.

Beneath the surface of liberal slogans in this novel published
between 1883 and 1897, one can perceive the increasingly expansionistic sentiments of Shiba Shirō. In the second chapter,
Yūran says to the Wanderer:

> As the sun climbs in the eastern skies, so is your country rising in
> the Orient. . . . Your country will take the lead and preside over
> a confederation of Asia . . . it is your country and no other that
> can bring the taste of self-government and independence into the
> life of millions for the first time, and so spread the light of civiliza-
> tion.[56]

As Ishida Takeshi has pointed out, by the time the second
chapter was published in 1885, Shiba's thought was departing
from his earlier emphasis on criticizing excessive governmental
authority to his later preoccupation with national power.[57] By
the end of the novel, Shiba used the argument of Japan's destiny
to bring enlightenment to the rest of the peoples of Asia as the
justification for military expansion.

The aspect of Pan-Asianism that had initially appealed to
Liang was the vision of an independent and "free" Asia united
on the basis of its "common cultural heritage" and "race." He
was also willing to acknowledge that Japan was further along
the path of modernization than China, and he translated faith-
fully the passage quoted above.[58] However, he was not willing
to accept the relegation of China to a servile position. He neg-
lected all mention of Han Kei as the servant of Yūran and
Kōren, and representing China—and introduced him only as a

patriot of China at the end of the second chapter.[59] Though this
effort was not carried through the entire translation,[60] it fore-
shadowed Liang's ultimate rejection of the novel.

In the final pages of the novel, Shiba Shirō discussed the
Sino-Japanese War of 1894–95. He laid the blame for the war
on Li Hung-chang's "lascivious desires." The Japanese government had sent soldiers with the best of intentions—to gain the
friendship of the Korean people—but was forced by circumstances into war. Speaking through Tōkai Sanshi, Shiba re-
counted how he had long advocated a policy of punishing China
for its insolence toward Japan, and of aiding the Korean people
in reform and independence, through occupation. He gloried in
the striking military superiority of Japan. He then gave a
lengthy discourse of various opinions. One dissenting voice
warned against the dangers of expansion, but such words were
mouthed by the "Speaker of the Position of Ruin" (Chinrinshi).
All others echoed the Wanderer's theme: the righteousness of
Japan's cause in leading other countries of Asia to enlightenment, through military occupation.[61]

Liang deleted this entire section. He blamed instead the
Japanese military in Korea for the war. They were guilty of
destroying, rather than helping, Korea's revolutionary spirit
and leadership. Liang concluded with a passage of his own
creation in which he argued that:

> At that time, Korea, confronted with internal difficulties and ex-
> ternal threats, asked China for help. It was natural for China to
> send an army to help. But Japan . . . was filled with ambitions and
> sought a cause for conflict in the East. . . . Seeing that China could
> be taken advantage of . . . Japan exploited the situation to create
> conflict with China. . . .[62]

Before the completion of this highly interpretive translation,
Liang had already abruptly terminated its publication in the
Ch'ing-i pao.[63] Nine months later, in November, 1900, he wrote

a poem speaking of how he had been mistaken in his admiration of Shiba Shirō.[64] When he reviewed the aims of the *Ch'ing-i pao* in its hundredth issue (December 21, 1901), he did not even pay lip service to the two earlier Pan-Asian principles.[65] His courtship with Pan-Asianism had lasted only a little over a year.

Shiba Shirō's expansionistic sentiments had provoked Liang's disillusionment with Pan-Asianism. The later portions of Shiba Shirō's book reflected in fact a broader change in the tone of Japanese Pan-Asianism after the war of 1894–95: in place of the earlier idealistic vision of cooperation and adventure, the emphasis of Japanese Pan-Asianism came increasingly to be on Japan's heavenly calling (*tenshoku*), regardless of the will of her neighbors. And there was a corresponding shift in attitude toward China—one characterized increasingly by scorn, by a picture of China as representing all that was backward and stagnant.[66]

However, even though Liang broke with expansionistic Japanese Pan-Asianism, some of the Western-inspired "liberal" values with which it was closely entwined remained to shape his thinking. Implicit in Liang's echoing of such Pan-Asian slogans as "liberty" and "equality" was a reinterpretation of the nature of the challenge posed by the outside world. When Liang earlier dubbed imperialism as a "barbarizing" encroachment by the West upon China, he had seen the challenge only in terms of superior wealth and power, and he had continued to treasure the values of his cultural heritage. Once he began to accept new values, however vaguely conceived and however different from their Western origins, he was acknowledging the fact that the modern West and Meiji Japan posed a total challenge to Chinese civilization, cultural as well as political and military. He was coming to a new conception of the meaning of imperialism.

Moreover, he continued to look to Meiji Japan for inspiration and guidance. Men such as Okuma, Kashiwabara, and Inugai were not overt expansionists, and they remained Liang's friends.

As late as 1910, Liang still wrote glowingly of his admiration for Okuma, and argued pointedly against those who advocated learning directly from the West rather than from Japan. "If we are sincere in our efforts and are good at learning," Liang emphasized, "then Japan is more than enough for us [to learn from]."[67] It was only with the shock of the Twenty-one Demands in 1915—issued under a government headed by Liang's long-time mentor, Okuma—that Liang ceased to look to Japan or Japanese thinkers for inspiration and guidance.[68] But the latter had long before then greatly influenced and shaped Liang's thinking. In fact, late Meiji society itself contributed to Liang's redefinition of the challenge posed by the modern West and Japan.

The Idea of a Modern Civilization

Japan in 1900 was a modern nation-state, and the first with which Liang had direct contact. He was much impressed with its educational system—universal elementary education had been introduced in 1872, and there were the great universities, including Waseda, with which Okuma and Kashiwabara were intimately associated.[69] Liang's admiration for Okuma was owing in part to the latter's role as an educator, and he wrote about Inugai's having impressed upon him the importance of a modern educational system.[70]

He also admired the freedom and independence that the Japanese press enjoyed, the more so because he himself for the first time was in an environment in which he could give free rein to his expressive pen. In the preface to his "Notes on Freedom," he gratefully pointed out that he had enjoyed the benefits of freedom of thought, of speech, and of the press.[71] In 1903, answering criticisms of corruption in the Japanese Ministry of Education's policy on textbooks, he pointed to the fact that the Japanese press was able to force the government to conduct a full inquiry into the case, an inquiry that might yet result in the resignation of the Minister of Education. This, he stressed, was clear evidence of the high level of development of "people's rights" in Japan.[72]

These aspects of Japanese society—a developed modern educational system and freedom of the press—were among the attributes of modern civilization that Liang could appreciate as positive virtues in themselves. He did not need to be persuaded of their relevance to national wealth and power. For him, they were not merely necessary means for China's survival, but desirable ends.

His attitude toward the outside world was changing. His earlier anti-Western racial feelings were replaced by a new outlook of a world community of equal nations. This is reflected in the following statement he made in 1901 on the occasion of the hundredth issue of the *Ch'ing-i pao*:

> There are journals of one individual; there are journals of one party; there are journals of one nation; and there are journals of the world. Those for which the aim is to further the interest of one individual or one company are one-man journals. Those for which the aim is the interest of one party are party journals. Those for which the aim is the interest of the citizenry are national journals. Those for which the aim is the interest of humanity are universal journals. . . . Where is the *Ch'ing-i pao* to be placed among these categories? It is between a party journal and a national journal. We hope that it will completely divorce itself from the limitations of a party journal, and will enter into the realm of a national journal, further endeavoring to become a universal journal.[73]

The internationalist sentiments expressed in this statement bear striking contrast to the Pan-Asian slogans that he wrote three years earlier in the first issue of the same journal.

The same attitude underlay his adoption of the Japanese term *bunmei* (*wen-ming*) in place of *fu-ch'iang*—wealth and power

—to express the goal of his program for change. Before 1898 he had spoken of reforms invariably in terms of their relevance to *fu-ch'iang*. His overriding concern had been to borrow Western political institutions to strengthen China.[74] But now he spoke instead of *wen-ming*, not in its classical sense of a civilized cultural condition, but in the Meiji Japanese meaning of "modernity" —it signified for him the desirable attributes of modern civilization, particularly the advancement of science, technology, material well-being, and liberal-democracy.

There were, according to Liang, three stages in the evolution of human civilization: the barbaric, the semicivilized, and the "modern" (*wen-ming*). Man in the barbaric stage led a nomadic life, had no knowledge of tools, no serious learning, feared natural calamities, and allowed himself to be subjected to the mercy and authority of others. Man in the semicivilized stage saw the flourishing of agriculture, and the establishment of states. But there was little real learning, and there was the lack of originality and creativity. The tendency was to follow the past rather than change it. In the "modern" stage, on the other hand, "Man classifies all natural phenomena and things into rules and principles. . . . He is not enmeshed in old customs; he is capable of self-rule. . . . There is only progress and no decline. . . . The development of commerce and industry are daily pursued so that all men may enjoy well-being."[75]

He now spoke of the West very differently. In the course of human history, he wrote, "the white peoples" alone "were able to spread *wen-ming*."[76] And it was England that he especially admired, because he saw that she possessed a liberal polity as well as national power. England, he pointed out, "was the first nation to have a modern polity, and her flag shines throughout the world."[77]

This was Liang's new outlook. The development of science, material well-being, liberal-democratic polities, and modern national power was the universal process of the contemporary world. It was an outlook that underlay Liang's new interpretation of the meaning of imperialism, and in turn, his new nationalism.

Meiji Japanese Social Darwinism[78]

For his new conception of imperialism, he drew inspiration from the Japanese social-Darwinist Katō Hiroyuki.

In both *Hundred Essays on the Law of Evolution*[79] and *Competition and the Rights of the Strong*[80] (the two books of Katō's that Liang read) Katō applied Darwinian categories to international relations. He began with the premise that human society obeyed the same laws of "struggle for existence" and "natural selection" as the biological world.[81] From this premise he leaped to his formula of *kyōken*, or "rights of the strong," pointedly rejecting the doctrine of "natural rights" (*tenpu jinken*), and asserted flatly that "not only in the biological world, but for human beings as well, . . . the only rights are those of the strong."[82] Applying this formula to nations, which he equated with organisms, Katō came to the following formulation of international Darwinism:

> The citizenry of superior knowledge will exterminate the citizenry of inferior knowledge; or it will conquer and enslave it, thus civilizing it gradually. The enlightened citizenry of today will definitely not grow out of useless humaneness and benevolence. Harming others, then, is a necessary condition of the biological world. It should be understood that this is nothing but the Law of Nature.[83]

Katō's ideas were very different from Herbert Spencer's. Katō was an ardent nationalist,[84] one who was very much concerned with the survival of the Japanese nation. By applying Darwinian categories to international relations, he warned of the dangers of imperialism and the necessity for Japan to be strong. At the same time, his formulation of international Darwinism made progress and modern civilization a universal property, to which Japan had as much claim as the West, so long as she could become fit. Finally, Katō's ideas also implicitly provided a rationale for Japanese imperialism. Spencer's concerns, on the other hand, lay elsewhere. For Spencer, "patriotism" belonged to societies of the "militant type," characterized by continual intertribal and international strife; it had no place in peaceful "industrial" societies.[85] And wars, though they played a contributory role in the progress of societies in the past,[86] were "positively demoralizing"[87] and "only further evils are to be looked for from the continuance of militancy in civilized nations."[88] Spencer abhorred imperialism; when he learned of the British instigation of the Boer War, he wrote, "I am ashamed of my country."[89]

Spencer's ideas on "militant" societies held more immediate relevance for Katō than his ideas on "industrial" societies and his rationalization of liberalism. Katō's formulation of imperialism as the struggle among entire citizenries evidenced the decisive influence of one notion in Spencer's discourses on societies of the "militant type": "To be in the highest degree efficient, the corporate action needed for preserving the corporate life must be joined in by everyone."[90] National power, in other words, was directly proportional to the degree of efficiency in utilizing the energies of the society. The idea was incidental to Spencer's concerns, but it became a central assumption for the nationalistic Katō.

Liang, like Katō, was intimately concerned with the question of the source of modern national power. Katō's nationalistic reinterpretations of Spencer thus held special relevance for him. He devoted one essay to each of Katō's two books discussed above and echoed Katō's ideas on the "Law of Evolution" and "rights of the strong."[91]

Katō's idea of competition among entire citizenries, especially, became the basis for Liang's new views on imperialism.

Liang first distinguished between what he called imperialism of "despotic states" and imperialism of "citizenries." The former reflected the ambitions of one man—it was the "oppression of the people by the monarch for the purpose of contending with other states." The latter type, on the other hand, "represented the struggle against another country by the individuals of one nation for their lives and property." It was much more powerful and would last much longer than the former.[92]

These ideas became fully developed in Liang's "The New Citizen." Since the sixteenth century, he wrote, the power of Europe had greatly expanded because of the growth of nationalism. "What is nationalism?" It was a situation in which "those people who share the same race, language, customs, and religion, come to look upon each other as compatriots, undertake self-government, and organize well-equipped governments for public welfare and national defense." In the last few decades, Liang continued, this nationalism had developed into "national imperialism" (*min-tsu ti-kuo-chu-i*). "National imperialism" was where "the strength of the citizens has developed so fully within that it must expand outwards." Its methods included the use of military power, commerce, industry, or churches.[93]

In this new Darwinian view, imperialism was seen as the necessary outcome of historical evolution. It represented the high point of the growth and expansion of European civilization, and was the agent for the spread of modern civilization. Liang's version of "national imperialism" was intended to convey the understanding he had acquired from Katō—the source of the immense power of European nation-states lay in the energies of Western societies.

If nationalism was the necessary precondition for the power of the modern nation-states, it obviously must be developed among the Chinese people in order for China to survive and maintain her sovereignty. The Chinese people, Liang wrote, had long known only of "the world under heaven" (*t'ien-hsia*)

THE NEW CITIZEN AND MEIJI JAPAN

but not of the nation (*kuo-chia*). They had known only their own
interests but not those of the nation. Today they must understand that one man alone was powerless; it was necessary to be
a member of the nation. They must know that their nation was
one among a community of contending nations and must give
their loyalty to their own nation.[94]

Katō's international Darwinism, then, became the basis for
Liang's new nationalism. In echoing Katō's ruthless language,
Liang intended to stress the dangers of imperialism and to
sound the call for an energetic and nationalistic Chinese nation,
so that she might survive in a world of rampant imperialism and
join in the universal march toward "modernity."

But there was a significant difference in emphasis between
Liang's ideas and Katō's. Katō's formulation of international
Darwinism had a twofold implication: it stressed the urgency of
Japan's national survival, but it could also be used as a rationale
for expansionistic Japanese nationalism. The realities of Liang's
world were different. There was nothing that could justify the
conception of China as a "modern" nation with a civilizing
mission in Asia. Liang's emphasis, in other words, was exclu-
sively defensive.

Having concluded that China must develop nationalism, the
next question for Liang was: how was this nationalism to be
fostered? Liang's answer was the establishment of constitutional
and representative government. He reasoned that popular
participation in the conduct of government would foster among
the people a sense of common identity with the nation.[95] He had
now fully rationalized his pre-1898 association of liberal- democracy with "wealth and power"—liberal-democracy would contribute to the growth of national power by fostering nationalism.

Liang did not stop here. Earlier he had pinned his hopes on
the adoption of such a government from above. The failure of
the reform movement of 1898 taught him to place his faith elsewhere, and his more sophisticated knowledge of the functioning

of liberal-democratic government made him more aware of some of the basic prerequisites for representative government.

Again, he called on Katō's doctrine of the "rights of the strong," which seemed to him especially pertinent. Before 1898, he had repeatedly used the Mencian ideal of "primacy of the people" to argue for democratic institutional reform as he had understood Western liberal-democratic thought largely in terms of the ideas of the Mencius.[96] Now he asked: what is the essential difference between the Mencian ideal and Western liberal-democracy?

> Someone asks: "Mencius is said to be the founding father of Chinese democracy. May I venture to ask whether the democracy of which Mencius spoke is the same as the democracy of which Western thinkers speak today?"
> I answer, "It is different! It is different! The democracy of which Mencius spoke concerned protecting the people and caring for the people. . . . Protecting the people is to treat them as infants. Caring for the people is the same as tyranny in that it invades the people's right to liberty. The people prize their independence; they treasure their rights. They are not to be interfered with."[97]

In other words, in the former ideal, the ruler took the initiative; the people had to wait for the benevolence of the ruler. In modern liberal-democracy, on the other hand, initiative for the establishment of liberal-democratic institutions and the guarantee of individual liberty came from the members of society. Therefore, the Chinese people must take it upon themselves to assert their rights. Thus, Liang echoed Katō's assertions that "the great Law of Evolution" dictated that the only rights were those of the strong.[98] His intention was to emphasize the need for the individual Chinese to assert his rights: "Rights can only be secured by each citizen's struggling for them, without giving way a single inch";[99] or, "He who wants to have the right of liberty must first seek to be strong."[100]

The difference between Liang's interpretation of social Darwinism and Spencer's thought is readily apparent. Spencer's emphasis was essentially deterministic—he saw himself as an objective scientist engaged in the explication of the necessary workings of an impersonal law; Liang, on the other hand, intended to stress the possibilities for man's control of his and his nation's destiny—his was a call to revolutionary action.

But Katō's idea of *kyōken* could serve quite a different purpose. The doctrine that only the "strong" were entitled to "rights" could argue for denial of "rights" to the "weak" no less logically than for the necessity of the "weak" to become "strong." Thus Katō used the doctrine of evolution to argue against "natural rights," and in 1874, and again in 1882 and after, to argue against the calls for liberal reforms that he deemed premature.[101] Liang himself would change after 1903 to a more cautious and gradualist emphasis[102] similar to Katō's, and would call upon Katō's translation of Johann Kaspar Bluntschli's (1808–81) *Allgemeines Staatsrecht*[103] to buttress his arguments.

The important point here is that in spite of the apparent differences from Katō in the immediate use to which Liang put the idea of *kyōken*, he drew two important ideas from Katō. First was Katō's formulation of international Darwinism and of imperialism as the expansion of entire citizenries. From this formulation Liang learned the important idea that modern national power stemmed from the energies of Western individuals and societies. Another was Katō's idea that representative government must be predicated upon certain definite qualifications of the people. This led Liang again to emphasize energetic assertion on the part of the people. And Liang called further upon Fukuzawa Yukichi (1835–1901) and Nakamura Masanao (1832–91), two of Meiji Japan's leading interpreters of English liberalism, to elaborate upon the necessary qualifications for a "new citizen."

Morals and National Power

Fukuzawa's abiding concern, as he put it himself in 1898, was to "elevate the moral standards of men and women of my land to make them truly worthy of a civilized nation." His moral program centered around the catch phrase "independence and self-respect" (*dokuritsu jison*) because "the independence of a nation springs from the independent spirit of the people. Our nation cannot hold its own if the old slavish spirit is so manifest among the people. . . ."[104]

Fukuzawa's idea that in order for Japan to acquire national dignity the Japanese people must adopt a new set of morals patterned after that of England was even more explicit in Nakamura. Nakamura translated Samuel Smiles' *Self-Help* (1859), a book that had most successfully propagandized Victorian morality. Smiles' book is something of a classic statement of the Victorian "gospel of work," abounding in exhortations to work, application, diligence, patience, perseverance, elevation of character, and so on. For Smiles, the book's purpose was to argue that "the spirit of self-help is the root of all genuine growth in the individual." As a subsidiary argument, he asserted that when this spirit of self-help is "exhibited in the lives of many, it constitutes the true source of national vigour and strength."[105] But in Nakamura's hands, the secondary argument became the most important one, for Nakamura was interested above all in finding the secret to England's striking national power. His translation bore the title *The Success of the Western Nations*; he emphasized in the preface to the book that the power of Western nations stemmed not from their armies, but "from their people's sincere belief in Providence, from their possession of the right of self-determination, and from the justice of their government and laws."[106] Nakamura's central emphasis was that the secret to

Western power lay above all in Western morality, and he meant to inculcate a new morality in his people.

This was the message that especially impressed Liang. Liang's predilection, and it was a Confucian one, was to view morals as the root of all things—where the root was sound, all else would be well. He harped on the theme that "modernity" had both "form" (*hsing-chih*) and "spirit" *(ching-shen)*. The "form" consisted of such things as political institutions, laws, and tools. The "spirit" on the other hand, had to do with the "spontaneous attitudes" (*yüan-ch'i*) of the people. The "spirit" was the more difficult to acquire, and, once acquired, the "form" would naturally follow. "True modernity," Liang concluded, was "nothing but its spirit."[107]

Thus he echoed repeatedly the ideas of Nakamura and Fukuzawa. He devoted one essay each to "independence"[108] and "self-respect."[109] He asked for spiritual originality and independence—"I have my own body and sense organs; I have my own mind. If I do not use them and just rely on the ancients . . . then I am but a mechanical and soulless wooden figure."[110] He also devoted one essay to "self-help" and credited Nakamura with having "stirred up the spirit of the people, making each Japanese youth possessor of the spirit of independence and self-respect."[111]

In short, the lessons Liang drew from Katō, Fukuzawa, and Nakamura led to the same conclusion—China must develop a new kind of individual Chinese in order to modernize. From Katō Liang learned that the immense power of modern nation-states stemmed from uniting the state with society. Liang concluded that this union could only be effected through the development of nationalism and representative institutions. But representative institutions, Liang learned from Katō, were predicated upon the existence of a politically conscious and active body of citizens. Liang further learned from Fukuzawa and Nakamura that the secret to Western power and progress lay in the distinctive character of its individuals. Liang therefore called for a new kind of Chinese citizen, one active, independent, and nationalistic.

Liang's fusing of ideas drawn from thinkers as widely different as Katō was from Fukuzawa and Nakamura becomes readily understandable in the perspective of the basic concern with developing a new kind of citizen. Katō, Nakamura, and Fukuzawa shared a common point of departure—the Meirokusha, of which they had all been members. This society, formed in 1873, had been dedicated to drastically reforming the character of the Japanese people. The shared assumption of all members of the society was that radical reform of the morals and "spirit" of the Japanese people was the first essential task for Japan's modernization.[112] Liang's Confucian predilection to view the morality, values, and attitudes of men as more important than all else rendered him readily receptive to such an idea.

Liang also had other reasons for choosing Nakamura and Fukuzawa as his mentors. England was Liang's ideal. In looking to Meiji Japan, Liang sought not so much to define his aims as to define the methods for achieving those aims. Fukuzawa and Nakamura, as two of Meiji Japan's leading interpreters of English liberalism, supplied the needed answer.

These diverse strands of ideas would be drawn together in 1902 and 1903 in "The New Citizen," a crystallized statement of Liang's program for China's modernization.[113]

"The New Citizen"

Liang's term for the "new citizen," *hsin-min*, was taken from the classic *Great Learning* but with a significant modification in usage. The *Great Learning* begins with the passage: "The way of the Great Learning consists in clearly exemplifying illustrious virtue, in loving the people (*ch'in-min*) [also read *hsin-min*, or renovating the people] and in resting in the highest good."[114] Elsewhere it is written: "If you can one day renovate yourself, do so from day to day."[115] Or, "In the announcement to K'ang, it is said, 'to stir up the new people' " (tso hsin-min).[116] Clearly, the message was intended principally for the ruler and his officials. But the *Great Learning* can also be interpreted as being intended for all men, especially if read in the context of the passage in the *Mencius* that "Every man can become a Yao or a Shun."[117] Indeed, the *Great Learning* contains the passage "From the emperor down to the people, all, without exception, must consider cultivation of individual character as the root."[118] Liang's usage of the term hsin-min was unequivocally in the latter interpretation. He wrote, "By hsin-min, I do not mean to suggest a distinction between a new person and the one who makes him new. Instead, I mean for each of our people to renovate himself."[119] His intention was to advance a new set of morals for the "new citizen" of a modern China. As he put it: "He who cleanses himself of the contaminating filth of the past is said to be renovating himself (tzu-hsin). Those who can rid themselves of the contaminating society of the past are called new citizens" (hsin-min).[120]

Liang then proceeded to exhort all Chinese to adopt a new system of values. His two themes were the "spirit" of "liberty" and nationalism. Each individual must trust in his own thoughts and not depend on the authority of the sages of the past; he must not be "the slave of custom," the "slave of his environment," or the "slave of his passions and desires."[121] Another aspect of this independent "spirit" was the "consciousness of rights." The "new citizen" must not wait to have his rights bestowed upon him by a benevolent ruler; he must actively seek their guarantee in law for himself.[122] The "spirit" of "liberty" included also an awareness of the importance of national sovereignty.[123] Every Chinese must understand that his nation's interests were also his own and offer his loyalty to the nation.[124]

In addition to "liberty" and nationalism, Liang advanced a host of other new values. The individual must cultivate physical, moral, and intellectual courage. He should possess a "spirit of adventure and the desire for improvement" (*chin-ch'ü mao-hsien*). This brought into play such traits as hope, earnestness, knowledge, physical, and moral courage.[125] The individual who possessed these virtues and persevered would succeed.[126]

The new Chinese citizen must also possess the civic virtues of the citizens of modern nations. He must have a sense of responsibility (*i-wu ssu-hsiang*), realizing that duty was the converse side of rights. He should be prepared to fulfill such responsibilities to his community as paying taxes and performing military service.[127] Liang also stressed "self-respect" (*tzu-tsun*), by which he meant respect for law, for one's fellow man, as well as self-reliance, pursuit of worthy aims, and a sense of responsibility toward one's community,[128] and he asked the new citizen to be economically productive, not a parasite depending upon others for his livelihood.[129] This same individual must cultivate self-discipline (*tzu-chih*)—a capacity for self-government as well as of control of his passions and desires so as to lead an orderly and constructive life.[130] He must cultivate a capacity for acting as a member of the community by developing his national consciousness and his regard for public welfare (*ho-ch'ün* and *kung-te*).[131]

The keynote of the essay was the call for active assertion. All of Liang's exhortations were placed in the framework of his adopted social-Darwinian categories. The Anglo-Saxons had proved to be the "fittest" in the world of "struggle for existence." For the Chinese nation to survive in the Darwinian international world, the Chinese people must become more fit and more like the Anglo-Saxons. They must turn from passive subjects of despotic rule into active citizens of a new nation.[132]

The central idea was that more than new armies, technology, industries, institutions, or laws, China needed a new kind of Chinese, with a new set of values. This idea was in turn founded upon a number of assumptions—the challenge of the West was no longer understood as merely a challenge of superior wealth and military power, but a total challenge, both root and branch. Imperialism was now understood not simply as hateful encroachment upon China but also as an agent for the spread of modern civilization, of universal progress toward modernity. And China's modernization was understood as not only necessary, but desirable. All of these ideas were new in the early years of the twentieth century; they would be commonplace by the time of the May Fourth intellectual revolution.

CHAPTER 4

Liberalism and Nationalism
in Liang Ch'i-ch'ao's Thought

Liang was also profoundly influenced by eighteenth and nineteenth-century English liberal thinkers. His writings, especially those between 1898 and 1903, abounded in references to Jeremy Bentham (1748–1832), John Stuart Mill (1806–73), Herbert Spencer (1820–1903), and to the favorite phrases of these men—"the greatest happiness of the greatest number," "liberty of thought and discussion," "struggle for existence," and "survival of the fittest."

But to call Liang a liberal—in the classical, not in the contemporary sense—is to suggest both too much and too little. "Classical liberalism" calls to mind at once the notion of "the state as passive policeman," the economic idea of laissez faire, and England of the late seventeenth, eighteenth, and the first half of the nineteenth centuries. As a cluster of ideas that obtained in a particular historical setting, "classical liberalism" could not but undergo substantive change when it crossed the boundaries of time and culture. In China, even more so than in continental Europe, classical liberal ideas were subjected to reinterpretations. Liang's "liberal" ideas were in fact a conglomeration of Confucian precepts and Western liberal ideas, welded together by the proclivities of Liang's mind and by the realities of Liang's world.

In analyzing Liang's "liberal" ideas, one of the first difficulties is that of language. Many of the categories used by Liang's liberal mentors were entirely new to him; he had to create a new vocabulary to convey these ideas. "Liberty" is one example—Liang's term *tzu-yu* was intended as an equivalent translation, but this equivalence cannot be taken for granted. To begin with, the root meaning of the Chinese *tzu-yu* is fundamentally different from that of "liberty." *Tzu-yu* in classical Chinese conveyed only the idea "to act as one wishes."[1] The English word "liberty," of course, has one meaning similar to this concept, but its basic meaning has to do with freedom from bondage or from arbitrary and despotic rule or control,[2] quite a different concept from the classical Chinese term. This one fact alone suggests that the historian of modern Chinese thought must be constantly on the lookout for interpretations introduced in the mere act of translation. In Liang's case, the first question must be: what exactly did he mean by *tzu-yu?*

Liang at first glibly entitled his random study notes "Notes on Freedom." These notes covered a wide variety of subjects, ranging from short essays on Gladstone, Bismarck, T'an Ssu-t'ung, Katō Hiroyuki, Herbert Spencer, and others to brief discussions of "self-help," self-confidence," "education," "heroes," and so on.[3] It was only in "The New Citizen"—most of which was written in 1902[4]—that Liang attempted to give a systematic definition of his conception of "liberty."

"Liberty," according to Liang, "is a universal principle, a necessary condition of life, and is applicable everywhere." There were four kinds of "liberty": political, that having to do with the relationship between the people (*jen-min*) and the government (*cheng-fu*); religious, pertaining to the liberty of the believers vis-à-vis the church; national, or the liberty of one nation vis-à-vis other nations; and economic, or the liberty of capitalists in their relationship with laborers, and vice versa. His own concern, Liang wrote, was primarily with "political" and "national" liberty, which he soon fused into "political liberty."

There were in turn six kinds of "political liberty": the absence of class privileges; the right of the citizens to a voice in government; the right of a colony to self-government and equal status with the "mother country"; the freedom of belief; national self determination; and the freedom of laborers from exploitation. (Liang, alas, was never a very clear or precise thinker.) Four of these six were not problems in China; only two were needed—popular participation in government and national sovereignty.[5]

Liang then went on to ask for independence and active assertion from every Chinese "citizen." He criticized above all the "slavish character" of the Chinese. One must not be the slave of the ancients; he should have his own thoughts. One should not be the slave of custom, of environment, or of one's desires. And Liang made clear why he asked for assertive and intellectually free "citizens"—such persons were necessary for China's progress and for her national survival. "Liberty," in other words, was desirable not only in and of itself, but because it would contribute to national power and survival.[6]

Such a conception of "liberty" suggests at once that a wide gulf separated Liang from his liberal mentors. The differences can be illustrated by the way in which Liang paraphrased and commented upon Bentham and Mill.

He apparently read not only secondary Japanese accounts of Bentham's thought, but also Japanese translations of several of Bentham's works, including the *Introduction to the Principles of Morals and Legislation*.[7] And he was sufficiently familiar with Bentham to give a generally accurate summary of the import of Bentham's ideas. But invariably he added his own commentary, rejecting, selecting, and reinterpreting portions of Bentham for his readers.

He had little use for Bentham's dogmatic utilitarianism—that pleasure is the only good, and pain the only evil; and the judgment of good and evil is exactly equivalent to the judgment of whether an action increases or diminishes the sum of human pains or pleasures. He rejected the doctrine as "unsuitable for use in China today."[8]

He praised, however, the Benthamite formula for the criterion to be used in legislation—"the greatest happiness of the greatest number." Liang put it this way: the implication of the formula was that "legislation that directly or indirectly benefits more than half the people should be adopted; that which brings harm to more than half the people should be discarded." This principle, it seemed to Liang, could not be disputed.[9]

Yet even here he had added his own interpretation. He certainly did not have in mind a "science of legislation," based on a precise calculus of pain and pleasure. Instead, Liang was simply asking that legislators be guided by considerations of "public interest," and "public interest" to Liang remained a vague notion, not a precise quantity. He likened the Benthamite formula to the Confucian idea of *jen*—humaneness.[10] What had impressed Liang about Bentham's formula was not the utilitarian "science" of morality but simply the category "the greatest majority."

The idea of the paramountcy of "the majority" was a new idea for Liang, and one to which he attached a great deal of importance. Before his exile to Japan he had repeatedly called upon Mencius to argue that the ruler and his officials were merely servants of the community, their task being to carry out the wishes of the people. But "the people" in his Mencian conception of democracy had remained an abstract category. Now he tended to substitute the more concrete idea of "the majority" for the category "the people." Even in commenting on Rousseau, he pointed out that the "General Will" must in practice be arrived at through the principle of majority rule.[11] Elsewhere he advanced the theory that history witnessed an ongoing process of the widening of the basis for political power, moving from minority rule to majority rule.[12] He suggested further that majority and minority interests were often at odds. In a utopian society, neither would have to be sacrificed for the other, but in the realities of his day, one must opt for the majority.[13]

Such a formulation suggests that Liang was more concerned with the welfare of Chinese society and of the Chinese nation than with the interests of individuals per se. The same point is evidenced in Liang's interpretations of Mill.

He first mentioned Mill in 1899 in the preface to his "Notes on Freedom":

> John Stuart Mill said, "In the progress of mankind, there is nothing more important than freedom of thought, of speech, and of the press." I have enjoyed the benefits of all three, and I thus name my book.[14]

Though Liang never devoted a separate essay to Mill, as he had to Bentham, Rousseau, and others, he made frequent references to him, and most extensively in an essay of 1902 entitled "On the Limits of Authority between the Government and the People." Here he quoted from Mill's Introduction to *On Liberty* and the essay was clearly inspired by Mill's ideas.[15]

The main concern of his essay, Liang stated, was with defining the limits of the authority of the government, and only secondarily with delineating the limits of the rights of the people.[16] Governmental authority should be limited according to the following formula: the government should undertake only those actions that individuals alone could not accomplish; and the government would interfere with the actions of individuals only where they encroached upon the rights of others.[17] This formulation, vague as it was, suggests that Liang was at this time inclined toward the classical liberal emphasis on limiting the power of the state.

But here the parallel ceased; there were fundamental differences between *On Liberty* and Liang's interpretation of it. Mill's principal concern in *Liberty* was to define a realm over which the individual would be sovereign. The Jacobin reign of terror and de Tocqueville's warnings about the dangers of democracy were real concerns to Mill. He wrote of his fear of the "tyranny of the majority," that "the inevitable growth of social equality and of the government of public opinion should impose on mankind an oppressive yoke of uniformity in opinion and practice."[18] "Liberty," to Mill, possessed a twofold justification —it contributed to the progress of society, and it provided the conditions under which an individual could develop to the utmost his individuality, which was "one of the elements of well-being."[19]

Liang did not share this concern. In the realities of his world, the oppression of "the government of public opinion" and the "tyranny of the majority" must have seemed distant problems indeed. For this reason, although he quoted from the passage on the tyranny of the majority in Mill's Introduction, he did not bother to comment on it. Elsewhere he stated that where minority and majority interests were in conflict, the majority must prevail.[20] Such an idea would have been anathema to Mill.

The basic point of divergence between Liang and *On Liberty* was that Liang could have little appreciation for "individuality" as an end in itself. To Mill the argument that liberty would best provide the conditions under which an individual could develop his individuality and attain personal happiness and well-being was one that needed no further justification; the "individual" was an absolute in itself. Liang's concerns, on the other hand, remained primarily national. The very category of "individual" was new to Liang and hardly an absolute that he could take for granted. Thus, while Mill's most frequently juxtaposed categories in *Liberty* were "individual" and "society," Liang spoke mainly of "people" and "government," even rendering "individual" and "society" as "people" and "government" when he paraphrased Mill. And he consistently placed his arguments for liberty in the context of national interest rather than individual well-being.[21]

If Liang's preoccupation was indeed principally with the Chinese nation, why then should he have been drawn to Mill? Why should he have seized upon "liberty," a Western value associated mainly with the individual, as an answer to China's ills?

To begin with, Liang's intellectual temperament was very similar to Mill's. Mill wrote of himself: "I had always a humble opinion of my own powers as an original thinker . . . , but thought myself much superior to most of my contemporaries in willingness and ability to learn from everybody."[22] Leslie Stephen commented that Mill's "real generosity of sentiment, and the obvious sincerity which comes from preaching what he practised," lent new force to his arguments for the old idea of liberty.[23] Stephen further noted Mill's "perfect intellectual honesty"[24] and stressed that Mill "was singularly candid, fair in argument, and most willing to recognize merits in others."[25] In other words, "liberty of thought and discussion" expressed for Mill not only an intellectual conviction but also, and perhaps even more deeply, the basic proclivity of his own mind.

Like Mill, Liang prided himself on his tolerance of different opinions and his willingness to alter his views. His motto was: "I care not if I challenge myself of yesterday with myself of today."[26] And he observed that the greatest contrast between himself and K'ang Yu-wei was that "K'ang was too fixed in his views while Ch'i-ch'ao was too ready to change his mind."[27]

His mind was in fact singularly free and flexible. He traveled with little intellectual baggage and no fixed itinerary, changing as the circumstances around him changed. His intellectual flexibility, in contrast to K'ang's rigidity, accounts for many of the differences between the two men. Liang had been dissatisfied with K'ang's "arbitrariness" from the very beginning of his days at K'ang's academy.[28] By 1897 he had come under the influence of Yen Fu and was ready to part company with K'ang —he rejected K'ang's efforts to "preserve the faith" (*pao-chiao*) and credited Yen with having smashed for him "the closed gourd of several thousand years."[29] Once in Japan, he openly challenged K'ang's efforts to "preserve the faith" and to make Confucianism a religion. His rationale was that preserving the faith would stifle the people's intellectual energies. And he exclaimed: "I love Confucius, but I love truth more; I love our ancients, but I love our nation more; I love my friends, but I love freedom more."[30] His subsequent writings called repeatedly for independence of mind and spirit and abounded in approbations for those who had contributed to the cause of liberalizing thought.[31]

He was like Mill in yet another respect. Mill saw himself as living in a period of transition, "when old notions and feelings have been unsettled and no new doctrines have yet succeeded to their ascendancy." This view of his contemporary intellectual world underscored for Mill the importance of freedom of thought and discussion—in order that all possible truths could have a hearing and be invigorated by the challenge of conflicting ideas.[32] Mill thought of his own role in this period of transition more as "an interpreter of original thinkers, and mediator between them and the public," than as a creator of new systems himself.[33] Liang's ideas were strikingly similar in this respect. Assessing his own role in recent Chinese intellectual history, Liang observed that his guiding principle had been that "as many doctrines of the world as possible should be brought into China freely." He himself had indeed been "too broad and had often been sloppy"—his ideas were "often hazy and general, or even simply wrong"; his methods had been "sweeping and crude." But he had "opened new ground" and might be considered one who heralded the new intellectual world.[34] Like Mill, Liang saw himself as living in a transitional period between the old intellectual world and a new one to come, and it was his faith that freedom of thought would best contribute to the shaping of the new world to come.

These similarities in temperament and conviction account for much of the appeal that Liang found in Mill. However, given Liang's preoccupation with the fate of the Chinese nation, he no doubt would not have espoused "liberty" so fervently if he had thought that "liberty" would conflict with his nationalistic aims. The question remains: why did Liang assume that representative institutions and liberty of thought and discussion were relevant to his nationalistic concerns?

His assumption that there was an identity of interest between his liberal ideals and his nationalistic concerns was founded on the social Darwinian ideas he had taken from Katō Hiroyuki. As noted earlier, the central message of Darwinian concepts for Liang was that the power of Western nations stemmed from the combined energies of Western individuals who had been motivated by competition and liberty. Applied to thought, Darwinian evolution meant the "survival of the fittest" ideas under the conditions of the free "struggle for existence."

The idea that energetic individuals would contribute to a dynamic society and that "liberty" would foster the development of such individuals was not original to Liang or to Katō. It was explicit in Mill, for example. Mill quoted from Wilhelm von Humboldt to argue that "from the union of these [freedom, and variety of situation] arise individual vigour and manifold diversity." Only a person who acted and thought independently would have an active and energetic character.[35] Nineteenth-century English liberalism was moreover closely entwined with Victorian morality and its "gospel of work."

The implications seemed clear and simple to Liang: England was strong; she had representative institutions and her writers emphasized liberty and energetic assertion. Meiji Japan had modernized successfully; she had adopted a constitution and representative institutions and some of her most prominent thinkers echoed the ideas of English liberals. The conclusion seemed obvious: "liberty" and a new morality patterned after Victorian England would foster the growth of energetic individuals, who would in turn assure the modernization and power of the Chinese nation. That was the central idea of Liang's "New Citizen."

But such a liberalism carried with it intrinsic weaknesses. What if it could be shown to Liang that representative government and the liberty of thought and discussion would not in fact contribute to national power? While "liberty" might indeed have contributed to the energy and power of England and America, there is no necessary connection between "liberty" and national power. The nineteenth century offered other models of power—Napoleonic France—and Bismarckian Germany, for example. Liang was probably correct in assuming that uniting the energies of society behind national goals was an essential ingredient of modern national power. But societal energies can be tapped in different ways, as the twentieth century has shown.

In fact, one might well argue that representative institutions and liberty of thought were utterly irrelevant to modern China's overriding concern—national sovereignty. The China of Liang's time was beset with internal strife and foreign aggression. And the "new citizen" for which Liang called remained a mirage. Under such conditions, representative government was hardly an effective means to national unity and rapid modernization. Thus, while Liang's classical liberal inclinations led him to emphasize the limitation of governmental authority, his nationalistic concerns increasingly demanded that he place first priority on a strong state. It was not long before Liang had to confront the tensions between his liberal and nationalistic sentiments.

The decisive year was 1903. Since 1898 Liang had espoused

liberal ideas with all the fervor accompanying new discoveries; by 1903, much of the novelty had worn off and Liang was better prepared to evaluate them critically. It was a year of new experiences for Liang. He traveled extensively through the United States, visiting nearly every major center of Chinese population—New York, Boston, Philadelphia, New Orleans, St. Louis, Chicago, Portland, San Francisco, Sacramento, and so on.[36] The experiences of that year drastically reshaped many of his ideas.

He was struck by the great differences between Chinese realities and the conditions he saw in the United States. Though not uncritical of what he saw—he pointed, for example, to the mistreatment of Negroes,[37] to the striking inequities in income[38] —he was on the whole impressed with the United States. The dynamism of the American economy, the striking growth of its national power, and the size and wealth of the great cities (which, by comparison, "made even Japan look poor") were among the things at which he marveled. And he could not help but make constant comparisons between the conditions in the United States and those in China. He was especially impressed with the fact that, by 1900, the United States had some 11,226 newspapers and journals commanding a total readership of about 15,000,000; even the most outstanding journals in China, he noted, could boast of a circulation of only several thousand.[39] Or again, when he visited the library of the University of Chicago, he noted that students had free access to the stacks. Told by the librarian that this policy could be followed because the university calculated that a policing system would cost more than the two-hundred-odd volumes lost each year, Liang exclaimed, "This one small thing, we Orientals cannot learn in a century!"[40]

His experiences with the American branches of the Society to Protect the Emperor only added to his disillusionment. He had gone to the United States at the invitation of the society, and one of his principal missions was fund raising. Here he encountered repeated frustrations. His reputation was enough to ensure enthusiastic receptions wherever he went, but he succeeded in getting only a modicum of financial support for his party's cause. One difficulty was that the society could boast of few concrete achievements. Another was the nature of some of the party's planned actions—K'ang was engaged at the time in a plot to assassinate the Empress Dowager with hired professionals. Such plans had to be kept secret, and secrecy was hardly the best way to make people open up their wallets. Even the small amounts Liang succeeded in raising did not always end up under his or K'ang's control; there was much organizational confusion within the party structure. Finally, Liang himself was constantly subjected to slanderous criticism from those not sympathetic to the party. The grit of political action soon proved to be too much for Liang, who had spent most of his life in his study. By the end of his trip, he was complaining to K'ang of the futility of his efforts—he wished he could work and die simply for a worthy and unambiguous cause.[41]

The conditions he observed among the American Chinese communities only convinced him further that his ideals were far removed from realities. San Francisco's Chinatown greatly distressed him. He pointed out that this community of twenty to thirty thousand actually had six newspapers and journals, and was indeed a far more literate community than any in inland China. Yet it was swamped with corruption, infighting, inefficiency, and poverty. These and other observations led him to conclude that the Chinese were qualified only to be members of family clans—they had neither national consciousness nor dignity of purpose; they were "noisy, inefficient, dirty, and lazy." The Chinese people "were simply not ready for democracy."[42]

Such observations placed him in direct opposition to the program of the revolutionaries. Sun Yat-sen and his followers

were carrying many of Liang's earlier ideas to their extreme
conclusions: increasingly the revolutionary program focused
upon republicanism as the panacea to China's ills—if only the
Manchu government could be overturned, republican democracy would follow and all would be well. Liang was by now too
sophisticated about liberal-democracy to accept such a program.

Whereas Sun tended to emphasize the form of institutions,
Liang had from the start stressed the necessary foundations of
democratic institutions. That was the main thrust of his "The
New Citizen"—a politically conscious and active citizenry was
the principal prerequisite for liberal-democracy. Precisely because he had placed his emphasis on the foundations rather
than the form of institutions, he realized more quickly than Sun
that democracy would be premature in China. By the end of
his trip to the United States he had become completely convinced that the new citizenry he envisaged was at best a distant
possibility; "liberty" could not be implemented overnight by
revolution.

Upon his return from the United States, his writings changed
abruptly in tone and emphasis. The last three chapters of "The
New Citizen" were written after his return.[43] In sharp contrast
to the earlier chapters, they focused on what was rather than
what ought to be. Liang reminded himself that his writings
could only reach "the smallest number of a minority of the
Chinese people."[44] The conditions among the overseas Chinese
only demonstrated further that the Chinese people simply did
not yet possess the necessary qualifications for modern citizens.[45]
And Liang repeatedly cautioned against rash action, argued
against the "destruction" that he had advocated earlier, and
called for gradualism.[46]

His authorities before 1903 had been such liberal thinkers as
Mill and Fukuzawa; he now needed a new authority to buttress
his new intellectual position. The one he called upon was

Johann Kaspar Bluntschli. Bluntschli, a Swiss jurist, politician, and political thinker, is a relatively minor figure in European history, but in Japan he was given national eminence by Katō Hiroyuki, who published a translation of his *Allgemeines Staatsrecht* (Public Law) in 1872.[47]

Bluntschli's ideas served the purpose of rationalizing Liang's post-1903 tendency to place first priority on a strong state. Liang echoed Bluntschli's theory of the State as an organic entity possessing a will, personality, development, and growth of its own—"a moral and spiritual organism, a great body which is capable of taking up into itself the feelings and thoughts of the nation, of uttering them in laws, and realising them in acts."[48]

Liang's arguments were now very different from those he had used earlier. According to him, he had used Rousseau's ideas— to which he had given a liberal-oriented interpretation—in the hope that they would serve as a bridge to a liberal-democratic and powerful China, but he had not achieved even a tiny portion of his aims. Worse, anarchistic tendencies had become rampant.[49] He was now ready to discard Rousseau. If Rousseau, he continued, had been the mother of nineteenth-century thought, Bluntschli was the mother of twentieth-century thought. Imperialism and international struggle had placed new demands upon nations—each nation must be united under a strong central government in order to survive in the international arena.[50] China's most urgent need was for organic unity and strong discipline; freedom and equality were at the moment of only secondary importance. He himself had earlier gone too far in his advocacy of liberty[51]—liberal-democracy could only function in matured nations, and the Chinese people did not yet possess the necessary qualifications to be citizens of a modern nation.[52]

He defined this proposition systematically two years later in a lengthy essay entitled "Enlightened Despotism."[53] Liang's starting premise was international Darwinism. Nations were organic units: those that were united and fit would survive; those torn by internal strife were unfit and would be destroyed.[54] Liang went on to assert that "what is fit, is good, even if it is bad; what is not fit is bad, even if it is good."[55] The primary criterion for judging the quality of a political system, then, was whether it promoted "fitness" for survival in the international arena. And Liang defined the term "enlightened" or *k'ai-ming* accordingly: "even if a governmental system nearly robs the people of the bulk or all of their liberty, it is a good system provided that it is founded on the spirit of meeting the exigencies of national defense."[56]

Liang's "enlightened despot" would be one who ruled in the interest of national survival and domestic tranquility. He would impose whatever laws and discipline necessary for these purposes and would be a desirable ruler so long as he followed the dictates of such considerations. Liang's chosen models of "enlightened despots" were Frederick II and Napoleon I.[57]

His liberal commitments had been pushed further into the future. "Enlightened despotism," he asserted, would be the transitional and preparatory phase to constitutional government. Under "enlightened despotism," a consultative assembly should be established to prepare for full-fledged representative government.[58]

Such ideas were indeed a far cry from Liang's pre-1903 emphasis on limiting governmental authority and on individual liberty. The change in emphasis had come as a result of his increasing realization that a hiatus separated Chinese realities from his liberal ideals, and that under such conditions "liberty" held little relevance for the goal of national power.

His new emphasis on a strong state under an all-powerful ruler underscores the basic concern of his earlier liberal sympathies. In a China that had suffered repeated humiliations and encroachments from the imperialist powers, he could not

help but be concerned first and foremost with the sovereignty
and survival of the Chinese nation. He could espouse his liberal
ideals only so long as he believed them to be in the interest of
national survival. Once he realized that China was ill prepared
for "liberty," he had to choose between his liberal ideals and
his nationalistic concerns. He opted for the latter—his liberal
goals were pushed into the distant future, and nationalistic considerations had come to dominate the foreground of his thinking.

CHAPTER 5

Reformer or Revolutionary?

Closely related to the conflicting tug within Liang between his liberal aspirations and his nationalistic sentiments was the indecision over whether to follow the route of revolution or of reform. He tried for a time to maintain the fiction that there was an identity of interest between revolution and reform and when he chose revolution over reform, as he did until 1903, he was never unequivocally committed to the revolutionary cause. After 1903, he inclined toward reform rather than revolution and at the same time his nationalistic concerns came to overshadow his liberal aspirations.

The battle within Liang between revolution and reform is well illustrated by "Hsin Chung-kuo wei-lai chi" (The Future of the New China),[1] his one attempt at writing a political novel. This short novel was written in colloquial style and was published in 1902 in his new journal, *Hsin hsiao-shuo* (The New Fiction).[2] The novel was intended to convey Liang's political views[3] and to pave the way toward a new literature that would help create a "new Chinese people."[4]

The story itself is at once fictionalized history and political discourse. It opens with the fiftieth anniversary of the Chinese "restoration" (*wei-hsin*), sixty years from the time of writing. China has been a republic for fifty years, beginning with the first president, one Lo Tsai-t'ien, the namesake of the Kuang-

84

hsü Emperor. On the occasion of this fiftieth anniversary, a certain Professor K'ung Hung-tao, a descendant of Confucius and one who had been active in the restoration movement, is lecturing on Chinese history of the previous sixty years. Professor K'ung begins his story with the founding of the "Alliance for Constitutional Government," which united the three principal forces for change in the nation: the revolutionary party, the Society to Protect the Emperor, and the secret societies. The alliance was not troubled by factional differences over the form of government; they had a common concern for the welfare of the nation and the people.

The alliance was founded by one Huang K'e-ch'iang, whose name suggests that he was a Han Chinese rather than a Manchu.[5] He later became the second president of the republic. He had been schooled in history and in the Lu-Wang school of Neo-Confucianism. Together with a disciple of his father's, Li Ch'ü-ping, Huang had then studied abroad, first at Oxford, and later at Berlin University, while Li went on to the University of Paris.[6]

The body of the story is set at Shanhaikwan, the gateway between Manchuria and North China. Huang and Li have just returned to China via St. Petersburg. Much aggrieved by the strength of Cossack influence beyond the Wall, they engage in a lengthy dialogue over the pros and cons of violent revolution.

The tone of the discussion is set by Li's opening remark: "Look at present-day China—can it be considered a Chinese China? Where among the eighteen provinces is there a place that is not within the sphere of influence of a foreign country?"

The dispute does not concern the objective of national sovereignty, which the two men share, but with how that sovereignty is to be attained. Li, the younger and more hot-headed of the two, argues: those in power today are responsible for the current state of affairs—they have been monstrous exploiters of the people but have been obsequious slaves of the foreigners. These Manchu rulers must go. The imperial order must be replaced by democratic government. This is the age of nationalism and democracy. To this, the more mature and cautious Huang replies: the Manchus have been assimilated; there is no need for a racial revolution. Huang is, moreover, skeptical of democracy: even in so-called democratic societies, power in fact remains in the hands of a few. Furthermore, the Chinese people are simply not ready for self-rule. Like children, they still require parental discipline and education. Revolution can only produce widespread destruction, and end in a return to despotic rule.

Huang's method would be different from Li's rash plan. He would put his trust in education, book writing, journalism, speechmaking, commerce, and industries, and on persuasion of those in power. China would first have to have a "sage ruler" assisted by a group of outstanding ministers. These men would expand the power of government even beyond that under the old imperial governments. They would speed China along the path of modernization and national power. Local assemblies would be developed under such a government and, "in a decade or two," the people would be enlightened and the nation sufficiently strong to institute rule by the majority. To all this Li rejoins: how can those in power be relied upon? True, the emperor is an enlightened and benevolent man, but he holds no power. To attempt to use persuasion on the existing bureaucracy would be like "asking the tiger for its skin!"[7]

At this point, the two men pour themselves another glass of whiskey with a touch of water, and after a little rest Huang begins: he objects to revolution because of his fear of foreign intervention. Violent revolution will create widespread disorder. Their commercial interests threatened, the powers will intervene. China will then really be carved up. Li objects once more: China already has but a semblance of sovereignty. Avoiding revolution will not keep China intact. On the other hand, if the patriotic and revolutionary spirit of the people can be awakened, China would be strong enough to withstand foreign aggression. Huang points out that all this is unrealistic, that revolution will bring not only external interference, but internal division—just look at the dissensions among the patriots today. The Chinese people are in fact not ready for revolution. Were they ready for the kind of vision Li held, then a revolution would not be necessary. Li now concedes that the Chinese people are indeed not ready for a republican revolution.

But, he points out, they are not any better prepared for the constitutional monarchy that Huang advocates. In any event, even if revolution is not possible, its advocacy will at least help equalize the power of radicalism with that of conservatism and make possible a compromise in constitutional monarchy. Li himself has not the qualifications to be a statesman such as Camillo di Cavour; he will settle for the role of Joseph Mazzini.

It is Huang who supplies the concluding remarks: "We must today try to unite the patriots of the nation and prepare and train the people. When the time comes to act, we can only adapt ourselves to the circumstances and act accordingly. But we will not easily resort to the path of destruction unless we absolutely have no other choice." With this Li agrees.[8]

From Shanhaikwan, the two men travel on to Port Arthur and Dairen. Here their nationalistic passions are stirred once more, as they encounter an old shopkeeper from their home province, Kwangtung, who tells them about Chinese sufferings at the hands of, alas, the Cossacks again. Asked by the young men why he does not leave and go back to his home province, the old man answers: "Do you think the Chinese bureaucracy's treatment of the people is any better? I am afraid that sometimes it is even much worse. What's more, conditions at court being what they are, our eighteen provinces will sooner or later be carved up by the foreigners. At that time, won't other places be just like this?"

In the evening, Huang and Li meet a young patriot from Chekiang, by the name of Ch'en Meng. Ch'en, it turns out, has been preparing himself for the future by studying Russian and learning about the territories leased to Russia. The three men go into a discussion of Russia's imperialistic designs on China, but conclude that Russia, governed by autocracy, is less of a threat than England, America, Germany, and Japan, where expansion is propelled by the sentiments and power of the people.

Liang never finished the novel. It ends with Huang and Li taking note of a patriotic poem, which had been written by a girl to rhyme with one they themselves had written on the wall of the inn earlier.[9]

This disjointed story tells more about Liang himself than about China's future. There is much wish fulfillment in the story: the successful union of all the forces for change in the Alliance for Constitutional Government, the peaceful transition to a republic, and China's rise to an exalted position in the international community by the time of Professor K'ung's lecture. More importantly, however, it tells about Liang's divided loyalties toward revolution and reform, separately represented by Li Ch'ü-ping and Huang K'e-ch'iang.

Li and Huang share some basic tenets: they are united in their nationalistic preoccupation with China's sovereignty; they share the aspiration for a strong and democratic China; they both take for granted that an active and nationalistic citizenry would be the fundamental prerequisite for a strong and democratic China.

Their differences are over means and over the conceptions each holds of the role he himself would play. Li, the more hotheaded of the two, would awaken the people's patriotic and revolutionary sentiments. The awakened Chinese people would together overthrow the men in power, establish democratic government, and all would be well. Li, then, would be the revolutionary publicist and a revolutionary of the people.

Huang, on the other hand, anticipates the necessity for a transitional phase, during which there would be a strong ruler assisted by capable ministers. Huang would expect himself to fill the role of one of the ministers, if not the chief minister. At the same time, Huang is hopeful that the divergent forces for change can be unified into a single political party, with himself at the helm. He could then assure a peaceful transition through constitutional monarchy to republic, and even become the president of the republic. Huang, in other words, would fill the role of a leading party politician or a statesman.

Liang compared Li to a Mazzini and Huang to Cavour. Elsewhere he depicted Mazzini as a man of the purest and loftiest of ideals. He awakened the Italian people with his writings and hence laid the foundation for a unified, new Italy.[10] Cavour, on the other hand, Liang compared to Chu-ke Liang: a man who systematically prepared himself for the tasks of a statesman. Cavour was finally able to do for Italy what Bismarck did for Prussia—"he unfettered the Italians and gave them freedom; he smoothed their path for them and educated them."[11] Liang urged his readers to adopt Mazzini or Cavour as their models.[12]

There can be little doubt that these contrasting self-concepts were constantly at war within Liang himself. Was he to aspire to be a Mazzini-Li Ch'ü-ping or a Cavour-Chu-ke Liang? Was he to favor revolution or reform? Was he to devote his energies to revolutionary writings to awaken the people or was he to prepare himself for the role of a statesman? Was he a young revolutionary hothead or a shrewd party politician who would unify divergent political forces? Could he, perhaps, be all these things at the same time?

His self-image, until 1903, was primarily that of a Li Ch'ü-ping, although he attempted also to play the role of the shrewd party politician who would unify the divergent forces for change, after the fashion of the Huang K'e-ch'iang of his novel.

He devoted most of his energies to publicizing revolutionary ideas. Almost immediately after he arrived in Japan, he established the journal *Upright Discussions* (*Ch'ing-i pao*). This journal appeared three times a week and Liang served as both editor and chief contributor—nearly every issue carried one or more contributions from him.[13] The *Upright Discussions* was succeeded after its hundredth issue by the *Journal of the New Citizen* (*Hsin-min ts'ung-pao*), which first appeared in February, 1902.[14] In all, Liang's published writings between the end of 1898 and the end of 1902 total about eight volumes, or an average of more than six thousand words each week.[15]

The revolutionary sentiments and ideas Liang expressed in these writings date back to 1897 when he joined the Academy of Current Affairs in Hunan. There, in the company of other like-minded young men, he had called for "political authority of the people" (*min-ch'üan*) and had sought to incite anti-Manchu feelings, by distributing, for example, the *Ten Days' Sacking of Yang Chou*—a record of Manchu brutalities in that city in 1645.[16] Once in Japan, he sought to instill in his readers the new, revolutionary ideas of nationalism, liberty, and "the new citizen." He continually leveled scathing criticisms against the existing government and called for "destruction."

He attempted also to build a personal following for the purpose of revolution. Among his colleagues at the Academy of Current Affairs in Hunan were two other men who had studied with him at K'ang's school, the Wan-mu ts'ao-tang—Han Wen-chü and Ou Chü-chia, both of whom were inclined toward revolution. There was also T'ang Ts'ai-ch'ang, who would become the central figure in Liang's plot for an armed uprising in 1900. Together Liang, Han, Ou, and T'ang constituted the core group of the more radically inclined among K'ang's followers.[17]

They regrouped in Japan after the conservative coup and Liang's exile. They were at first constrained by K'ang's presence in Japan, but K'ang was forced to leave Japan in March, 1899, as a result of diplomatic pressures exerted by the Ch'ing court.[18] Almost immediately after his departure, Liang and his followers gathered in open defiance of K'ang. In July, Han, Ou, and another one of their fellow students from the Wan-mu ts'ao-t'ang, Lo Jun-nan, met at the resort town of Enoshima with eight others: Li Ching-t'ung and Ch'en Kuo-yung, who were on the staff of Liang's journal, the *Upright Discussions*; Mai Chung-hua, the brother of Mai Meng-hua, who had worked closely with Liang on the *Current Affairs (Shih-wu pao)*; Chang Hsüeh-ching, who, according to Feng Tzu-yu, was known for his contacts with secret societies; Liang Ch'i-t'ien, a cousin of Liang's; and Liang Ping-kuang, T'an Hsi-yung, and Huang Wei-chih, all new recruits to the cause from among the overseas Chinese in Japan. The twelve men pledged themselves as sworn brothers.[19] Though the precise purpose of the meeting is not known, some indication of the tenor of the group is given by Feng Tzu-yu's account of a letter that was sent to K'ang around this time by Liang and twelve others, substantially the same as the Enoshima group, but including T'ang Ts'ai-ch'ang, who had now joined up with the group in Japan. They urged K'ang to retire.[20]

Another important component of Liang's personal following was the group of his former students at the academy in Hunan. Eleven of them—Li Ch'ün, Chou Hung-yeh, T'ien Pang-hsüan, Li Ping-huan, Ts'ai O, Ch'in Li-shan, Ts'ai Chung-hao, and Lin Kuei rejoined Liang in Tokyo, enrolling in the upper level Ta-t'ung School that Liang established that fall.[21]

This was the following with which Liang tried to effect an alliance with Sun Yat-sen. The story of Liang's contacts with Sun is by now well known;[22] here it suffices to say that Liang first met Sun in the early spring of 1899. Subsequently, and especially after K'ang had been forced to leave Japan—K'ang had refused to have anything to do with Sun—Liang maintained close contacts with Sun. The two are said to have joined in publishing two issues of a journal entitled *Secret History of China (Chung-kuo mi-shih)*, and to have begun to develop plans for a merger of the two groups, a merger in which Liang was to be second in command to Sun. According to Feng Tzu-yu, Han Wen-chü, Ou Chü-chia, Chang Hsüeh-ching, and Liang Ping-kuang were those among Liang's followers who most actively sought this alliance.[23]

The plans of Liang's group to break out of the confines of K'ang's leadership and to join with Sun were dealt a severe blow toward the end of 1899. K'ang apparently still held considerable sway over his erstwhile disciple—alarmed by reports of Liang's activities, he ordered and was able to force Liang to leave immediately for Hawaii on the business of their organization, the Society to Protect the Emperor (Pao-huang Hui).[24]

Liang's tenuous alliance with Sun was quickly broken, as distance brought to the surface fundamental differences between the two men. For Liang, the programmatic differences between Sun and K'ang—between overthrowing the dynasty to establish a republic and "restoring" the Kuang-hsü Emperor to establish constitutional government—were differences over means, not ends. They were similar to the differences between the Li Ch'ü-ping and Huang K'e-ch'iang of his novel. Ideologically Liang held consistently to the position that the foundations of democratic institutions—an active and nationalistic citizenry—were of primary importance. The form of government, whether republic or constitutional monarchy, was a matter of expediency, not of principle. A Li Ch'ü-ping and a Huang K'e-ch'iang shared common aims and should have no difficulty working together. Liang himself wavered easily between the two. Thus, he appealed on the one hand to Sun to adopt the banner of "restoration" in the coming uprising. Since in 1900 there was considerable public outcry against an attempt by the Empress Tz'u-hsi to depose the Kuang-hsü Emperor,[25] Liang argued that "restoration" would be the more expedient slogan.[26] On the other hand, he urged K'ang to avail himself of the talent of all factions and groups.[27]

He himself tried to use the support of both sides. Sun had given him a letter of introduction to his brother Sun Mei, a useful entree to the local Chinese community. Liang was able to turn this contact to good advantage. He even got Sun Mei himself to assume the leadership of the Maui branch of the Society to Protect the Emperor.[28] And he was able to raise eighty to ninety thousand dollars from the local Chinese communities for his plot to "restore" the emperor.[29]

In Sun's eyes, Liang's behavior was nothing short of outrageous duplicity. Anti-Manchu revolution was for Sun no mere matter of expediency, but the very heart of his program; he tended to see republicanism as the panacea to China's ills. Liang, he thought, was using him to rally support to a diametrically opposed cause. Thus, while Sun no doubt seemed to Liang intransigent, Liang appeared unpardonably devious to Sun.

There were other sources of tension between the two men. Sun had not received much of a classical education—most of his schooling had been in Hawaii and Hong Kong; Liang, on the other hand, was an accomplished classical scholar and a holder of the *chü-jen* degree. Moreover, Sun drew most of his support from the have-nots and secret societies among the overseas Chinese communities, while Liang's appeal was primarily to the more well-to-do and established elements in those communities. This aspect of the differences between the two is well illustrated by the following account by contemporary Japanese police observers of the struggle between the two groups for control of the Ta-t'ung School in Yokohama. The issue, in January, 1899, was over the election of the president and officers of the school. On January 15, members of the "K'ang faction" met and decided to restrict the election to some two hundred of the most prominent members of the local Chinese community. On the seventeenth, "Sun's faction" called for a general election opened to all. At the scheduled meeting on the evening of the seventeenth, "hired hoodlums" of the "Sun faction" disrupted the meeting by force. Important members of the school then met and decided to entrust the selection of officers to the board of the Overseas Chinese Association. The new officers thus elected were almost entirely of the "K'ang faction" and the results were then announced at a meeting of over three hundred "upper-class" Chinese.[30] Differences such as these might have been worked out in time if Liang and Sun had been able to maintain cordial personal relations. The divisions in 1900, however, produced the rift that soon turned into an irreconcilable gulf, and precluded any genuine cooperation between the two men in subsequent years.

The tightly knit group that Liang had gathered around himself also suffered from his absence. We find Liang lamenting early in 1900 that several members of the Enoshima group had quickly lost heart upon returning to China.[31]

The final blow to Liang's group came with the abortive failure of the plot to "restore" the Kuang-hsü Emperor. The plans were ambitious and elaborate—K'ang and Liang, and the Society to Protect the Emperor, were to supply the funding; T'ang Ts'ai-ch'ang would raise an army of some 20,000 in the Yangtze Valley, cooperate with Chang Chih-tung, then Governor General at Wuchang, and declare the independence of the south. The hope was to "restore the Kuang-hsü Emperor," move the capital to the south, and establish constitutional government. The group even formed a skeletal parliament on the basis of the Tzu-li Hui (Society for National Independence), which T'ang had established in Shanghai the year earlier.[32] Liang himself placed particular emphasis on the Kwangtung-Kwangsi area and planned to use a mercenary army of 500 Japanese and 500 Filipinos,[33] no doubt with the hope of coordinating with Sun's planned Waichow (Hui-chou) uprising.[34]

He also tried to enlist the support of the Japanese government, and even offered to join the allied forces bound for Peking to lift the Boxers' seige on the legation quarters.[35]

Liang pitched all the meager resources and support he wielded into this plot. The remnants of the Enoshima group and some of the students of the Academy of Current Affairs supplied most of the leadership; at least five of the students from the academy who had rejoined Liang at the upper level Ta-t'ung School in Tokyo—T'ien Pang-hsüan, Li Ping-huan, Ch'in Li-shan, Ts'ai Chung-hao, and Lin Kuei—followed T'ang back to China to participate in the planned uprisings.[36] And members of the Enoshima group manned the top-level coordinating positions. Han Wen-chü and Ou Chü-chia served at the head-quarters of K'ang's Society to Protect the Emperor at Macao. Mai Chung-hua, Huang Wei-chih, and Lo P'u were responsible for coordinating activities in Tokyo. Chang Hsüeh-ching and Liang Ping-kuang were assigned to the Kwangtung-Kwangsi area. Liang himself was responsible for raising funds in Hawaii, and maintained close contacts with all phases of the movement, making repeated recommendations with respect to strategy and personnel.[37]

The entire plot, however, suffered from internal dissension and consequent confusion. K'ang and his closer followers could never quite cooperate wholeheartedly in this scheme in which his "rebellious" disciples played such a prominent role. K'ang was apparently able to retain control over the society's head-quarters in Macao, which meant that communications between Liang and party headquarters virtually broke down.[38] Liang, on the other hand, wielded much more influence over the Tokyo branch of the society, and sent most of the money he was able to raise back to Tokyo.[39] This kind of internal dissension easily made for confusion and distrust and the two sides were soon accusing each other of bad faith.

The movement itself ended a total fiasco. The hoped-for

support in Kwangtung-Kwangsi and the plans to engage foreign mercenaries never materialized. At Hankow, T'ang Ts'ai-ch'ang had to postpone repeatedly the planned uprising when support funds failed to arrive. On August 22, the day before the uprising was finally scheduled to take place, Chang Chih-tung arrested T'ang and his followers. T'ang was executed, together with three of the students from the academy: Lin Kuei, T'ien Pang-hsüan, and Li Ping-huan.[40]

Liang, for his part, had bungled badly. He was able to raise about eighty to ninety thousand dollars but managed to send only forty-four thousand of it back to Tokyo and Macao, and that belatedly.[41] The tardiness was excusable—it was due to the necessity for obtaining permission from the local authorities, something that the Ch'ing consulate in Hawaii managed to delay.[42] But the loss of a substantial portion of the funds was not —Liang was apparently carried away with wild dreams of raising "ten million dollars" through an American contact. He had hoped to go to the mainland himself, but there was at the time widespread scare of a bubonic plague and San Francisco authorities, quickly associating race with disease, forbade the entry of any Chinese. Liang entrusted some twenty-thousand dollars to his contact man, from whom he never heard again.[43]

The disastrous failures of 1900 cost Liang his entire support base. The Enoshima group fell apart; the students from the Hunan Academy could not forgive Liang for his part in the failure of the plot and the consequent deaths of T'ang and of their fellow members. Ch'in Li-shan, for example, one of the few survivors of the Hankow plot, severed all relations with Liang as well as with K'ang.[44] And Liang had managed to alienate both of the groups he had hoped to unite—K'ang and the more conservative elements in the Society to Protect the Emperor could never forget Liang's "rebellious" actions; Sun and the revolutionaries were convinced of Liang's duplicity and bad faith. Liang came out of the disastrous "restoration" movement almost completely isolated. He had bungled badly, both as a revolutionary and as a unifier of divergent political forces.

After 1900, Liang continued for two years to advocate revolution and to devote himself to spreading new ideas, impelled by his conviction that the attitudes of the people lay at the very basis of any hope for a new and modern China. He soon reached the zenith of his career as a publicist, his influence extending to virtually all members of a new generation of intellectuals. But he was not satisfied with only this role. By 1903, he felt keenly that he had engaged in little more than "empty talk." Unable to rally any personal support and yet impelled by the desire to do something concrete and tangible for China,[45] he turned increasingly away from the self-image of a Mazzini-Li Ch'üping to that of a Cavour-Huang K'e-ch'iang. Thus we find that by 1902 when he wrote "The Future of the New China," his sympathies were already very much on the side of the more mature and calculating Huang K'e-ch'iang.

The decisive change came finally during his travels through the United States in 1903, and can be pinned down to a period of a few months during the spring and summer of that year. As late as April 15, he wrote to Hsü Ch'in, a close personal friend and one of the inner circle among K'ang's followers, that although he was willing to accept other criticisms of himself made by K'ang and others, he could not abandon the idea of revolution. "Every time I read the news," he wrote, "I feel strongly the urge to act. I deeply believe that China must have a revolution. I harbor this cause ever more deeply today."[46] Yet, on August 19, he wrote to Chiang Kuan-yün, who was carrying the burden of sustaining the *Journal of the New Citizen* in Liang's absence, that "having witnessed during the past few months the chaos and decadence of the revolutionary party, I dare the less again to advocate revolution."[47]

During this period Liang felt his isolation more keenly than ever before. For one thing, the dissensions among the society that had emerged during the fiasco of 1900 returned to plague him in 1903. There was considerable dissatisfaction with Liang's conduct among those at the society's headquarters in Hong Kong and Macao. The issue came to a head in the early months of 1903, when the faction, with the support of K'ang, moved to establish a new joint stock company. Without prior consultation with Liang, they demanded that he incorporate the monies in two of his enterprises—the *Journal of the New Citizen* and a company dealing in translated books that Liang had established earlier—into this new joint stock company. Liang's response was, on the one hand, to argue for a president of the new company who he would find palatable and, on the other hand, to call for expansion of the stock issue of his own translation company. The latter move was interpreted by those at the society's headquarters as an attempt to undercut the new joint stock company. Disagreements soon led to malicious slander, and Liang found himself the target of repeated scoldings by K'ang and of vehement personal attacks by the Hong Kong–Macao faction. He was eventually forced into a position of having to apologize to those in Hong Kong.[48] The entire episode no doubt left wounds that could never completely heal.

His experiences in the United States offered no solace. The main mission of his trip was to raise money and to establish new branches for the society, but he soon despaired over the lack of serious commitment among the overseas Chinese communities and the meagerness of his accomplishment for nearly a year of feverish activity.[49]

It was thus with considerable mental anguish and a growing sense of the futility of his own efforts that he reached the pessimistic conclusions about his liberal program described in the last chapter. Convinced that China had not the requisite leadership or people for democracy, and convinced further that liberal-democracy held little relevance for the immediate and overriding concern of national sovereignty, he turned increasingly toward an emphasis on a strong state. And his own self-conception was fast changing from that of a Li Ch'ü-ping to a Huang K'e-ch'iang.

The volume of his writing declined substantially after 1903. From 1898 to 1902, his average output had been nearly two volumes per year; he wrote an average of less than one volume each year between 1903 and 1912.[50] His *Journal of the New Citizen* suffered as a consequence: until July, 1903, the *Journal* appeared regularly and punctually every two weeks; after July, 1903, however, it appeared only irregularly, suspended for periods of several months at a time. The *Journal* finally stopped publication after 1907, during which Liang had managed to produce only three issues.[51] The volume of his writings declined further after 1912, and he did not regain his productivity until after 1917, when he finally withdrew from the political arena to give his full attention to scholarship.

The tone of his ideological writings also changed abruptly. The last portions of his "The New Citizen," written after his return from the United States, repeatedly cautioned against rash action and "destruction." He called upon Bluntschli's theory of the State as an organic entity to buttress his arguments in favor of gradual reform and against revolution, and he engaged in a heated debate with the revolutionary *Min-pao* over the pros and cons of violent racial revolution. His own position was summed up in the phrase *K'ai-ming chuan-chih*, or "enlightened despotism." An "enlightened despot," assisted by capable ministers, would speed China along the path of modernization and national power, after the fashion of a Frederick II or Napoleon I.[52]

Increasingly, the conception of himself as a statesman came to dominate much of his thinking and activities. His writings focused on concrete issues, especially in the areas of finance and economics, and on government and constitutional law. He paid special attention to China's currency problem and to the issue of foreign loans, as in "The Currency Problem in China,"[53] "Discussions on Currency Regulations,"[54] and "Foreign Loans."[55] "Introduction to Constitutional Government"[56] and "Personal Views on China's Parliamentary System"[57] are representative of his contributions to the area of government and constitutional law. Liang was in fact preparing himself for the time when he would be called upon to head the government of China.

This shift in his self-concept is also shown in his other writings. Before 1902 he had presented to his readers as models of action such figures as Mazzini, Madame Roland,[58] and "The Hungarian patriot Louis Kossuth,"[59] now he wrote about men such as Kuan Chung[60] and Wang An-shih.[61] As he confided in a letter to his brother in 1909, "The more I have studied political problems during this past year, the more convinced I am that there can be no hope for China's future unless I return to take the reins of government."[62]

The stance that he took in the strike involving some 8,000 Chinese students in Japan in late 1905 and early 1906 is indicative of his changed view of himself and his new ideological position. Chinese students were on that occasion protesting an ordinance issued by the Japanese Ministry of Education.[63] The ordinance, issued on November 2 and entitled "Regulations Governing Public and Private Schools that Admit Chinese," was ostensibly a purely educational measure aimed at redressing a variety of abuses and problems that had emerged in connection with the presence of enormous numbers of Chinese students in Japan.

As the students surmised, the new regulations were actually designed to give the Chinese and Japanese governments stricter control over the selection and behavior of Chinese students in Japan. The regulations included the following provisions: 1. The Japanese private and public schools concerned must require a letter of introduction from Chinese authorities in

Japan as a part of the application for admission from a Chinese student. 2. These schools must require a letter of approval from Chinese authorities in Japan when a Chinese student applied for transfer to another school or for withdrawal from a school. 3. These schools are to require their Chinese students to live in dormitories or in boardinghouses supervised by the schools and are to supervise their outside activities. 4. These schools are not to admit a student who had been dismissed by another school for "bad character and conduct."[64] The fact was that the Ch'ing government had become greatly alarmed at the spread of revolutionary sentiments among the Chinese students in Japan and had sought the cooperation of the Japanese government to restrict the flow of dissident students to Japan and to control more closely student activities. The Japanese government, for its part, had issued the ordinance as part of an over-all effort at the time to befriend the Ch'ing government.

Chinese students saw in the ordinance a double enemy—the repressive and corrupt Manchu government, which many wished to overthrow, and the imperialistic Japanese government now acting in cooperation with the Manchu government. Revolutionary and nationalistic sentiments were joined in the protest against the ordinance. On December 5, some three-hundred student leaders met and passed a resolution calling for a strike to demand that the regulations be rescinded. Groups of monitors were organized to maintain order and to implement the strike, which soon involved virtually all Chinese students in Japan.

The nationalistic sentiments of the students were further intensified by hostile and blatantly anti-Chinese comments in the Japanese press. On December 9, Ch'en T'ien-hua, one of the organizers of the newly founded revolutionary T'ung-meng Hui and a leading writer of the revolutionary camp, jumped into the sea to protest one of such comments—the *Asahi Shimbun*, on December 7, charged the Chinese with being "self indulgent and base" (*hōjū hiretsu*). Ch'en's suicide moved "several" thousand Chinese students to resolve at a meeting on the following day to resort to the most drastic action open to them—to pick up and return to China. A total of perhaps two thousand did go back in protest. The strike itself continued into the middle of January.

Liang was no longer in tune with the sentiments of the young. On December 26, the *Journal of the New Citizen* carried a lengthy article by him on the issues of the strike;[65] the tone of the article was didactic, legalistic, and defensive. Many of the students, Liang argued, had misread or misunderstood the regulations, which were actually directed more at the schools admitting Chinese students than at the students themselves; the regulations carried more advantages than disadvantages—they were stronger in their restrictions on abuses by Japanese schools than in restrictions on the freedom of Chinese students; to ask for a rescinding of the regulations was senseless, for it was legally impossible. Liang conceded that the original intentions of the regulations might indeed have been directed against the Chinese students and that they might have been formulated in conjunction with Chinese authorities, but he insisted that the actual effect of the regulations amounted to only slight inconveniences for the students. Liang appealed to calm, to reason, even to Wang Yang-ming. And he was consciously defensive—he acknowledged that he was espousing a most unpopular position, and that in arguing against the strike, he was doing what "was tantamount to declaring war on the entire student community."[66] All this was a far cry from the Liang whose writings had inspired an entire generation of young Chinese thinkers. The irony was that Liang should have so soon afterward found himself on the opposite side of those whom he had so profoundly influenced.

The student strike marks a turning point in the contest between reformers and revolutionaries for the allegiance of the

Chinese students abroad. Sun's Society to Revive China (Hsing Chung Hui) had not been able to gather much support from the intellectuals; the T'ung-meng Hui, however, founded on August 20, 1905, managed to attract several of the outstanding intellectuals of the time, including Chang Ping-lin and Wu Chih-hui, and younger men such as Sung Chiao-jen, Ch'en T'ien-hua, Hu Han-min and Wang Ching-wei. As the strike showed, the revolutionaries were now riding the crest of the tide. Liang, having realigned himself with K'ang's ideological position, had lost the initiative.

He was now completely identified with the cause of orderly reform from within the existing structure. During the course of 1905, he maintained frequent contacts with reform-minded notables at the court, especially Tuan-fang, who had become one of the leading advocates of reform at the capital. Tuan-fang was calling for constitutional government and amnesty for K'ang and Liang. Liang reportedly drafted memorials totaling more than 200,000 words for Tuan-fang.[67]

Liang was not optimistic about these efforts, however. In "Enlightened Despotism," he was projecting a preparatory or transitional period of "at least ten to fifteen years" before constitutional government could become practicable in China.[68] But Japan's surprising victory in the Russo-Japanese War changed the political atmosphere at the capital and brought the unexpected decision by the court to follow Japan's example in political modernization. On September 1, 1906, the Empress Dowager decreed that plans and preparations were to be made for constitutional government.

The move brought a change in the emphasis and tone of Liang's writings, as he took on the other side of the role of a Huang K'e-ch'iang—the party politician. In contrast to the moderate and pessimistic tone of his writings of the two preceding years, he called now for immediate establishment of constitutional government, veering from his "establishmentarian" tones to address "the people" once more: he charged the government with full responsibility for virtually all of China's ills, with "murdering annually tens of millions of people." "The people" must not put up with such a situation any longer; they must rise to supervise the government through representative institutions.[69] Liang exhorted like-minded individuals to join with him to form an organization to give expression to popular sentiments against despotism, to educate the people politically, and to dispel the belief that the people were not yet ready for constitutional government.[70] He himself was planning to establish precisely such an organization.

This organization was to be completely respectable. Liang sought the endorsement of such leading officials as Yüan Shih-k'ai and Chang Chih-tung,[71] and of eminent Manchus such as Shan-ch'i (Prince Su) and Tuan-fang.[72] He also solicited the support of leading local gentry, including Chang Chien and Cheng Hsiao-hsü.[73] He himself would manipulate from behind the scenes; neither he nor K'ang, since they were still on the wanted list of the court, would have any formal association with the organization.

He ran into difficulties from the very start. He had counted on the support of Yang Tu, one of the most influential persons in the Chinese community in Japan. But a variety of complications soon arose—between Yang and Hsü Fo-su, who had come to Japan to study in 1905 and had quickly developed a very close personal relationship with Liang; between Yang and Chiang Kuan-yün, the fourth key person in the planning stages of this organization. There was much squabbling over the precise structure and the position each was to occupy. In the end, Yang split from the group and formed his own organization.[74]

Liang's organization was finally inaugurated in Tokyo on November 17, 1907. It bore the appropriately innocuous name of Political Information Society (Cheng-wen She). Its membership, boasted to be 1500 strong, consisted largely of the moderate Chinese in Japan.[75] When Liang moved the headquarters of the society to Shanghai a few months later, he hoisted Ma Liang, an elderly scholar known more for his scholarship than his politics, to the position of "Director." The office of president was left vacant for the time being—Liang had pledged it to K'ang in his efforts to secure K'ang's financial backing for this venture.[76]

The declared purpose of the organization was to ensure, through peaceful and orderly means, a speedy transition to constitutional government. More specifically, the club's constitution called for: (1) the early convening of a national legislative body and the institution of responsible government; (2) the establishment of the "rule of law" and the independence of the judiciary; (3) the development of local self-government; (4) the equality of China with foreign nations.[77]

Another one of Liang's hopes was for the club to serve as a rallying point for a broad base of moderate opinion in order to counter the growing influence of the revolutionaries. Liang was keenly aware of the spread of revolutionary sentiments among the Chinese students in Japan. He knew that the T'ung-meng Hui, in spite of its organizational weaknesses, held greater appeal than did his own group. He pointed out to K'ang, for example, that "the struggle against the revolutionaries" was "the first order of business" for them, of even higher priority than the battle against the government.[78] Liang no doubt overstated this point for K'ang's benefit, but he himself unquestionably shared some of these sentiments, and continued to give much of his energy to the heated debates with the revolutionary *Min-pao*.

Liang tried at the same time to develop other bases of power within China. One plan called for the establishment of a journal and a school in Hankow—the journal would rally support to his cause; the school would train men for the future.[79] The other plan involved the intricate game of court politics—he had at first sought the cooperation and support of Yüan Shih-k'ai; when it became clear that Yüan was hostile to his cause, Liang plotted with K'ang to remove Yüan from power. They hoped to alienate Yüan from the Empress Dowager with the help of eminent Manchus such as I-k'uang, Shan-ch'i, T'ieh-liang, Tsai-tse, and Tuan-fang.[80]

The focus of the open activities of the society was on pressuring the court through petitions for an early convening of parliament. Numerous constitutional associations had sprung up in the provinces after 1905 and Liang attempted to coordinate these local organizations into a national movement for constitutional government. According to Carsun Chang, who headed this effort, at least three thousand signatures had been secured by the end of March (1908) and Chang hoped that there would be tens of thousands.[81] The petition was submitted in July; its lists of signatures were led by the names of prominent members of the Association to Prepare for Constitutional Government in Kiangsu, Cheng Hsiao-hsü, Chang Chien, T'ang Shou-ch'ien, and others. The Constitutional Association in Hunan and the Self-Government Association in Kwangtung also participated.[82] In addition, Liang's society sent a telegram in the names of its membership to urge that parliament be convened in three years.[83]

These efforts were supplemented by another petition that K'ang submitted in the names of some two hundred overseas branches of his Constitutional Party.[84] This petition made even more far-reaching demands than the others: K'ang asked for (1) immediate convening of parliament and implementation of constitutional government; (2) getting rid of all eunuchs; (3) eradicating Manchu-Han differences—the court would adopt the designation of Chung-hua for the nation; (4) moving the capital to south of the Yangtze River.[85]

All this proved to be too radical for the court. On August 14, an imperial decree banned the Political Information Society and ordered the arrest and punishment of its members.

Liang had failed once more. He had elected to side with the existing government against the revolutionaries. In the process, he found himself caught in the crossfire from both sides; for the T'ung-meng Hui and the revolution-minded students, Liang was more than ever the enemy of the revolutionary cause; to the court, he represented an unacceptable radical threat.

The society fell apart as soon as it was banned. After all, its very rationale was legitimacy; it could not long survive the decision that it was illegitimate by those very people on whom it had gambled.

Liang's other plans were no more successful. The plan to build a local base in Hankow never materialized. The efforts to use leading officials to further the cause of constitutional monarchy backfired—Yüan Shih-k'ai urged the banning of the society.

In the meantime, however, the domestic constitutional movement was fast gathering momentum. The provincial assemblies were established in October, 1909, and before the first session closed, Chang Chien, in his position as Chairman of the Kiangsu Assembly, called for a national congress of these assemblies to expedite the establishment of constitutional government. Liang immediately instructed Hsü Fo-su to join in and to help coordinate another national petition movement.[86] The congress, which convened in Shanghai, sent thirty-three representatives to Peking to present its petition for an early convening of parliament. This petition denied, the constitutionalists went on to organize a second petition under the capable and dedicated coordination of Sun Hung-i. Presented in June, 1910, this second petition included the support of a variety of other organizations—educational, commercial, overseas Chinese, and so on. Again denied, Sun and others coordinated a third movement, this time on a still larger scale with the support of several of the provincial military governors. The court finally compromised, shortening the period of preparation for constitutional government from nine years, as had been stipulated in the Outlines of a Constitution promulgated in 1908, to six years.[87]

Liang and Hsü now joined with the other constitutional forces in the nation to try once more to form a national organization. The plans were ambitious: this new organization would unite all the diverse constitutional groups in the nation into a single national organization that would serve as the basis for a full-fledged, modern political party. Established on June 4, 1911, the Society of the Friends of Constitutional Government (Hsien-yu Hui) was the constitutionalists' most ambitious effort yet at political organization: branch offices were established for nearly all of the provinces, and the society's membership included virtually all the chairmen and vice-chairmen of the provincial assemblies.

But the society was not to survive the revolution. Formed on the basis of an uneasy alliance among Liang's group, the group around Sun Hung-i, and the supporters of Chang Chien, it was racked from the start by factional divisions.[88] The three groups were united only by their common commitment to the search for a peaceful transition from dynastic rule to constitutional monarchy. When the court failed to cooperate and the revolution could no longer be forestalled, the membership of the society split apart, some in antipathy to the revolution, others in varying degrees of sympathy with it. The result was that Liang and the constitutionalists would not be able to bring a unified organization to bear on the course of republican politics.

On a different front, Liang continued also with the game of court intrigue. Even after the Political Information Society was banned, Liang persisted in his efforts to destroy Yüan's power and influence. The opportunity came with the death of the Kuang-hsü Emperor on November 14, and of Tz'u-hsi on the following day. Tsai-feng, the father of P'u-i, the new child emperor, and brother of the deceased Kung-hsü Emperor, became the Prince Regent. Liang and K'ang now plotted to use the relations they had established with Shan-ch'i to influence Tsai-tse, whom they believed held the confidence of Tsai-feng.[89] Yüan was in fact dismissed in December, but it is doubtful that the efforts of K'ang and Liang made any substantial difference, since the jealousies over Yüan's power among many of the influential Manchus dated from much earlier.

After the outbreak of the Wuchang uprising, Liang plunged once more into feverish political maneuverings.[90] This time his plans centered around Tsai-ta'o, another brother of the deceased emperor and Commander of the new Imperial Guards established in 1908. In addition to Tsai-t'ao, Liang had an important contact in General Wu Lu-chen, Commander of the Sixth Division stationed in Paoting. Liang had known Wu since at least 1900 when Wu had been a follower of T'ang Ts'ai-ch'ang. Wu had in fact followed T'ang back to China in 1900 to join in the planned uprising but had managed to escape to Japan.[91] He had afterwards attended the Japan Army Officers' Academy, graduating in 1902. Through Wu, Liang tried to enlist the support of two other young military officers stationed in the vicinity of the capital—Chang Shao-tseng, Commander of the Twentieth Division, and Lan T'ien-wei, Commander of the Second Mixed Brigade. Chang and Lan were fellow graduates of Wu's from the Officers' Academy.

The outlines of Liang's plot can be reconstructed from a letter he wrote to Hsü Ch'in on October 29.[92] He hoped that Tsai-t'ao would be able to effect a coup at the capital and depose the ruling clique under I-k'uang, who had become Prime Minister in the new cabinet established in April, and Tsai-tse, Minister of Finance in the same cabinet. Liang would have Tsai-t'ao become the Prime Minister and convene parliament immediately. The Emperor would adopt a Chinese (Han) name, as would all Manchus. Thus, the steam would be taken out of the revolution and national unity and order could be maintained. Military support for this scheme was to come chiefly from Wu, with, Liang hoped, the cooperation of Chang and Lan.

On the same day that this letter was written, Lan and Chang did stage what has come to be known as the Luan-chou revolt. Ordered by the court to lead their armies south, they had instead presented the court with twelve demands, asking for the convening of parliament within the year and for the institution of the system of a responsible cabinet. Shansi, it so happened, declared independence on the same day, and the court found itself threatened by a march from both east and west. Tsai-feng and I-k'uang acceded to the demands. On November 1, they dissolved the "royal cabinet" and asked Yüan to take over as Prime Minister. On November 3, the court approved the draft constitution prepared by the Consultative Assembly.[93]

Liang was sufficiently encouraged by all this to decide to leave for Dairen on November 6, hoping to play a central role in the new government. He thought he would be in a strong bargaining position against Yüan if he could secure the backing of Wu, Lan, and Chang. By the time he arrived on November 9, however, the situation had changed. Wu had been assassinated on November 6. Liang now pinned his hopes on contacting Chang and Lan. But Yüan moved quickly to consolidate his power—Chang was promoted to a sinecure and Lan had to escape to Shanghai. Before long, Yüan succeeded also in forcing Tsai-t'ao to resign from his command of the Imperial Guards.[94] Liang had no choice but to return to Japan to await a more propitious moment to return to China. When he did, late in 1912, he would find Yüan in full control and he himself would have to operate from an assembly devoid of real power.

Liang's position in 1912 was indeed a far cry from the hopes he had expressed in "The Future of the New China." Neither his political organization nor the T'ung-meng Hui held the real power to guide the destiny of the nation. That power, in 1912, lay with Yüan Shih-k'ai. But Yüan was hardly Liang's image of an "enlightened despot"; nor was Liang quite Yüan's image of a Chu-ke Liang. Even in the impotent National Assembly, Liang would be far overshadowed by the revolutionaries.

The irony is that the discussion between Li Ch'ü-ping and Huang K'e-ch'iang should have proved to be truly prophetic. China was not prepared for a republican revolution, as Huang pointed out. On the other hand, Huang's hopes that those in power could be persuaded to implement constitutional government was no more realistic, as Li had argued. Both Huang and Li had believed in the necessity for an awakened citizenry. That citizenry, in 1912, remained a mirage. China simply had no room for either a Li Ch'ü-ping or a Huang K'e-ch'iang.

CHAPTER 6

National Politics*

The revolution of 1911 was the joint work of the new parties and the provincial and regional armies. The T'ung-meng Hui supplied the spark in Wuchang, which set aflame the divisive forces in the nation. The first revolutionary base, Wuhan, was secured by an alliance between the T'ung-meng Hui forces and the local assistant commander, Li Yüan-hung. T'ung-meng Hui forces then led, forced, or persuaded the armies of the lower Yangtze valley to join the revolution, and Nanking became the second revolutionary stronghold. Within a month, all provinces except Chihli, Honan, Shantung, and the Northeastern provinces declared independence, and the provincial constitutionalists joined with the revolutionaries or the local military commanders against the dynasty. What finally sealed the fate of the dynasty was the desertion of Yüan Shih-k'ai and his Peiyang Army.

As the diverse forces set about the task of establishing a na-

* The subject of national politics during the early republican period still awaits detailed, monographic study. The framework presented below, into which I have placed Liang's activities and thought during the period, can only be a very tentative way of looking at the complex developments of the period. I have tried to break away from the biases of the Chinese writings on the subject by emphasizing the realities of the power configuration of the time.

tional government, it was clear that Yüan's was the strongest power base in the nation. The Peiyang Army was undeniably the most powerful military force in the country. And, once it had been decided that Yüan would head the new national government and that Peking would be the seat, Yüan gained other advantages. His power could be brought to bear directly on dissidents in the government. He held, moreover, legitimacy—anyone who opposed him was open to the charge of opposing the central government. He also held legitimacy in foreign eyes, and that meant access to foreign loans and a far stronger financial position than any potential challenger to his power. But Yüan had to be careful to retain the support of his own Peiyang Army, which, as the mutiny of the Third Division in Peking on February 29, 1912[1] and the events of 1916 would show, was by no means unconditionally loyal to him. Of greater threat, of course, were the other power bases in the nation.

The T'ung-meng Hui's influence was concentrated in the lower Yangtze Valley, especially the provinces of Kiangsi, Anhwei, Hunan, and Kiangsu, and Kwangtung, where Hu Han-min was the military governor. The party also wielded some power in nearly all the other southern and southwestern provinces, but complicated factional divisions pervaded all the provinces and localities under its influence and it was racked from the start by internal divisions. The fact was that the T'ung-meng Hui was a loosely knit conglomerate of many diverse interests, not a centralized organization.

The third major center of power was grouped around Li Yüan-hung and Wuhan. Although Li's power was not comparable to that of either Yüan or the T'ung-meng Hui, he had the advantage of being a "middle roader," one with whom either side could ally itself. He could thus play a pivotal role in the close balance between Peiyang and T'ung-meng Hui power.[2]

Other provincial bases also figured in the arena of national politics during the early republican years. Yen Hsi-shan in

Shansi, Shen Ping-k'un in Kwangsi, and the Northeastern provinces, for example, were not closely aligned with any of the major power centers. If united behind one or the other, however, these "unaligned" provinces could tip the scale decisively.

As a group, the constitutionalists emerged from the revolution weaker than any other. If the T'ung-meng Hui suffered from a lack of centralized organization, the constitutionalists had no unified party to speak of at all. K'ang and Liang's Constitutional Party had failed miserably; their final efforts in 1911 to secure a power base had been abortive, as had so many of their earlier attempts. The two men themselves were divided by irreconcilable differences and hovered on the verge of an open break. Neither one had more than a handful of personal followers, his ideas, and his personal reputation to draw upon for power and influence. Provincial constitutionalists such as T'ang Hua-lung in Hupei and Sun Hung-i in Chihli had indeed played important roles in the events of the revolution[3] and had wielded considerable influence in their respective localities and provincial assemblies, but were relatively insignificant in the national power configuration when compared with the men who controlled strong armies. Others, such as P'u Tien-chün, who emerged briefly into the limelight in Szechwan during the revolution, were soon pushed aside in the ensuing power struggles. Perhaps the two strongest constitutionalists were Chang Chien, who held considerable financial and personal influence,[4] and T'an Yen-k'ai, who emerged as the military governor in Hunan. But neither Chang nor T'an could command the support of a sufficiently large segment of the constitutional forces in the nation to bring about even the semblance of a national organization. As a group the constitutionalists lacked the unity to enable them to challenge on their own the powers of Yüan Shih-k'ai or the T'ung-meng Hui.

The ideologues of the revolution also figured in the national power configuration. Had the revolution been a mere dynastic rebellion, China might simply have disintegrated immediately into military satrapies and there would be no need to account for the role of ideology, but it was made in the name of nationalism and democracy. In the immediate aftermath of the revolution, all sides were agreed upon the need to institute a national and a constitutional government and the ideological appeal of such a government permitted otherwise powerless men—Liang Ch'i-ch'ao and Sung Chiao-jen—to play prominent roles in the national government. As the ideologues of the revolution, they carried considerable force of legitimacy. The "republican mandate" in 1912 was the ideologues' to confer, and a military figure who wished to make pretensions to legitimacy must have the support of at least a significant segment of this new intellectual elite. The ideologues, moreover, could claim privileged and expert modern knowledge and no government in twentieth-century China could long survive without such knowledge. But their influence was dependent upon the continued appeal of national and constitutional government.

Constitutional government in 1912 and 1913 was predicated on the theory that somehow constitutional legality would serve as the final arbiter in factional disputes. The diverse political interests in the nation would be brought to one table to hammer out their differences, to develop a workable balance of power, and to make national decisions in accordance with constitutional prescriptions. And all sides contended for representation and influence in the new legislative bodies.

The composition of the legislative bodies in fact closely paralleled the existing power configuration. In the absence of political parties with popular bases of support, representatives to the legislative bodies were simply chosen by the established powers in each of the provinces. The Nanking Provisional Assembly (Ts'an-i yüan) consisted primarily of delegates sent by the military governors of the provinces that had declared independence.[5] Membership in the expanded Peking Provisional

Assembly, which first met on April 12, 1912, after the seat of
the national government had been moved from Nanking to
Peking, was similarly determined by the military governors and
the provincial assemblies.[6] In the permanent legislature (Kuo-
hui) convened on April 8, 1913, membership in the upper house
was again determined by the provincial assemblies. The lower
house was theoretically elected directly by popular vote, but
there can be no doubt of the decisive influence of the established
powers within each province.[7]

The T'ung-meng Hui, as might be expected, secured the
largest numbers in the legislative bodies. It did suffer in 1912
from factional splinterings—many of its members joined with
Chang Ping-lin's Chung-hua Min-kuo Lien-ho Hui (later the
T'ung-i Tang), Li Yüan-hung's Min She, Ts'ai O's T'ung-i
Kung-ho Tang or one or several of the plethora of small political parties that sprang up after the revolution—but it still
managed to secure forty-plus seats in the 120-seat Peking Provisional Assembly. The party's influence reached a new height
in August, 1912, by the acquisition of the bulk of the membership of the T'ung-i Kung-ho Tang and several other smaller
parties. This new conglomerate Kuomintang, under the capable leadership of Sung Chiao-jen, counted among the members of its senate the military governors of the provinces of
Kiangsi (Li Lieh-chün), Hunan (T'an Yen-k'ai), Kwangsi
(Shen Ping-k'un), Anhwei (Po Wen-wei), Kwangtung (Hu
Han-min), Shansi (Yen Hsi-shan), and T'ang Chi-yao, who
would in 1916 emerge the strongest military figure in Yunnan.
And the party succeeded in winning overwhelmingly in the
elections of late 1912 and early 1913—it secured 269 seats out
of 596 in the lower house (Chung-i yüan), and 123 out of 274
in the upper (Ts'an-i yüan).[8]

The chief contender to the T'ung-meng Hui in the Peking
Provisional Assembly was the Kung-ho Tang. This party was
formed on the basis of an alliance between Li Yüan-hung's

Hupei-centered Min She and several of the major constitutional groups, especially Chang Chien and his faction in the
T'ung-i Tang. The Kung-ho Tang secured the second largest
numbers in the elections to the permanent legislature—120
seats in the lower house and 69 in the upper.[9]

The national government in 1912, in other words, was
founded on a precarious relationship among the existing centers
of power. Yüan occupied the office of president while the Kuomintang controlled the majority in the legislature. Constitutional issues and frictions between the president's office and the
legislature were more than ideological contests; they were direct
reflections of the struggle for power between the two major
power centers in the country. Vice-President Li Yüan-hung
and the constitutionalists allied with him occupied the middle
position in this delicate relationship, and could make their
weight felt as a pivotal force.

It was against this background that Liang had to formulate
his strategy of action. He was first of all determined to play a
prominent role in the new national government. After all, he
had tried for nearly two decades to influence the course of national events and had systematically prepared himself for the
day when he might be in a position to implement some of his
ideas. He was, moreover, understandably convinced that his
were the right answers and that he was as well qualified as anyone to direct the course of his nation. As he had confided to his
brother in 1909, he felt that there could be "no hope for China's
future" unless he "returned to take the reins of government."[10]

But he had no power base of consequence. Ts'ai O, the Military Governor in Yunnan, was the only military figure in the
nation to whom he had been close—Ts'ai had been his student
at the Academy of Current Affairs in Hunan. That contact
would prove to be important in 1916, when Yunnan spear-
headed the resistance to Yüan's monarchical movement, but in
1912, Yunnan was but a far-away province with little conse-

quence in national politics. Liang's influence in the new political parties was similarly limited. He had tried in 1911 to organize an umbrella organization for the diverse constitutional
groups in the country, the Society of the Friends of Constitutional Government (Hsien-yu Hui), but the society could not
survive the revolution. Many members joined with Li Yüan-
hung's Kung-ho Tang or with one of the other parties. The only
two groups that looked to Liang for leadership were the Kung-
ho Chien-she T'ao-lun Hui led by the Hupei constitutionalist
T'ang Hua-lung and the Hopei constitutionalist Sun Hung-i,[11]
and the Kuo-min Hsieh-chin Hui, organized by Chi Chung-
yin, one of Liang's close personal followers.[12] Neither group
held much influence in the Peking Provisional Assembly. Under these conditions, Liang could hope to influence national
events only by allying himself with one or another of the major
power centers—Yüan, Li, or the T'ung-meng Hui.

His first decision was to work with Yüan. Hsü Fo-su and
Carsun Chang, his two closest followers, both urged him to do
so. They reasoned that Yüan was clearly the strongest power
in the nation and was bound to be at the center of any national
government.[13] When Sun Yat-sen himself resigned in favor of
Yüan and the Nanking Provisional Assembly unanimously
elected Yüan Provisional President, there was no longer any
question of the role Yüan was to play in the national government. Liang, like Sun, Huang Hsing, and Sung Chiao-jen,
early perceived that Yüan was the only one capable of imposing
a semblance of unity on the nation.

The question was not whether to accept Yüan, but how to
work with him. Sun and Huang chose not to participate in the
national government. Sung's plan was to institute the "cabinet
system," to vest administrative powers in a cabinet headed by
a premier and responsible to the legislature. Yüan as president
would then be able to wield only very limited powers.[14] Sung
was counting on legislative means, backed by his party's power

in central and south China, to realize his aims, but Liang could harbor no such illusions. Unlike the T'ung-meng Hui, his party was powerless. And he was not willing to think in terms of co-operating with the T'ung-meng Hui. None of his followers even suggested such a possibility; they took for granted that coopera-tion would be precluded by the personal and ideological differ-ences between Liang and the T'ung-meng Hui leaders and their long-standing feuds.[15] Moreover, a double alliance with Li Yüan-hung and with Yüan offered far better prospects for him to exert more decisive influence.

The style of his cooperation with Yüan is reminiscent of his self-image as the Huang K'e-ch'iang of his political novel, "The Future of the New China." Liang obviously had hopes that Yüan might somehow prove to be an approximation of his ideal of an "enlightened despot," one who would unify the na-tion and bring about modernizing reforms. He himself might fill the role of a Camillo di Cavour as Yüan's chief adviser on strategies of modernization. By the early spring of 1912, we find Liang unabashedly addressing Yüan in a series of letters as the "enlightened ruler." Trying in these letters to establish his own possible role as an indispensable adviser, he counseled Yüan on financial policies and advised him to develop a moderate political party to counterbalance the influence of the T'ung-meng Hui in the legislature. He even drafted a constitution for Yüan. And he pointed again and again to the role that he him-self might play in Yüan's service.[16]

Yüan, for his part, no doubt well understood the value of Liang's support. Liang still had a tremendous reputation as a publicist and his support would greatly enhance the prestige and apparent legitimacy of Yüan's government. Liang, more-over, might be a crucial moderating influence on the increas-ingly hostile legislature. Yüan perhaps also appreciated Liang for his expertise in law and finance, on which Liang had pub-lished extensively during the last years before the revolution.

He therefore reciprocated fully Liang's approaches, returning Liang's flattering references by addressing him as the worthy man whose advice and help he earnestly sought.[17] Upon Liang's return to China in November, 1912, Yüan treated him with the utmost courtesy and supplied him with a monthly stipend of 3,000 *yüan*. He also pledged 200,000 *yüan* to the support of the moderate conglomerate party that Liang was trying to develop.[18] And he would twice appoint Liang to official posts.

The alliance with Yüan was one side of a two-sided strategy Liang was following. A Huang K'e-ch'iang was not only a statesman, but a party politician as well, and Liang was not so naïve as to pin all his hopes on his influence on Yüan. He sought to capitalize on his personal reputation and his contacts with the constitutionalists to develop a substantial following in the legislature. Such a following would be his basis for pressuring Yüan, should such pressures be necessary.

Here again he had to play the game with only very limited assets. Hsü Fo-su had early suggested that he join simply with Li Yüan-hung's Min She,[19] but Liang intended to wait for a moment when his own bargaining position could be stronger. Throughout the course of 1912, his followers in the Kung-ho Chien-she T'ao-lun Hui and the Kuo-min Hsieh-chin Hui negotiated with Li Yüan-hung's Kung-ho Tang for a possible merger of the groups. But the discussions never got very far— T'ang Hua-lung and Chi Chung-yin wanted to have Liang either at the helm of the new party or in the number-two position, a rather high price considering the limited influence of Liang's two parties.[20] In August, the T'ao-lun Hui and the Hsieh-chin Hui merged into the Min-chu Tang.[21] Liang was hopeful that his personal popularity would greatly boost the influence of this party in the forthcoming elections to the legislature.

He was in 1912 indeed one of the best known and most

widely respected of the ideologue-politicians. The fact that he had been identified with the opposition to the cause of republican revolution had not seriously tarnished his reputation as a publicist and his support was a prize that all groups sought to win. Thus, when he arrived in Tientsin on November 13, 1912, after fourteen years of exile, he was wooed by all sides: some members of the Kuomintang tried to enlist his support; Chang Chien waited for three days to see him; and he was immediately at the center of the ongoing efforts to create a large, moderate party.[22] When he reached Peking two weeks later, he was inundated with speaking engagements and interviews. He was so elated with all this attention that he spoke of how he was receiving a much more impressive welcome than that which had been extended to Sun, and that the Japanese papers were correct when they identified him as the most popular man in the nation. He wrote to his daughter that everyone was surrounding him as "the milliard stars are in attendance to the North Star," and that while Sun's speeches only made people laugh, his moved them deeply.[23]

But he had far overestimated his own influence on the existing power configurations in the nation. The Min-chu Tang managed to secure in the elections only sixteen seats in the lower house and eight in the upper house.[24] Liang complained bitterly that the triumphant Kuomintang had defeated his side by "intimidation and bribery."[25] He was now forced to join with Li Yüan-hung's Kung-ho Tang from a much weaker bargaining position than he had hoped to have, and in February he formally became a member. On May 29, the Min-chu Tang was finally merged with the Kung-ho Tang and the T'ung-i Tang into the Chin-pu Tang. Li Yüan-hung was the head of the new party; Liang was only one of its nine executive members.[26] But he had little choice: the Chin-pu Tang was his only prospect for significant influence in the legislature.

His ideological stance at this time is best reflected in a speech he gave before the Kung-ho Tang on May 19: he was opposed to the methods of the Kuomintang, which he charged with being a "rowdy party"; he pointed to the dangers of "mob rule" and "anarchy," and insisted upon the necessity of working within existing possibilities; with respect to Yüan, he declared that although "our party is not satisfied with a single measure of the Provisional Government," "we force ourselves to support this government," "in order to await the formation of a permanent government and to attempt gradually to reform the government." His guiding principle would be to "calmly and watchfully supervise" the government, and not "needlessly maintain hostility toward it."[27]

This stance was entirely consistent with his stated ideas and beliefs. He had since 1903 been convinced that his "new citizenry" was at best a distant ideal and that therefore full-fledged liberal-democratic government was as yet premature. His "enlightened despotism" had been intended to serve a dual purpose—to unite the nation under a strong central government in order to withstand foreign aggression, and to implement reforms that would gradually lead to full-fledged constitutional and representative government. The extremists in the legislature seemed to him to be making the very same mistakes of a Li Ch'ü-ping in calling for the overthrow of the existing government before the nation was prepared to institute anything in its place. His own model of action at this time was the more realistic Huang K'e-ch'iang. He would work within the limits of existing possibilities and since Yüan was the only man capable of uniting the nation and exerting strong central leadership, he would have to work with Yüan. At the same time, he would use parliamentary pressures and persuasion to set Yüan onto the "enlightened" path of modernization and eventual liberal-democracy.

He was also playing an intricate game of power. His aim was to maximize his influence in national affairs, and this he had to try to do from an essentially powerless position. The close personal relationship with Yüan meant possible opportunities to implement his ideas, for Yüan was after all the man who made the appointments and carried out national policy. It also meant a power base from which he could maximize his influence in the Chin-pu Tang since Yüan, in addition to being at the head of the government, was also a source of funding for the party. And influence in the Chin-pu Tang was itself a means to maximize his influence on Yüan. By aligning himself with a group that interposed itself between Yüan and the Kuomintang, he was in a position to play upon the delicate balance of power between the two. It was much the same shrewd strategy that Li Yüan-hung was using.

The power configuration upon which Liang's strategy of action was predicated, however, was fast changing by the beginning of 1913. The elections generated a heated political atmosphere; some of the parliamentarians were advocating that the seat of the legislature be moved from Peking to Nanking; and the issues of a responsible cabinet and of centralized governmental authority as opposed to a loose confederation of provinces were also subjects of debate.[28] The parliamentary experiment in 1912 had not satisfied anyone: Yüan and many of the military governors had grown weary of the unwieldy legislative body; many members of the Kuomintang had been antagonized by Yüan's high-handed measures during the preceding year; the more moderate parliamentary elements were critical of Yüan or the Kuomintang, or both. It was in such an atmosphere and in the elation over the Kuomintang victories at the polls that Sung Chiao-jen reached the decision to try to remove Yüan from power completely. As Wu Hsiang-hsiang shows, Sung by this time was planning to have Li Yüan-hung elected as president, and to institute "cabinet government" under a premier elected by the lower house. Sung himself was of course the most likely candidate for the position of premier.

In February and March, Sung began openly to criticize Yüan and called for a "party cabinet" and "cabinet government."[29] All this proved to be too much for Yüan, and on March 20, Sung was assassinated.

The precarious relationship between Yüan and the Kuomintang now broke down. Rumors spread quickly that Yüan was behind the assassination, and by April 25, investigations led to the release of telegrams and documents that clearly implicated Yüan. Some of the Kuomintang members went south, while others planned to seek Yüan's impeachment.

Legislative means proved to be inadequate. Weakened by the loss of its most capable leader, the Kuomintang was not able to command a clear majority in the legislature. In fact, the balance between the Kuomintang and the Chin-pu Tang was now so close that the legislature was almost completely paralyzed. While Kuomintang members sought legislative action on Sung's murder, Liang and the Chin-pu Tang favored leaving the matter entirely to the courts, with the result that the case was never taken up.[30] Another example of legislative paralysis involved Yüan's loan of 25 million pounds from the Five Power Banking Consortium, for which he had not sought legislative approval. Most of the Kuomintang members were insistent upon holding to legislative prerogatives and called for revocation of the loan contract, but Liang and the Chin-pu Tang maintained that since the loan was already an accomplished fact, the important thing was not the procedural technicality but legislative control over the funds borrowed. Again the legislature failed to act.[31]

In the meantime, Yüan continued with his assault on the power base of the Kuomintang. In June, he moved to relieve key Kuomintang military governors from their posts—Li Lieh-chün in Kiangsi, Po Wen-wei in Anhwei, and Hu Han-min in Kwangtung. In July, Li began the "second revolution," in Kiangsi, and was soon joined by Hung Hs'ing, who rose in hearby Nanking. But the other military governors sympathetic to the Kuomintang were unable to act together, and the main battles were fought over Kiangsi and Nanking. By September Yüan had crushed the rebel forces and brought the lower Yangtze valley under Peiyang supremacy.

During the course of this "second revolution," Yüan arbitrarily dismissed several Kuomintang representatives from the legislature, imprisoned eight others, executed two, and terrified the remainder into silence or disavowal of their Kuomintang affiliations.[32] Through all this, Liang could only meekly ask Yüan to distinguish between the extremist minority in the Kuomintang from the more moderate majority.[33]

The full implications of the crushing defeat of the "second revolution" for constitutional government itself did not become clear until several months later. For the moment, the fate suffered by the Kuomintang must have seemed to some Chin-pu Tang members more a blessing than a curse, for the parliamentary balance had now been tipped in their favor. In September, the Chin-pu Tang reached the height of its influence with the formation of the Hsiung Hsi-ling cabinet, known as the "cabinet of talent" or the "Chin-pu Tang cabinet"—in addition to Hsiung, who was concurrently Premier and Minister of Finance, the cabinet included three other prominent members of the party: Chang Chien as Minister of Agriculture and Commerce, Wang Ta-hsieh as Minister of Education and Liang as Minister of Justice.

Liang finally had an opportunity to try to implement some of his ideas. As Minister of Justice, he aimed above all to establish the independence of the judiciary. He urged that the respective areas of authority between the law courts and the military authorities be delineated clearly and that any interference by military officials with the courts be forbidden. His rationale was that the rule of law was integral to any modern nation. "To cultivate the rule of law," it was necessary to instill in all the "respect for the law," which in turn required the full independence of the judicial system from arbitrary encroachments.[34]

His approach was characteristically gradualist. While he warned against rashly innovative action, he was also against abolishing the new law courts, even though they functioned imperfectly, and he argued against Yüan's desire to revert to the old legal system. Liang would build the new judicial system upon the existing structures. Where no new law courts yet existed, he would have local administrative officials continue to oversee judicial functions until a fully developed new legal system could be established. He would strengthen the new legal system gradually with the help of funds from the central government's tax revenue, the establishment of an institute in the capital to train judges, and a host of other measures designed to improve its efficacy.[35]

Even while Liang was trying thus modestly to reform the legal system, the issue of constitutional government itself was coming to a head. The Committee to Draft the Constitution had been constituted at the end of June. The Kuomintang managed to command a majority in this committee, partly because of internal divisions in the Chin-pu Tang. As the committee proceeded with its work during the subsequent months, the irreconcilable differences between the parliamentarians and Yüan soon came into focus. The committee was insistent upon following the precedent of the Provisional Constitution of 1912 and maintaining genuine legislative checks upon executive authority. Yüan, on the other hand, was equally determined to arrogate to his own office much greater powers than those provided in the Provisional Constitution. In particular Yüan sought full powers over appointments and the making of treaties, and requested emergency legislative and budgetary powers.[36]

When the committee refused to budge, Yüan acted swiftly. On November 4, the day after the completed draft was presented before the committee as a whole, Yüan ordered the dissolution of the Kuomintang. By early morning of the fifth, the Peking military police had confiscated the membership certificates of 98 representatives of the upper and 252 of the lower house, and revoked the membership of another 34 representatives of the upper house and 54 of the lower. When the two houses tried to meet on the fifth, they could no longer form a quorum.[37] On January 10, 1914, Yüan formally dissolved the legislature. On May 1, he proclaimed a revised constitution, giving himself dictatorial powers, and thus ending the first parliamentary experiment.

The ease with which Yüan was able to put an end to the legislature of 1913 attests to the weakness of constitutional government in early republican China. Constitutional government had been instituted in the immediate aftermath of the revolution because the revolutionary calls for democracy were backed by the power of the Kuomintang in central and south China. When Yüan succeeded in destroying that power base, only ideological appeal remained to sustain the parliamentary experiment, and even that appeal had worn thin by 1913; the parliamentary forces had discredited themselves through their incessant factional struggles.

Liang, no less than the Kuomintang, was rendered powerless by the disastrous failure of the "second revolution." The Chin-pu Tang could no longer make its weight count as a pivotal force and effectively check Peiyang military power. Liang's experiences in his role as minister of justice only told of his powerlessness. His struggle for judicial independence from military authority was but an extension of the by now hopeless struggle for constitutional government.[38] He resigned on February 20, 1914, a short five months after he had assumed office.

But Yüan was determined to keep Liang in his government. It is true that Liang in 1914 was by no means as "popular" as he had been in 1912. Ideologues and politicians in general had been discredited in the eyes of many people. Liang himself had several times been the object of attack by segments of the press: he had been suspected of involvement in the assassination of Sung,[39] and he was now charged with complicity in the dismissal of the Kuomintang.[40] Although he no longer carried as much weight of "public opinion" as he had earlier, he was still widely recognized as one of the outstanding experts of modern knowledge. Yüan was now proposing to use him in such a capacity—to head the Bureau of Currency. In fact, Yüan did not accept Liang's resignation from the Ministry of Justice until the day after he had appointed Liang to the new post.[41]

As for Liang, his reaction to Yüan's dissolution of the legislature was mitigated by the fact that he himself had found results of the elections to that legislature bitterly disappointing, had disapproved of the behavior of many of the parliamentarians and had been totally disgruntled with the legislature's inability to rise above factional strife.[42] After all, even without Yüan's interference, it is doubtful that the legislative body of 1913 could have functioned effectively. Perhaps even more important was Liang's continued desire to serve his nation, to do, as Ting Wen-chiang put it, "as much as possible within the limitations of existing circumstances."[43] And Yüan was shrewdly offering him a post that promised such a possibility in an area in which he was deeply involved—he had written extensively on China's currency problems[44] and had served as a member of the legislative committee on the currency system.[45]

On March 10, Liang assumed his new post, with the aim of standardizing and stabilizing China's disorderly currencies. He would first adopt a silver standard, as a transitional step toward a gold standard. The silver tael would be replaced gradually by a silver dollar of standard, government-prescribed weight. The rapidly devaluating provincial paper currencies would be absorbed by honoring them at par value for the purchase of government bonds. A limited amount of government exchange notes would be issued to help finance the cost of standardizing currency.[46]

His first concrete step was to promulgate a new set of currency regulations.[47] Yang Ju-mei, in his *Finance in Republican China*, attributes to this set of regulations the beginnings of currency reform in republican China, pointing out that the new standard currency did begin gradually to replace the old media of exchange during 1914 and 1915.[48]

Success was very limited, however. The regulations themselves confronted an immediate stumbling block in the protracted disputes over the standard weight to be adopted for the new silver dollar. Liang had also suggested that the central government itself take the lead by adopting the new currency for purposes of taxation and government spending, but the Customs Office, the chief source of government revenue of the time, refused to change from the tael to the new dollar in its transactions. Liang's regulations never achieved the full efficacy that they might have had.[49]

The other measures he advocated ended stillborn. He soon discovered that his office held little power over established bureaucracies and authorities. He was in fact sitting on a sinecure, as the *Shen pao* reported on December 16.[50] He finally left his post on December 27, once again disheartened by the realities of the early republican government. His own assessment was that he had not been able to do anything, that his policies "ended as nothing but policies on paper." "I have been brandishing my brush on his matter for a decade," he wrote, "yet today I end only in empty words."[51] The Bureau itself was subsequently abolished.

Yüan tried to persuade Liang to stay, for he now had other things in mind and he needed Liang's support. At about the same time that Liang resigned from the Currency Bureau, he was invited to a dinner by Yüan's son, K'e-ting. The younger Yüan spoke at length during the dinner about the evils of republicanism and tried to get Liang to agree that monarchy would suit China best. But Liang objected strongly, and warned of the domestic and international dangers involved in such a move.[52] He then tried to dissuade the older Yüan, pleading before him the case for constitutional government: public opinion, Liang argued, was against monarchy. Yüan must not incite the people's wrath. He must observe the law of the land, set an example for the officials and the people, encourage the expression of public opinion, and work toward popular participation in government.[53] Naïve and academic ramblings, Yüan must have thought.

Friendly appearances were maintained for a few more months, even though the two men were now fast moving toward an open rupture in relations. Yüan denied that he had any intention of making himself emperor. In July he even appointed Liang to a new Committee for Drafting a Constitution. Liang accepted, but he was already expecting harsh reprisals from Yüan and had moved into the Tientsin concession areas for his own safety.[54]

On August 19 came the establishment of the Ch'ou-an Hui, ostensibly a body devoid of political implications and organized for the sole purpose of academic study of the pros and cons of monarchical government. The Ch'ou-an Hui quickly arrived at the conclusion that since republicanism had failed to operate effectively in China, monarchy was the only answer. Liang immediately wrote an essay to refute the arguments of the Ch'ou-an Hui: the people had not even begun to recover after the immense sufferings wrought by the revolution; a retrogressive change could only breed further disorder; moreover, a change in the form of the polity could hardly significantly alter the quality of government, which was dependent on the men in government and on the political maturity and capability of the people.[55] Yüan tried in vain to quash the publication of this essay by offering Liang 200,000 yüan.[56]

Liang was now planning to resist Yüan's monarchical scheme by the force of arms. The day after the formation of the Ch'ou-an Hui, he met with Ts'ai O to discuss plans for the anti-monarchical movement. In October, Tai K'an, a key figure in Kweichow, came to Tientsin at Ts'ai's bidding and the three men conferred on the strategy of the movement.[57] Yunnan was to serve as the spearhead of resistance to Yüan. It would also set an example for provincially initiated reforms—since Liang could foresee no quick and easy victory over Yüan, he was prepared to pin his hopes on local reforms.[58]

In December, Liang left for Shanghai to prepare for the movement. He tried to enlist Japanese help in funding and arms and to raise money from the overseas Chinese and the Shanghai community. He also sent Huang Su-ch'u, one of his trusted followers, to solicit the support of Feng Kuo-chang, who was now based in Nanking. Huang had contacts with two of Feng's men. And Liang maintained close contacts with all phases of the movement and repeatedly offered advice on strategy.[59]

On December 25, Ts'ai O declared the independence of Yunnan; Kweichow followed suit a month later. In February, Lu Jung-t'ing sent word to Liang that Kwangsi would rise upon Liang's arrival.[60] Lu was anticipating complications within his own province and from Kwangtung, and calculated that Liang's presence and help would be an asset.[61] Liang left on March 4, disguised as a Japanese and traveling via Hong Kong, Haiphong, and Hanoi.[62] Lu declared independence on the fifteenth, while Liang was still en route, with a text drafted by Liang and sent under their joint names.[63]

On March 22, Yüan recanted his earlier "acceptance" of the throne, but by this time the antimonarchists were demanding his complete ouster. The Kuomintang fragments in Kwangtung managed to persuade Military Governor Lung Chi-kuang to declare that province's independence on April 6.[64] Chekiang, Szechuan, and Hunan soon joined with the rebels. Yüan made a belated effort to placate the rebel forces by calling for responsible government, but he could not now command even the support of his long-time lieutenants, Feng Kuo-chang and Tuan Ch'i-jui. On June 6, the entire issue ended abruptly—Yüan died.

The antimonarchists had triumphed not so much by force of ideology or the power of the men committed to republicanism as by the divisiveness among the military powers in the nation. Ts'ai O and Yunnan had only supplied the spark. Men such as Lu Jung-t'ing in Kwangsi or Lung Chi-kuang in Kwangtung were not unequivocally aligned with either Liang's group or the Kuomintang, but were acting in their own interests. Yüan's power had grown too great and threatened the independence to which the provincial military figures had grown accustomed. Even Yüan's own lieutenants, such as Tuan Ch'i-jui and Feng Kuo-chang, preferred not to see him in a position of undisputed power.

The power configuration had changed considerably since 1912. Tuan was now the most powerful figure in the Peking area. Feng controlled Nanking, the center of the lower Yangtze Valley. Li Yüan-hung still held his base in Wuhan. These were now the three most powerful men in the nation, a fact that was reflected in the new national government—Li became Acting President, Feng Vice-President, and Tuan the Premier. As for the parliamentary forces, they were even weaker than they had been in 1912. The Kuomintang did not recover in 1916 its earlier base of influence in the lower Yangtze Valley. It was more than ever dependent on the whims of individual military governors in the south and southwest. Liang might have had a base in Yunnan, if Ts'ai O had remained supreme in that province, but T'ang Chi-yao was emerging the strongest figure in Yunnan, and T'ang was far less sympathetic to Liang than Ts'ai had been.

For the moment, however, the nation returned once more to

the form of constitutional government. The parliamentary forces succeeded in restoring the Provisional Constitution of 1912. On August 1, 1916, the legislature of 1913 was reconvened in Peking.

A new atmosphere seemed to prevail among the reconvened parliamentarians. The old political parties were gone, and in their place had risen a plethora of new "cliques" (*hsi* or *p'ai*), "clubs" (*chü-lo-pu*), and "societies" (*hui* or *she*). The prevailing sentiment was summed up by the slogan of the erstwhile Chinpu tang—"a-partyism" (*pu-tang chu-i*). Many seemed to have hoped that the reconvened legislature would rise above partisan differences to concern itself with national issues.

But the old alignments were in fact modified only very slightly. The Kuomintang used the appellation Society to Confer on Constitutional Government (Hsien-cheng Shang-chüeh Hui), and consisted now of three factions: a left wing known as the 1916 Club (Ping-ch'en Chü-lo-pu) and representing the China Revolutionary Party (Chung-hua Ke-ming Tang), the tightly knit revolutionary organization started by Sun Yat-sen in 1914; the T'ao-yüan faction made up of radicalized members of the Chin-pu Tang, such as Sun Hung-i; the center and numerically largest K'e-lu faction, led by Chang Chi and consisting chiefly of earlier followers of Sung Chiao-jen. Most of the Chin-pu Tang members, after a brief separation into two factions, were regrouped into the "Research Clique" (Yen-chiu Hsi).[65]

Liang was for a time uncertain about whether to plunge himself once more into the torrent of national politics. He was painfully aware of the futility of his own efforts during the preceding years. As he pointed out to his followers, their group had tried to operate without "a foot or an inch of power base." In the end they had done little more than "waved their empty fists and made noises for others."[66] His sense of distress was aggravated by a number of personal tragedies during the spring and summer of 1916. T'ang Chüeh-tun, one of his closest friends and followers, was murdered by Lung Chi-kuang's underlings on April 12.[67] In May, Liang learned of the death of his father[68] and in July, he heard that Ts'ai O was ailing.[69] He now spoke more and more of withdrawing from public life to devote himself entirely to the task of "educating society."[70]

But once again his desire for political action overrode his sense of despondence. In the heat of the victory of the anti-monarchical movement, he could temporarily forget the futility of his earlier actions. He also shared with many other parliamentarians the hope that important lessons had been learned from the failures of the preceding years and that constitutional government could perhaps operate more effectively henceforth. He would try the game of power once more.

He could have allied himself with any one of the three major powers in the nation. Li Yüan-hung asked him in July to head the Secretariat of the President's office and offered him a monthly stipend of 2,000 yüan.[71] Feng Kuo-chang was courteous and Liang, for his part, tried to influence the composition of the new cabinet through Feng,[72] but even as he maintained contacts with Li and Feng, his choice was Tuan Ch'i-jui. His calculations were undoubtedly much the same as those which had prompted him to choose Yüan in 1912: Tuan was the strongest of the three and was wielding most of the power in the national government. By October Liang was secretly reporting to Tuan through Chi Chung-yin on the affairs in Kwangtung-Kwangsi and was receiving instructions from Tuan for his actions.[73]

On January 6, he arrived in Peking and immediately became embroiled in the leading national issue of the day—China's policy in the World War. On February 1, Germany announced her submarine blockade of the seas. The American, British, and Japanese governments now solicited China's entrance into the war.[74] Tuan favored declaring war against the Central Powers, and the majority of the legislative members were inclined to go

along with this policy, the only exception being the radical 1916
Club. Thus the two houses passed by wide margins on March 10
and March 11 the resolution calling for severing relations with
Germany.[75]

Liang was among the leaders of those who advocated a declaration of war against the Central Powers. He believed that
participation in the war would enhance China's international
prestige, would strengthen her financial position, and would
mean automatic cancellation of the indemnities owing to
Germany and Austria-Hungary. China could, moreover, bar-
gain for concessions from the Allies on customs valuations and
obtain extensions on indemnity payments. The increased customs revenues and the savings from the indemnity payments
could then be used to build up China's gold reserves—and the
general devaluation of gold under wartime conditions presented an unusual opportunity—which could in turn be used
to help stabilize China's currencies. Liang was hoping to follow
up on his earlier efforts as head of the Bureau of Currency under
Yüan.[76]

But the issue of foreign policy quickly became a contest among
the various power groups. Even before the legislature had voted
for severing relations with Germany, Tuan had precipitously
instructed Chang Tsung-hsiang, the Chinese ambassador to
Japan, to proceed with negotiations for Japanese concessions.
Many of the parliamentarians saw in Tuan's move a conspira-
torial scheme to strengthen his own power base with Japanese
help and the more radical among them wanted to use the
foreign policy issue to topple Tuan's cabinet. Tuan attempted to
pressure these dissidents into submission—on May 10, the legislative session was surrounded by a mob of over 3,000, ostensibly representing "public opinion" in favor of declaring war.
The move served only to turn more of the parliamentarians
against Tuan. The representatives adjourned their meeting to
protest against the attempted interference. When President Li,

in spite of pressures from those military governors who supported Tuan, refused to dissolve the legislature and ordered instead Tuan's replacement, Tuan had to step down.[77]

The combined powers of the legislature and Li were able to
force Tuan's resignation, but they were not able to come up
with a realistic alternative. Li's power was not sufficient to sustain the national government. Li turned in desperation to
Chang Hsün, the Military Governor of Anhwei, but Chang
had different plans. On June 13, he forced the dissolution of the
legislature and his armies entered Peking on the following day.
Two weeks later, Chang announced the restoration of the
Hsüan-t'ung Emperor, P'u-i. Thus ended the second parliamentary experiment.

The legislature in 1916–17 was after all only a shadow of
what it had been earlier. In 1913 it had been based on the
Kuomintang power base in central and south China, and could
only be destroyed when Yüan's forces crushed that power base.
But in 1916–17, the legislature resided in a power vacuum and
was therefore even more easily dispensed with.

Chang Hsün's power was also incapable of sustaining the national government. Chang apparently hoped to isolate Tuan
with the support of Li and Feng Kuo-chang, but the restoration
gesture turned nearly everyone against him, and Chang's forces
were no match for the anti-restoration forces led by Tuan. Tuan
returned to power once more, and Li, for his miscalculations,
had to resign in favor of Feng as Acting President.

Liang had again chosen the winning side. Upon receipt of
the news of restoration, he immediately sent a circular telegram
to argue against restoration: the leaders of restoration were
foolish bookmen and greedy militarists. They had no appreciation of the realities of politics. How, for example, were they
going to finance their government? They argued that republicanism had not worked. True, but that was the fault of the
men in government, not of the system. How could a return to

the imperial system alone improve the quality of government? Moreover, such a step could only breed autocracy, and, in turn, revolution.[78] Liang himself personally joined with Tuan's army in Tientsin to participate in the campaign against Chang.[79]

His reward was another opportunity to try "to do as much as possible within the limitations of existing circumstances." On July 17, he became Minister of Finance in Tuan's new cabinet. He was now in a position similar to that in 1913 when he joined the "cabinet of talent." The new cabinet consisted of two other members of the "Research Clique," both of them Liang's close associates—T'ang Hua-lung as Minister of the Interior and Lin Ch'ang-min as Minister of Justice.[80] His party was again preponderant among the parliamentarians in Peking, especially since many of the Kuomintang representatives left to join Sun Yat-sen's military government in Canton.

In his new capacity, Liang hoped to carry out the plans he had formulated in connection with the issue of declaring war against the Central Powers. The Allies did in fact agree to a five-year extension on the Boxer indemnities in return for China's entrance into the war. This meant, as Liang pointed out, a savings of about $70,000,000 in China's customs revenues during the next five years. Liang's hope was to use this sum to pay off China's debts and to build up her gold reserves. The general devaluation of gold at the time, he argued, presented a special opportunity for liquidating loans computed on the basis of the gold standard and for building up China's gold reserves to prepare for adopting the gold standard.[81] He proposed to make two new loans: one of 10,000,000 yen from the Four Power Banking Consortium and another of 20,000,000 yen from Japan. Both loans would be used to purchase gold for immediate deposit in foreign banks to serve as security for the newly standardized currency.[82]

Liang was widely criticized by his contemporaries and by

later scholars for the loan of 20,000,000 yen from Japan.[83] This loan was one of the group of eight loans from Japan concluded between January 20, 1917, and September 28, 1918. These eight loans came to be known as the "Nishihara loans," so called because they were not negotiated through normal diplomatic channels but through Nishihara Kamezō, a personal representative of Prime Minister Terauchi Masataka.[84] From the start, the loans became an emotionally charged issue. It was the stated policy of the Terauchi cabinet to support Tuan and contemporary opinion was quick to see "conspiracy" and "selling-out" in the loans.[85]

While it is true that the Japanese conceived the loans as a means of establishing Japanese supremacy in China, the loans themselves did not carry exacting terms. The China policy of the Terauchi government was fashioned after the experiences in Korea of Terauchi, Nishihara, and Shōda Kazue. Terauchi had served as Governor General in Korea, Shōda as president of the Bank of Korea, and Nishihara, manager of a joint Korean-Japanese textile firm. The three were together known as the "Korean Group" (Chōsen gumi), with which the Japanese government's China policy was now identified. They were opposed to the methods of the Okuma cabinet, which had sought direct military and economic concessions from China through the Twenty-one Demands, and they had risen to power on the wave of discontent that led to the fall of the Okuma cabinet. Their theory, well represented by Nishihara, was that the best way to secure Japan's supremacy in China was to develop Sino-Japanese economic cooperation rather than to seek territorial and economic concessions.[86] The actual terms of the loans, therefore, were very favorable: the interest rate was low; there was no commission charge and no demand of any security.[87]

The fault of the loans lay not so much in "selling out" as in the purposes to which they were put. It was Liang's hope that the funds would be used to stabilize China's currencies, but in fact they were used only for military expenditures. As Liang pointed out in his report to President Feng and Premier Tuan: the funds were used up by (1) increases in the routine expenditures of the army and navy, (2) the strengthening of various provincial armies, and (3) the "pacification" campaign against the military government in the south. Such expenditures, he continued, were flagrant abuses of the terms of the loan contract, which had explicitly stipulated that the funds were to be used for building up China's gold reserves.[88] The fact was that there could be no meeting of interests between Liang and the military men in power. Liang's first priority was for reforms that he deemed to be in the interest of the nation's modernization. Tuan and Feng's choices, on the other hand, could hardly have been other than for the strengthening of their own positions; they could not otherwise maintain their precarious hegemony over the multifarious contending military factions. The limited funds available to the central government could not serve both purposes at once. Liang resigned in November, a short four months after he had assumed office.

His parliamentary activities could only come to a like ending. He had hoped that the reconvened legislature would shed itself of earlier partisan strife and find a way to operate under existing conditions, but it proved to be no more able to do so than it had been in 1913. Once again Liang hoped that a more moderate legislature consisting principally of his own "Research Clique" might at least be able to maintain some semblance of constitutional government. Accordingly, he supported Tuan's call for a reorganization of the legislative body.[89] But the results of the "elections" of July, 1918, shattered even those last hopes: the reconstituted legislature only reflected more realistically the existing power configuration. The powerless Research Clique won a mere twenty seats. The thin veneer of national and constitutional government had finally been stripped from the government in Peking and China was in the period of full-fledged warlordism. Liang and other ideologues of the revolution could no longer figure prominently in the political arena. Liang himself withdrew from public life to devote his full attention to education and scholarship.

He had done about as well as could be expected under the circumstances. Starting from an essentially powerless position, he managed to play a remarkably prominent role in the national government. He understood well that the first prerequisite for the national government was military power and he managed always to choose the winning side, first Yüan, then Tuan. He also understood the power configuration of the time and succeeded in maneuvering himself into positions where his support and service were actively solicited by the men in power. He came much closer to having a real opportunity to implement his ideas than a man such as Sung Chiao-jen.

His failures tell the other side of the story. His relationships with Yüan and Tuan symbolized the conflict between ideology and military power in early republican China. Essentially powerless, Liang had finally little more than the force of persuasion to help him realize his aims. The lesson of his failures was that drawn by Sun Yat-sen and Mao Tse-tung in the 1920s: ideology must be rendered sufficiently powerful to bend the army to its aims, and perhaps the only effective formula was to have a tightly knit political organization with its own army. Liang's was one early story of the futility of the efforts of individual liberal reformers in twentieth-century China.

CHAPTER 7

Syncretism and Liberalism

The May Fourth intellectual revolution came in the midst of widespread disillusionment with political realities. The failures of national and constitutional government convinced many intellectuals that more fundamental and sweeping changes were necessary. As republican government degenerated into war-lordism and the hiatus between realities and aspirations widened, intellectuals were increasingly alienated from the political scene. Few paid any attention to questions of political action, of how to get from what-was to what-ought-to-be. The orientation of the intellectual revolutionaries was chiefly theoretical. And the mood was radical. The new cries were for a "new youth," a "new literature," or a "new culture." The search was for a completely new China.

The call for a new China was the climax of intellectual tendencies a century old. In the 1840s, men such as Wei Yüan and Lin Tse-hsü called for the strengthening of China's maritime defenses in the face of superior Western firepower. By the 1870s, the "self-strengtheners" were to call for new commerce and industries, deemed to be inseparable from military power. By the 1890s, some reformers turned their emphasis to political institutions in their quest for ways to close the gap between Chinese and Western power. After the abortive Hundred Days' Reform, some thinkers went on to challenge the entire moral

141

fabric of Chinese civilization, and Liang Ch'i-ch'ao was among the first to call for new Chinese "citizens," with new moral values. Still, China found herself at the mercy of imperialistic encroachments in the 1910s, and the intellectual revolutionaries were now calling for total change.

The sweeping changes in the climate of intellectual opinion between the 1890s and the 1910s are well reflected in the contrast between the central intellectual issues of the day. In the 1890s, the question had been: what does China need to adopt from the West? By the 1910s, the tables had been turned. The question was: what, if anything, can be salvaged from Chinese civilization? The advocates of "wholesale Westernization" held the initiative. Their enemies were not so much archconservatives who believed in the superiority of Chinese civilization, but modernizers or syncretists who called for a synthesis of the best of China and the West.

Liang took his place among the syncretists, as indeed his record of the two preceding decades would lead us to expect. He had, since 1902–1903, favored gradualism, in opposition to more radical and revolutionary change. In action, he had shown himself to be always inclined to follow a "middle road," to position himself between the established authorities and the forces of radical change. His choices in the 1910s and 1920s were the same: to tread the middle path between radical iconoclasts and conservative traditionalists. And he was able to find in postwar intellectual currents in Europe confirmation for his syncretic inclinations.

He sailed for Europe on December 23, 1918. In the course of his year's stay in Europe, he tried to learn firsthand about the civilization that he had studied from a distance for so long. In England, he attended a session of the House of Commons and visited Oxford and Cambridge. On the continent, he toured Italy, Switzerland, Germany, and Holland. In Paris, where he

spent most of his time, he rode an airplane to "an altitude of
500 kilometers," met Henri Bergson, Woodrow Wilson, and a
score of other eminent philosophers, statesmen, and litérrateurs.
He also attended lecture courses in history, politics, and modern
literature.[1]

He was handicapped linguistically. He had tried his hand at
several foreign languages, but he was never able to devote much
time to language study and had made significant progress only
with Japanese. On board ship to Europe, he struggled with
French, but with little success.[2] In Paris, he turned his attention
to English and boasted by the end of his stay of being able to
get the general idea out of English books and newspapers. He
had studied English by his own methods, however, and in the
end could neither speak nor understand spoken English.[3] He
himself acknowledged this linguistic handicap and that he
would have gained "more than ten times as much" from his trip
if he had had a knowledge of the European languages.[4]

He was able to learn about European thought only through
the help of his younger companions: Carsun Chang, Chiang
Fang-chen, Liu Ch'ung-chieh, Ting Wen-chiang, Hsü Hsin-liu,
and an attendant, Yang Wei-hsin. Chiang had studied in
Germany, Chang and Ting in England and Germany, and Hsü
in France. Ting knew English and German well, and Hsü was
completely fluent in French and served as Liang's interpreter
in Paris. These men also possessed varied background, training,
and interests: Chang and Chiang had worked closely with Liang
in his political activities; Chiang was a soldier by profession but
was now undertaking a study of the Renaissance; Chang's interests were in philosophy, with a special focus on Bergson, socialist
ideas, and the new idealist currents of thought; Liu was a
diplomat by profession and Ting was a trained scientist whose
interests encompassed history and philosophy as well. As a
group they were ten to fifteen years younger than Liang and

belonged to the generation of thinkers who came to maturity in and after the May Fourth period. They served as Liang's antennae in Europe.[5]

Liang enthusiastically plunged into his new studies with the help of these younger companions and was, as he wrote to his brother, "determined to be a student on this trip."[6] The result was a panoply of impressions that sparked a reevaluation of his earlier ideas about the West. As he put it:

> I am unable to predict the course of the changes my mind is undergoing. In the past five months, I have met people of all descriptions; I have heard ideas of a variety of schools and observed all kinds of conflicts in interests. I am dazzled by paintings and sculptures that capture the inner spirit in the presentation of the outward form, moved by kaleidoscopic and bustling social phenomena and feasted with magnificent and changing natural scenery. Given my nature which is rich in feeling and my desire for continual improvement, try to imagine the stimulations I am experiencing! I feel that my mind is daily fermenting and that it will undergo a great revolution. But what the product of that revolution will be, I am still unable to tell.[7]

The aftermath of this "revolution" of the mind is recorded in Liang's "Impressions from My European Journey."[8]

For two decades Liang had shared with his classical liberal mentors a faith in world-wide progress. When he echoed the individualistic liberalism of John Stuart Mill and Jeremy Bentham, and Spencerian Darwinism as reinterpreted by Katō Hiroyuki, he meant to convey that inordinate striving of Western individuals that he thought to be the very source of modern Western civilization. With Spencer and Bentham he shared the belief that individual competition and "enlightened" pursuit of self interest had contributed to the inexorable progress of the modern world. If it was what Benjamin Schwartz calls "the

Faustian character of the West"[9] that he perceived, then it was the character symbolized by Goethe's Faust who found salvation rather than the tragic Faust of the original legend.

The First World War and its consequences, which he now witnessed firsthand, led him to question his earlier faith. The road of inexorable progress had somehow led the West to the abyss of World War I. What, he asked, went wrong in the West? Had not unmitigated Darwinian struggle led to this disastrous holocaust? And he found that the postwar intellectual climate in Europe mirrored his own doubts. Spengler's *The Decline of the West* was enjoying wide sales in this same year, 1919.[10] It was also apparent that social Darwinism was in disfavor. Already in the 1890s, in what Stuart Hughes calls "the revolt against positivism," advanced European thinkers had turned against the assumptions of social Darwinism.[11] In America, the vogue of Spencerian Darwinism was likewise a dead letter by the end of the war.[12] The west, Liang commented, had rejected the view of Darwinian struggle in favor of Kropotkin's "mutual aid."[13]

Liang was now prepared to discredit the West of the late nineteenth and early twentieth centuries. Like some of his European contemporaries, he tended to lump Darwinism together with a host of other doctrines. As Stuart Hughes points out, the late nineteenth-century critics tended to use the word "positivism" interchangeably with "materialism," "mechanism," and "naturalism," all of which they regarded with equal disfavor. What they opposed was "the whole tendency to discuss human affairs in terms of analogies drawn from natural science."[14] Liang similarly found in Darwinism, naturalism, materialism, and positivism what he called "the materialistic and mechanistic view of life." According to him, such a view of life led in its extreme form to the "perverted ideas of Nietzsche," which were in turn mated to militarism and imperialism. This view of life represented the type of morality in which "altruism was considered to be the morality of slaves," and "annihilation of the weak the natural duty of the strong." And together such doctrines accounted for the coming of the war.[15]

Addressing his own contemporaries more directly, Liang concluded his "Impressions" with an essay entitled "The Dream of the Omnipotence of Science." Here he simply equated science with positivism. The Europeans, according to him, "have dreamt the dream of the omnipotence of science, but today they are declaring the bankruptcy of science." In fact, he continued, this was "the key to the present changes in the intellectual currents in Europe." Europeans were aware that their "dream" had led to a disregard for man's spiritual life and had bred the unmitigated pursuit of wealth and power that ended in the holocaust of World War I. China must not make the same mistake.[16]

Liang might have gone on from this point to draw new inspirations from the latest currents of thought in Western Europe. After all, it was fashionable in the May Fourth period to show that one was abreast with the latest in the West, and the Liang of the early 1900s would probably have done just that: he would have become the expert advocate of new Western ideas. But the more matured Liang had other concerns. The iconoclastic and radical mood of the young intellectual revolutionaries genuinely raised for him the specter of crass positivism, or what D. W. Y. Kwok has called "scientism."[17] They forced Liang to take stock of an issue that was long overdue in his own intellectual development: given that China must modernize—and Liang no longer needed to argue for that since it was so widely taken for granted among the May Fourth intellectuals—what was to happen to Chinese civilization? Had China really nothing to offer to the modern world, as so many of the revolutionaries were inclined to believe?

Liang was simply too old and too much aware of the force of historical continuity to believe in a program calling for wiping the slate clean. His personal inclination was to favor syncretism. And here again he could find Western authorities for his position. By the time of Spengler's *The Decline of the West*, cultural relativism had gained considerable currency in Western Europe. The primacy of Western history was no longer taken for granted and alien civilizations were considered by many to be of equal value.[18] According to Liang, the American journalist Frank Herbert Simonds (1878–1936) told him that "Western civilization is bankrupt," and that the West was looking to Eastern civilizations for salvation.[19] Liang also quoted Étienne Boutroux, who, he said, impressed upon him the need for every people to develop its indigenous culture and to combine the unique qualities therein with those of other cultures. Boutroux had read some translated Chinese philosophical works and had "invariably found them to be extremely profound."[20] Liang's self-appointed task in the May Fourth period was precisely to discover the "unique qualities" of Chinese civilization in order to fuse them with "the better qualities" of the West.

But what was he to look for? Liang understood only too well that he could not approach his own cultural heritage without preconceptions. He must first redefine or reaffirm what he considered to be of value in Western civilization, and present his ideal of the new China. Only then could he search for complementary values in Chinese civilization.

He chose, first of all, to reaffirm his liberal faith. The second half of his "Impressions" contains an essay entitled "The Self-Awakening of the Chinese."[21] Here he restated his belief in the centrality of men and of the human spirit—more important than the question of what kind of institutions or technologies was the question of what kind of man the new China should have. And his message was addressed to the youth. His call was for the young people to develop to the utmost their individual abilities. Only then could they contribute to the cause of the nation and of mankind. And he chose once more to emphasize the central importance of freedom of thought—only under conditions of free thought could individuals develop their potential.

As for the form of government, he reaffirmed his belief in constitutional and representative government as the ideal for China. Although it was true that it had failed miserably in China, it had failed only because she was not ready for such government. The basic failure of both the Kuomintang and of his own side was that they were not really representative—they had no popular bases of support. The parliamentarians of his own side had tried to work within the limits imposed by the existing governmental structure. But they had "in the end only been used by others without being able to implement any reforms."[22] The Kuomintang, on the other hand, had sought to overthrow the military men in power, but their only recourse in that effort had been other military men and they had only contributed to the further proliferation of warlords. He stressed once more the primary importance of the foundation of democratic institutions—an awakened citizenry.

But if the essay was in many ways a reaffirmation of the ideas contained in "The New Citizen," it also differed substantially from that earlier program. The radical and impatient mood of "The New Citizen" was replaced by calmer notes and an insistence on gradualism. Two decades of political action had tempered Liang's impatience. He was no longer hopeful, as he had been in 1899–1902, of instant results, and was prepared to bide his time until more favorable conditions had developed. "The national movement we are working on now," he wrote, "can only be realized twenty or thirty years from now."[23] Let us not be impatient, he continued, we must pin our hopes on the youth; they will in time be able to shoulder the heavy burdens if only they have the will and will train themselves for the task.

Gone also was the Darwinian verbiage of "struggle for existence" and "survival of the fittest." The keynote of individualistic assertion was replaced by an emphasis on cooperation.

"The greatest failing of the Chinese people is their lack of the ability to organize and their lack of the spirit of the rule of law."[24] As individuals, the Chinese were the equal of any American or European. As a group, however, they simply could not work together. What was needed was a set of agreed-upon rules and principles among the Chinese so that they could develop the ability to organize. And Liang advocated particularly the development of local self-government and professional organizations as concrete steps toward developing the organizational ability of the Chinese people.

The absence of the Darwinian framework affected also the tone of Liang's nationalism. "The New Citizen" had called urgently for the "spirit" of nationalism as the only way to develop modern national power. Liang had underscored the urgency of that call by depicting the international community as a jungle of teeth and claws. His tone was now entirely different. The call was for "a nation with a cosmopolitan spirit" (*shih-chieh chu-i te kuo-chia*). Nationalism must not lose sight of individual rights or of international cooperation. The goal of the future was to develop individuals who would not only contribute to the well-being of the nation but also to the general advancement of human civilization.[25]

Liang was affirming a substantially different liberal faith from that which he first espoused in "The New Citizen." Gone now was any reference to liberalism as an effective path to national power, of liberal institutions as providing the best environment for the release of individual energies behind national ends. Liang had in fact since 1902 and 1903 learned to dissociate the liberal program from the goal of national power. What he was reiterating was his faith in the liberal program as a value in and of itself, the intrinsic desirability of "liberty of thought" and "constitutional and representative government."

His tendency in 1918 and after was the reverse of that after 1902. He had then pushed his liberal commitments to the more

distant future because of his realization of their essential ir-
relevancy to the more urgent goal of national power. But the
international picture looked very different to him in 1918. He
was convinced that the era of imperialism had passed, that the
West had learned the lesson of the tragic consequences of international Darwinism. That meant also that China's sovereignty
was no longer as urgent an issue as it had been at the turn of the
century. China could perhaps afford the luxury of pursuing
universal, human goals without the constraints of considerations of national survival.

He had compromised his liberal ideals after 1902 and 1903
also because of his desire for concrete political action. What he
observed of Chinese realities had persuaded him that the liberal
program was as yet impracticable and he had followed the
model of "enlightened despotism" for more than a decade, a
decade that had ended in frustration and his resignation from
an active political career. He was now convinced that more
time was needed to develop the proper prerequisites for modern
government in China. Once more he was speculating on what
ought to be, without the constraints of what was. It was a
tendency that reflected the general mood of the May Fourth
period.

The main emphasis of "The Self-Awakening of the Chinese"
was finally on the central issue of the day: the place of Chinese
civilization in the modern world. Liang's instructions to the
Chinese youth were that they must, on the one hand, avoid the
simplistic position of those who said that "Western learning can
all be found in China." On the other hand, they must be equally
suspicious of those who were "intoxicated with things Western
and deprecate everything Chinese." The direction Liang
pointed to was: "to enrich our culture with Western culture and
to enrich Western culture with our own culture, so that they
might fuse into a new culture." In searching for "the best" in
Chinese civilization, care must be taken to distinguish the transi-

ent elements and conditions from the "fundamental spirit." The youth of China "must first have an attitude of respect for their own culture," they must then study it with "Western methods of research," and, as a final step, bring Chinese culture together with other cultures to create a new culture.[26] Liang himself would turn to his cultural heritage for values to complement his stated liberal ideals.

He devoted the bulk of his efforts during the final decade of his life to the study of Chinese history. He wrote a full-length essay on the history of verse writing in China, a detailed commentary on K'ung Shang-jen's "Peach Blossom Fan," and biographies of such figures as T'ao Ch'ien, Chu Shun-shui, and Tai Chen.[27] His three most important works were in "intellectual history"—*History of Chinese Political Thought in the pre-Ch'in Period, Intellectual Trends in the Ch'ing Period,* and *History of Chinese Thought in the Last Three Hundred Years.*[28] He also began plans for "A History of the World," "Our National History," "A History of China," and "A Cultural History of China."[29] Within this panoramic sweep of interests, his focus was especially on the classical period—in addition to the study of classical political thought, he did several studies of individual schools and thinkers, including "Philosophy of Lao Tzu," "Confucian Philosophy," "Confucius," and "Commentary on the Mo Ching."[30]

He was well aware of the fact that he approached the past with the preoccupations of the present. The aim of historical study, according to him, was "to reevaluate the past" in order to give it "new value" (*chia-chih*). There were two kinds of values—the "ephemeral values that depreciate as their time passes," and "the permanent values that appreciate with the passage of time." The latter were the ones that had to be defined and reevaluated for their contemporary relevance.[31]

The organizing conceptions of his historical studies were defined in a series of lectures he gave in 1926–27 on "How to Study Chinese History." He distinguished three kinds of intel-

lectual currents: 1. The mainstream (*chu-hsi*); "It is created and
organized by the Chinese people themselves; it is valuable and
authoritative; it contributes to world culture." The two main-
streams in Chinese history were classical thought and Sung
Neo-Confucianism. 2. The auxiliary current (*p'ang-hsi*); "It is
an imported current of thought which, after having been di-
gested and absorbed, . . . develops into a second mainstream."
Examples of this second category were Buddhism of the Sui-
T'ang period and Western thought in modern times. 3. The
tributary stream (*jen-hsi*): "It is the successor to a mainstream.
It consists of organizing and elaborating upon the mainstream." Examples of this category were the development of
classical thought during the period between Han and early
T'ang, and the developments of Neo-Confucian thought during
the Ch'ing period.[32]

Liang then went on to draw an analogy between modern
China and the Sung-Ming period. "Neo-Confucianism," he
wrote, "was the product of a fusion of a highly developed
auxiliary current with the mainstream of Chinese thought."[33]
China was now due for a third mainstream, the product of a
synthesis of indigenous ideas with those absorbed from the West.
Therefore, present-day Chinese must earnestly study and seek
to understand Western thought. Only then would they know
that their past learning was inadequate. At the same time, they
must systematically study their own cultural heritage. They
would then know that Western learning alone was also inadequate for solving Chinese problems. Thus would genuine
interaction take place to result in the creation of something
new.[34]

He himself was perhaps in a position comparable to the two
Ch'eng brothers and Chu Hsi. He pointed out that Chu Hsi
and the two Ch'engs both soaked in Buddhism for several years,
"hoping thereby to discover truths about life, but were finally
unable to satisfy their desires." They therefore returned to

Chinese classical learning. "But they had already been deeply
influenced by the Buddhist canons they had studied." . . . when
they looked anew at classical texts, it was as if "they had donned
binoculars or microscopes"—"even that which had contained
nothing now came to contain something."[35] The analogy Liang
intended was obvious: he himself had soaked in Western
thought for a number of years and was now returning to classical texts and finding new things in them. Perhaps he too could
launch the Chinese intellectual world into a new mainstream,
just as the two Ch'engs and Chu Hsi had done.

For the task of reevaluating his classical legacy, Liang in-
voked once more the Kung-yang doctrines that he had rejected
as early as 1899. The *Spring and Autumn Annals*, he stated, was
not merely history but contained Confucius' political ideals. The
text must be read for its "hidden and subtle meanings." The
latter were preserved in the Kung-yang and Ku-liang commentaries, Tung Chung-shu's *Deep Significance of the Spring and
Autumn Annals* and Ho Hsiu's commentaries on the *Kung-yang
Commentary*. The central idea of the *Spring and Autumn Annals* was
that of the "three ages," and Confucius' ideal society was that
of the "great community" (*ta-t'ung*), as given in the "Li yün."[36]

Liang was not making a simple return to the intellectual
position he had held before 1898. Formerly Kung-yang doctrines had been for him not only useful, but true, to be taken
literally. He was now turning to those same doctrines primarily
because of the flexibility they permitted him in reevaluating his
classical heritage. "When I was young," he wrote, "I thought
that their [the Kung-yang school's] ideas were the real ideas of
Confucius. Only in recent years have I realized that these ideas
were only a tool intended to serve as a bridge for transformation
in thought."[37] And Liang, as the designer of that bridge, could
restrict and guide traffic as he saw fit.

The value he singled out was *jen*. *Jen* was the same as "compassion toward one's fellow men" (*t'ung-ch'ing hsin*). All men

naturally felt compassion toward those close to them. To act in accordance with *jen* was to extend that compassion toward other men, ultimately to all of humanity. *Jen* could be expressed passively or actively. In its passive form, it followed the maxim "do not unto others what you would not have them do unto you." In its active form, it followed the principle that "if one seeks his own fulfillment, he will also seek the fulfillment of other men," for "to elevate mankind is to elevate oneself."[38]

Jen also stood for a political ideal. The purpose of government was "the elevation of the moral character of the citizens," "to broaden and develop each individual's feeling of compassion." The method of *jen* government was education, for "politics is education, and education is politics." The ideal community of *ta-t'ung*, then, was a community in which each individual's sense of "compassion" had been developed to the utmost.[39]

One value of *jen* in the contemporary world was that it could "harmonize" "individualism" and "public spirit," the conflicts between which were "a problem common to the modern world."[40] Liang again used a classical analogy: Yang Chu advocated extreme self-interest while Mo-tzu called for extreme self-sacrifice. The two positions were "harmonized" by Confucius through the use of "reciprocity" (*shu*)—he who pursued his self-interest would also seek to fulfill the interests of others.[41] While "the modern West built societies on a competitive spirit," "the spirit of *jen*" emphasized concession and compromise.[42] The same applied to the tensions between "nationalism" and "cosmopolitanism"—the "spirit" of *jen* transcended the boundaries of states; it was pacifist and condemned military aggression.[43] Thus *jen* would redress what Liang deemed to be an excessive emphasis on Darwinian assertion.

Even more relevant was the way of thinking expressed by *jen*. The way in which Confucius "harmonized" the two extremes of "egotism" and "altruism" was characteristic of his "middle way" (*chung-yung*) of thinking, according to Liang. This "middle way" meant to avoid extreme positions, "leaning neither to one side nor the other, but always taking an attitude of compromise and concession."[44] It was founded on an analogy of truth with nature. Confucius "was one who most admired the ways of nature. He thought that nature's unique quality rested in its intrinsic ability to harmonize." And "*chung-yung* was Confucius' emulation of nature's way of harmonization."[45] What this meant was a view of truth as consisting of multifarious parts: some apparently in conflict, others distinctly complementary, and yet somehow together constituting the greater harmonious whole that was nature. One must therefore maintain the "total" view and avoid identifying himself completely with one extreme or another. Liang even called upon the *Book of Chuang-tzu* to buttress this view. The "T'ien-hsia" chapter, according to him, correctly pointed out that Confucianists alone among the classical schools of thought retained "the total view of the ancients" (*ku-jen chih ch'üan*), whereas all the other schools were one-sided or perceived only one part of the whole.[46]

In the contemporary setting, the "middle way" was essentially the "liberal" way. Liang argued that since Confucius always maintained that the view of both extremes contained one side of truth and that truth was as many-sided as was nature, he was always tolerant of other opinions. He was never exclusive or dogmatic, but was "one who most respected freedom of thought."[47] By the same token, to apply the "middle way" in political action meant to avoid extreme positions and to occupy the "liberal" center. Again Liang used an analogy from the classical period: the Taoists were analogous to present-day anarchists and occupied the extreme left of the political spectrum; the Legalists were similar to present-day statists and occupied the extreme right; the Confucians were the ones who occupied the center of the political spectrum.[48] They alone had caught a glimpse of the principles of democratic government in their ideals of humane government and "primacy of the people." They understood the meanings of government "of the people" and "for the people," even though they failed to grasp the concept of government "by the people."[49]

Was he not stretching Confucianism just a bit far? No, Liang maintained, for Confucius spoke of *shih-chung*, which should be read as "applying the middle way in accordance with the passage of time and changes in circumstances." The term *chung-yung* itself conveyed the idea of applying (*yung*) the "middle way" (*chung*). And *shih-chung* must be interpreted in the light of Mencius' reference to Confucius as the "timely" sage—i.e., the sage who adapted the "middle way" to changing circumstances. In fact, *shih-chung* contained the fundamental and "unique character of Confucius' thought."[50]

In other words, the bridge that Liang tried to build between tradition and modernity was one that was intended to join Confucianism with liberalism. It was a bridge that permitted passage only to the traffic that promised to support or complement his stated liberal ideals, and the principal vehicle to gain passage was the reinterpreted "middle way." This middle way argued for liberalism—it rested on an analogy of truth with nature and therefore supported intellectual tolerance and diversity; it called for avoiding extreme positions, for concession and compromise, and therefore supported the gradualist position of the liberal political center. *Jen* in particular would serve to balance liberalism in what Liang deemed to be its excessive emphasis on the pursuit of individual and national self-interest. And, on the central intellectual question of the day—the place of Chinese civilization in the modern world—the middle way argued for a syncretic position. It would temper the intellectual mood of the May Fourth period, its craze for isms and its inclination toward extreme and simple positions. The attitude of the middle way toward the confrontation between Chinese and Western civilizations was that each represented one side of a

greater truth, in the same manner as *yin* and *yang* each constituted one part of the larger whole, nature.

Liang's own motto in the May Fourth period was in fact the
middle way. In the contemporary debates over science and
metaphysics,[51] for example, Liang rejected the extreme positions of both of his younger friends, Carsun Chang and Ting
Wen-chiang. Chang equated science with materialism and
claimed the domain of metaphysics for Chinese civilization.[52]
Chang, Liang said, was wrong in separating spirit from matter.
Ting, on the other hand, was also mistaken in his position that
"science can perhaps systematize and unify metaphysics in the
future." Thus, "while Chang deprecated science, Ting's excessive faith in the omnipotence of science was a like error."
Liang's own position was what he considered to be the middle
way—"life is a result of the union of the two sides—spirit and
matter—of a man's life."[53]

In 1924 he summarized his position toward the issues raised
by the intellectual revolution in an essay entitled "Against
Isms." In it, he stressed the complexity of human life and his
belief that truth could not be represented by any one ism alone.
The most important isms of the day, according to him, were
"idealism" and "materialism." The former denied the existence
and influence of material conditions, but man's mind was
actually limited and influenced by nature, by other people, and
by his heredity. As for the latter, "whether it emphasizes the
essential importance of heredity, or of environment, or even if
it be the narrowest view of economic determinism," it contained
one portion of truth. But only one portion, and Liang would not
subscribe to any dogmatic ism.[54]

As one contemporary, Wu Chih-hui, pointed out, Liang "opposed on the one hand the conservatives and, on the other hand,
he tried to restrain those who advocated rapid advance. He
thought that this was the way to carry out his 'middle way.' "[55]
Wu was being sarcastic, but he was correct in his description of

Liang's intellectual position within the spectrum of the May Fourth period. Unlike the Sinocentric Ku Hung-ming or Liu Shih-p'ei, who had no use for Western civilization, Liang chose to reaffirm his liberal values and attributed to Western civilization "one side" of truth. It was to his credit that he avoided the more simplistic position of a man such as Carsun Chang, who equated science and the West with materialism and Chinese civilization with metaphysics. Unlike also the radical iconoclasts such as Ch'en Tu-hsiu and Wu Chih-hui, who had no use for Chinese civilization, Liang's attitude was syncretic. Insofar as the dominant current of the time was iconoclastic, Liang chose to address himself primarily to the intellectual revolutionaries.

In the midst of the impatient clamor of the May Fourth period, Liang's was in fact one of the few sober and calm voices. While others flaunted their newly acquired ideas, Liang engaged himself in serious historical scholarship in an effort to find answers to China's needs. While others were prepared to settle for all-encompassing panaceas, Liang insisted upon the complexity of truth and the need for intellectual diversity. In the general confusion caused by the telescoped parade of all the isms of the modern world, Liang was among the few to call for patience and time.

But if his sobriety was his strength, it was also his weakness. Convinced that the era of imperialism had passed, he relegated his nationalistic concerns to secondary consideration. But China had yet to confront the greatest imperialistic challenge of her modern history—Japanese aggression—and the urgency of national survival was greater in the 1920s and 1930s than it had been in the 1890s. The immediate need was for an effective combination of an ideology of modernization with sufficient military power to unify the nation and implement that program. In such a context, Liang's moderate and gradualist stance rendered him irrelevant.

The Chinese intellectual world of the 1920s was in fact passing him by. Many thinkers were turning their attention to social and economic questions, but Liang persisted in his emphasis on the spirit and attitudes of men. Class analysis he dismissed by maintaining that China had no class divisions comparable to those in the West and that future conflicts that might arise between capitalists and laborers could be resolved simply by the spirit of cooperation and the middle way.[56] Nor could he understand some of the new thinking on social organization. His liberal commitments rendered social engineering unthinkable and he could offer little more than patience and education as a program. He dismissed Communist ideology simply as crass materialism that reflected the morality of "doing unto others what you would not have them do unto you."[57] He could not understand the effectiveness of the Communist program as an instrument of organization and revolution. The irony was that it was Mao Tse-tung who, more than anyone else, became heir to Liang's central perception that a new kind of Chinese was the most fundamental requirement for a new and modern China. The difference was that Mao's "new citizenry" would be created not by "liberty" and the "middle way," but by radical revolution.

CHAPTER 8

Modern Chinese Liberalism

The hindsight that informs us of the failure of Liang's liberal program must not blind us to the tremendous appeal that program held for Chinese intellectuals. Liberal ideals were in the limelight of the Chinese intellectual and political scene for nearly three decades, from the 1890s until the 1910s. The ideal of liberal-democratic government won its first advocates among the reformers of the 1890s who sought institutional change as a means to national survival. It continued to hold the allegiance of reformers and revolutionaries alike in the first decade of this century. K'ang Yu-wei and Sun Yat-sen disagreed violently over the means of change, but they were alike in their faith in constitutional and representative government. The appeal of the liberal program reached its height in the immediate aftermath of the revolution of 1911, when China chose to wrestle with the problem of divisive power interests through constitutional and parliamentary means. Though party politics were quickly discredited as parliamentary government proved to be unable to fulfill the task set for it, "democracy" remained to become a battle cry of the intellectual revolution and continued to claim the allegiance of many Chinese intellectuals. The liberal program ceased to figure significantly as a political force before 1920, but subsequent Chinese governments have nevertheless sought to maintain the appearances of "democratic government." The fact is that much of China dreamed the liberal-democratic dream for more than two decades.

Liang was undoubtedly the most eloquent and influential spokesman for the liberal program of his time. His story tells about the character of modern Chinese liberalism and about its strengths and weaknesses as a guide to political action in twentieth-century China.

Liang's liberalism was a mixture of selected Confucian, Meiji Japanese, and Western ideas, all reinterpreted according to his personal predilections and concerns. It was no mere Western transplant, based on intellectual rejection of his "Confucian heritage" and simple espousal of "Western" values and ideas. For China and the West did not represent mutually exclusive wholes to Liang, but each a complex range of intellectual alternatives. The persistence in Liang's mind of a Confucian predilection to view morality and attitudes of men as more important than all else and the role that Kung-yang ideas played in the shaping of his thought demonstrate both the influence and adaptability of the complex of ideas that made up Liang's Confucian heritage. For Confucianism as a system of ideas was by no means a fixed quantity—it could lead to the reformist position of a Chang Chih-tung, the racialist-revolutionary position of a Chang Ping-lin, the Sinocentric position of a Liu Shih-p'ei, or a host of other positions, as well as to the liberal position of Liang. Liang's receptivity to Meiji Japanese influence and his selective use of Western ideas similarly demonstrate the inadequacy of the category of "Western impact." The fact is that Liang chose his ideas from a wide range of Western and Meiji Japanese intellectual options and reinterpreted those ideas in accordance with his own inclinations much as he did with Confucianism.

The mixture constituting his liberalism was also a dynamic and changing one, in which the diverse components continually interacted with and reshaped each other. For example: Kung-

yang Confucian ideas claimed his total intellectual allegiance
in the early 1890s. But his commitment to "liberty of thought"
soon led him to reject the dogmatic claims of K'ang Yu-wei.
By the late 1910s and after, he called upon Kung-yang precepts
only as a means, a way to permit him maximum flexibility to
reinterpret Confucianism to suit his own syncretic purposes. At
the same time, however, the holocaust of World War I and the
extremist tendencies of the May Fourth intellectual revolutionaries led him to reemphasize what he deemed to be a basic
Confucian orientation toward compromise and moderation.
And he greatly qualified his earlier acceptance of the message
of national and self-assertion that he had drawn from social
Darwinism. Other changes, discussed below, stemmed from the
conflicting tugs of his nationalistic and liberal concerns, and
from the tensions generated by the wide gap between his ideals
and observable realities, between his aspirations and the exigencies of political action.

The heart of his liberal program was the idea of the "new
citizen." It was an idea born of a convergence of diverse influences—Liang's Confucian stress of the morality and attitudes
of men above all else; his attachment to the classical-liberal
ideal of "liberty of thought," an ideal with which he readily
identified because of his own mercurial intellectual temperament; an assumption dating back to the 1890s that liberal-
democracy would be an effective means to national power; the
idea current in Meiji Japan that an awakened citizenry would
generate the necessary societal energies for liberal-democracy
as well as for national power; and Japanese and Western writings on the morality and values of classical liberalism. The
"new citizen" rested on the assumption that any program of
change must begin with the modernization of the attitudes and
values of the people. Liang called especially for a free, nationalistic, and active "new citizen" who would possess a variety of
other moral and attitudinal attributes that he deemed neces-

sary for modern citizens. Such a citizenry, as he understood it, would ensure not only the realization of liberal-democratic government but also a strong, new China.

Like his liberal ideas, Liang's style of action was a mixture of old and new elements. He conceived of two alternative roles for himself, separately represented by the characters Huang K'e-ch'iang and Li Ch'ü-ping of his political novel, "The Future of the New China." Li was the idealistic revolutionary-publicist—he would awaken the people and lead them in a spontaneous revolution. Huang was the shrewd and practical statesman-politician—a combination of a modern party politician with the Confucian statesman who would be a wise advisor to a good ruler. Huang was one who would play the game of power and attempt to reform China from within the limits of existing possibilities. Until 1903, Liang's self-conception was primarily that of a Li Ch'ü-ping. From 1903 until 1917, he was guided principally by the self-image of a Huang K'e-ch'iang.

The weaknesses of such a program are best reflected in Liang's own experiences. Even as he tried to fill the role of a Li Ch'ü-ping, he could not long avoid the realization that his "new citizenry" could not be created overnight, that it was at best a distant ideal. Observable realities persuaded him that the aims of a Li Ch'ü-ping were unrealistic and premature. And the exigencies of national survival seemed to Liang to demand not revolutionary destruction, but a strengthening of the existing central government. He turned therefore to the model of action of a Huang K'e-ch'iang. He would try to call as much as possible upon the new constitutional forces in the nation, but he was too realistic to pin all his hopes on those forces alone. He realized that the men who wielded the power were those in control of the armies. He would therefore attempt to gain the trust of a military strong man and seek to guide him along the path of liberal democracy and modernization, by the force of persuasion and whatever parliamentary pressure he could muster. These ideas formed the basis of his opposition to the revolutionaries after 1903 and of his subsequent cooperation with Yüan Shih-k'ai and Tuan Ch'i-jui. His efforts were a prototype of later efforts by individual liberal-democrats— K'ang Yu-wei's alliance with Chang Hsün in 1917, Sun Yat-sen's attempts to work with the southern warlords, and the "good government" experiment of 1922, to name only a few examples.

But constitutional forces and persuasion alone were thin threads indeed to pull in the arena of republican power politics. By the 1920s, men such as Sun Yat-sen and Mao Tse-tung were turning to a different formula of power and action—a tightly knit party, mass organizations, and a party-army. The Kuomintang, and even more so the Chinese Communist Party, were the ones to forge a successful combination of ideology and power in the 1920s and after. And they were to control the destiny of China. Liang, however, could not think in such terms. His liberal as well as Confucian orientation to compromise and moderation and his personal preferences for intellectual freedom rendered him unwilling to think in terms of dogmatic ideologies. He retreated to his liberal-Confucian program of education to create a "new citizenry." He persisted in his hope that a "new citizenry" could be created gradually by education and that, once realized, this "new citizenry" would somehow generate the necessary power to translate his ideals into reality.

It was a vain hope. By the 1920s, the liberal program receded from the limelight of the Chinese intellectual and political scene. Many of its would-be adherents turned to other paths or to a complete withdrawal from political action. Still, Liang's conviction that China's modernization must begin with a transformation of the attitudes and values of the people remained to shape subsequent Chinese thought. But intellectuals of the 1920s and after were coming to different conceptions of the proper values and attitudes for the Chinese citizenry. The search was for more effective and efficient means to create a "new citizenry."

Notes

Abbreviations Used in the Notes

KMTKK   Nihon Gaimushō, "Kakumeitō kankei" (Pertaining
to the Revolutionary Party), in *Kakkoku naisei kankei
zasshū: Shina no bu* (Miscellaneous Collection Pertaining to the Domestic Affairs of Foreign Countries: China), vols. 1 to 4. Unpublished documents.

NP   Ting Wen-chiang, ed., *Liang Jen-kung hsien-sheng nien-
p'u ch'ang-pien ch'u-kao* (First Draft of a Chronological Biography of Mr. Liang Ch'i-ch'ao), 3 vols.
(Taipei, 1958).

YPSCC   Liang Ch'i-ch'ao, *Yin-ping-shih chuan-chi*, 103 volumes
in 24 books, in *Yin-ping-shih ho-chi* (Collected Works
and Essays of Liang Ch'i-ch'ao), 40 books. (Shanghai, 1932).

YPSWC   ———. *Yin-ping-shih wen-chi*, 45 volumes in 16 books, in
Yin-ping-shih ho-chi.

CHAPTER 1

1. NP, p. 434.

2. The most complete edition is *Ying-ping shih ho-chi* [Collected
Works and Essays of Liang Ch'i-ch'ao], 40 books.

3. The nine journals were: *Chung-wai kung-pao* [Chinese and
Foreign News] (daily, May–November, 1895; circulation, ca.
3,000); *Shih-wu pao* [Current Affairs] (thrice monthly, Aug. 8, 1896–
Aug. 8, 1898, 66 issues [Liang was the editor until the 52nd issue];
circulation, ca. 12,000); *Ch'ing-i pao* [Upright Discussions] (thrice
monthly, Dec. 23, 1898–Dec. 31, 1901, 100 issues; circulation, 3,000–

4,000); *Hsin-min ts'ung-pao* [The New Citizen] (twice monthly, Feb. 8, 1902–Nov. 20, 1907, 96 issues; circulation, ca. 10,000); *Hsin hsiao-shuo* [New Fiction] (irregular, Nov., 1902–Oct., 1905, 10 issues; circulation?); *Cheng-lun* [Political Discussion] (monthly, Sept., 1907–July, 1908, 7 issues; circulation?); *Kuo-feng pao* [The National Spirit] (thrice monthly, Jan., 1910–June, 1911, 52 issues; circulation, ca. 6,000); *Yung-yen* [The Justice] (twice monthly, 1912–1914, 29 issues; circulation, ca. 10,000); *Ta Chung-hua* [The Great Chung-hua Journal] (monthly, Jan., 1915–Dec., 1916, 24 issues; circulation ?); Cf. Chang P'eng-yüan, *Liang Ch'i-ch'ao yü Ch'ing-chi ke-ming* [Liang Ch'i-ch'ao and the Revolution of 1911], pp. 254–321, and Ko Kung-chen, *Chung-kuo pao-hsüeh shih* [A History of Chinese Journalism], pp. 125–27.

4. "Ch'üan-hsüeh p'ien" [Exhortation to Learn], *in Chang Wen-hsiang kung ch'üan-chi* [Complete Works of Chang Chih-tung], *chüan* 203:3. Cf. de Bary et al., eds., *Sources of Chinese Tradition*, p. 748. This formula is better known in the form of the catch-phrase: "Chinese learning in substance; Western learning in application."

5. This point has been made by numerous scholars. Hu Shih, *Ssu-shih tzu-shu* [Autobiography at Forty], pp. 47–48; Hsiao Kung-ch'üan, *Chung-kuo cheng-chih ssu-hsiang shih* [A History of Chinese Political Thought], pp. 770–71; Ts'ao Chü-jen, *Wen-t'an wu-shih-nien* [Fifty Years of the Literary World], p. 67; Chang P'eng-yüan, *Liang Ch'i-ch'ao yü Ch'ing-chi ke-ming*, passim.

6. Ibid., pp. 296–97.

7. "Pien-fa t'ung-i" [On Reform] YPSWC 1:54.

8. "Hsin Chung-kuo wei-lai chi" [The Future of the New China] YPSCC 89:1–57.

9. Cheng Chen-to, "Liang Jen-kung hsien-sheng" [Mr. Liang Ch'i-ch'ao], p. 351. Cf. Hu, *Ssu-shih tzu-shu*, p. 50.

10. Ibid., pp. 50, 52.

11. Cheng, "Liang Jen-kung hsien-sheng," p. 351.

12. "Hsin shih-hsüeh" [New History] YPSWC 9:1–31.

13. "Lun Chung-kuo hsüeh-shu pien-ch'ien chih ta-shih" [General Trends in the Development and Changes in Chinese Thought] YPSWC 7:1–103.

14. Hu, *Ssu-shih tzu-shu*, pp. 52–53.

15. Ku Chieh-kang, *Ku-shih pien* [An Examination of Ancient History], preface, pp. 11–12.

16. Ch'en Tu-hsiu, "Po K'ang Yu-wei chih tsung-t'ung tsung-li shu" [Disputing K'ang Yu-wei's Letter to the President and the Premier], p. 1.

17. Snow, *Red Star Over China*, p. 133.

18. Chou Shih-chao, "Ti-i shih-fan shih-tai te Mao chu-hsi" [Chairman Mao at the Time of the First Normal School], *Hsin kuan-ch'a* 2, no. 2 (January 25, 1951): 10. I am indebted to the late Professor Hsia Chi-an for calling my attention to this article.

19. Hu, *Ssu-shih tzu-shu*, p. 52.

CHAPTER 2

1. The above is based on NP, pp. 1–15.

2. Ibid., pp. 15–16.

3. Ibid., p. 16.

4. P'i Hsi-jui, *Ching-hsüeh li-shih* [A History of Classical Learning], p. 73.

5. Ibid., p. 88.

6. For a discussion of the history of classical learning in Han, see Tjan Tjoe-som, *Po Hu T'ung: The Comprehensive Discussions in the White Tiger Hall*, pp. 82–176. Tjan goes into the important question of the relationship between the New Text school and the apocryphal texts of Han. Cf. Honda Shigeyuki, *Shina keigaku-shi ron* [A History of Classical Learning in China], pp. 143–236. For a brief and simplified discussion of key differences between the Old and New Text schools (from a point of view not restricted to differences between the two schools in Han), see Chou Yü-t'ung, *Ching ku chin wen hsüeh* [New and Old Text Classical Learning].

7. Hsiao Kung-ch'üan, *Chung-kuo cheng-chih ssu-hsiang-shih* [A History of Chinese Political Thought], pp. 293–300; cf. Fung Yu-lan, *Chung-kuo che-hsüeh-shih* [A History of Chinese Philosophy], pp. 502–45.

8. Fung, *Chung-kuo che-hsüeh-shih*, pp. 538–39.

9. For a full discussion of the *san-t'ung* theory of Tung, see Woo Kang, *Les Trois Théories Politiques du Tch'ouen Ts'ieou*, pp. 136–61. For the influence of the *san-t'ung* theory on K'ang, see K. C. Hsiao, "K'ang Yu-wei and Confucianism," *Monumenta Serica* 18 (1959): 142–43.

10. Hsiao, *Chung-kuo cheng-chih ssu-hsiang-shih*, p. 298.

11. On mysticism in Mencius' thought, see Fung, *Chung-kuo che-hsüeh-shih*, pp. 163–66.

12. On the influence of Yin-yang thought on Tung, see ibid., pp. 497 ff.

13. Hsiao, *Chung-kuo cheng-chih ssu-hsiang-shih*, pp. 293–97.

14. Ibid.

15. Ibid., p. 307.

16. Uno Tetsujin, *Chūgoku kinsei jugaku shi*, trans., Ma Fu-ch'en, *Chung-kuo chin-shih ju-hsüeh shih* [A History of Confucianism in Recent China] 2: 412 ff.

17. Ch'ien Mu, *Chung-kuo chin san-pai-nien hsüeh-shu-shih* [A History of Chinese Thought in the Last Three Hundred Years], pp. 523–25.

18. Uno, *Chūgoku kinsei jugaku shi* 2: 412 ff.; cf. Hsü Shih-ch'ang, *Ch'ing-ju hsüeh-an* [Selected Writings of Ch'ing Scholars], *chüan* 73.

19. Arthur W. Hummel, ed., *Eminent Chinese of the Ch'ing Period*, p. 519; cf. Hsü, *Ch'ing-ju hsüeh-an, chüan* 73.

20. Ibid.; Liang Ch'i-ch'ao, "Ch'ing-tai hsüeh-shu kai-lun" [Intellectual Trends in the Ch'ing Period] YPSCC 34:54.

21. Ch'ien, *Chung-kuo chin san-pai-nien* . . ., p. 527.

22. Ho Hsiu wrote the *Tso-shih kao-huang* [The Incurable *Tso Commentary*], *Ku-liang fei-chi* [The Maimed *Ku-liang Commentary*], and the *Kung-yang mo-shou* [The Invincible *Kung-yang Commentary*]. Cheng Hsüan challenged each of these in turn with his *Chen kao-huang* [A Cure for the Incurable Disease], *Ch'i fei-chi* [Rehabilitation of the Maimed], and *Fa mo-shou* [Sacking of the Invincible Defense]. Though Cheng's training and views encompassed both the Old and New Text schools, his writings undoubtedly contributed to the final demise of the New Text school. (See Chou's introduction to P'i, *Ching-hsüeh li-shih*, pp. 2, 142–49.)

23. Ch'ien, *Chung-kuo chin san-pai-nien* . . ., pp. 527–28; Cf. Hsü, *Ch'ing-ju hsüeh-an, chüan* 75.

24. Hummel, *Eminent Chinese of the Ch'ing Period*, p. 518; cf. Liang, "Ch'ing-tai hsüeh-shu kai-lun" YPSCC 34: 5.

25. Hsü, *Ch'ing-ju hsüeh-an, chüan* 73. Chuang's *Ch'un-ch'iu cheng-tz'u*, for example, was not published until 1827, some forty years after his death (Hummel, *Eminent Chinese of the Ch'ing Period*, p. 207).

26. Hsü wrote, "Liu was given the office of a department director of the Board of Ceremonies, and occupied the post for twelve years. He constantly applied the principles of the classics to decide upon puzzling problems and was respected at the time" (*Ch'ing-ju hsüeh-an, chüan* 75; cf. Hummel, *Eminent Chinese of the Ch'ing Period*, p. 518).

27. Kung, at the age of 28 *sui*, studied Kung-yang learning under Liu (Ch'ien, *Chung-kuo chin san-pai-nien* . . ., p. 532). Wei first met Liu and Kung in 1814 in Peking (Hummel, *Eminent Chinese of the Ch'ing Period*, p. 850), and in 1830, joined Kung and Lin Tse-hsü in organizing a poetry club (ibid., p. 432).

28. Liang attributed to Kung and Wei the beginning of the tendency among nineteenth-century New Texters to apply classical learning to practical affairs ("Ch'ing-tai hsüeh-shu kai-lun" YPSCC 34: 55–56).

29. Ch'ien, *Chung-kuo chin san-pai-nien* . . ., pp. 534–51; cf. Hummel, *Eminent Chinese of the Ch'ing Period*, pp. 531–34; Liang, "Ch'ing-tai hsüeh-shu kai-lun" YPSCC 34:54, where Liang pointed out that Kung used Kung-yang ideas to criticize absolutist government. Cf. Hsiao, *Chung-kuo cheng-chih ssu-hsiang-shih*, p. 658. In his "P'ing-chün p'ien" Kung wrote, "The people's hearts are the basis of the world's conditions, and the conditions of the world are the basis of the fate of the ruler. If the people's hearts die, then the world's conditions will deteriorate and the fortunes of the ruler may be interrupted. The ruler who plans for his own interests will plan for the interests of the people's hearts and the world's conditions" (*Kung Tzu-chen ch'üan-chi* [Collected Works of Kung Tzu-chen] 1: 78).

30. For an excellent discussion of Wei's thought, see Nomura Kōichi, "Shinmatsu Kōyōgaku no keisei to Kō Yū-i no rekishiteki igi" [The Development of Kung-yang Thought in Late Ch'ing and the Historical Meaning of K'ang Yu-wei], *Kokka Gakkai zasshi* 71, no. 7: 705–65; 72, no. 1: 32–64; 72, no. 3: 256–320. Part 1 is devoted largely to Wei. See especially 71, no. 7: 738–58; cf. Ch'ien, *Chung-kuo chin san-pai-nien* . . ., pp. 529–32.

31. Hsiao, "K'ang Yu-wei and Confucianism," pp. 106, 113.

32. For the periodization of K'ang's early intellectual life, see ibid., pp. 103–16.

33. Drafts of the *Ta-t'ung shu* were written in the 1880s. The final version was done in 1901–2 (ibid., pp. 107–12). For a short summary of the contents of this book, see "Ch'ing-tai hsüeh-shu kai-lun" YPSCC 34:58–60; cf. Thompson, trans., *Ta T'ung Shu: the One World Philosophy of K'ang Yu-wei*.

34. For a short summary of the arguments in the *Hsin-hsüeh wei-ching k'ao* and an assessment of its impact, see "Ch'ing-tai hsüeh-shu kai-lun" YPSCC 34: 56–57.

35. Ibid., pp. 57–58; cf. Hsiao, "K'ang Yu-wei and Confucianism," pp. 166–69.

36. The linking of the *san-shih* to the *hsiao-k'ang* and *ta-t'ung* of the "Li yün" was K'ang's contribution to Kung-yang thought. He first made the link in 1898 (ibid., p. 115). These ideas were formalized in 1902 (ibid., pp. 1, 116, 151–54).

37. "Ch'ing-tai hsüeh-shu kai-lun" YPSCC 34: 58–60.

38. Hsiao, "K'ang Yu-wei and Confucianism," pp. 101, 133–34, 178–79.

39. "Ch'ing-tai hsüeh-shu kai-lun" YPSCC 34: 61.

40. "Hsi-hsüeh shu-mu piao hou-hsü" [Postscript to *A Catalogue of Books on Western Learning*] YPSWC 1:128.

41. "Ch'ing-tai hsüeh-shu kai-lun" YPSCC 34:60.

42. For example, see Hou Wai-lu, *Chung-kuo tsao-ch'i ch'i-meng ssu-hsiang shih* [A History of Enlightened Thought in "Early Modern" China], pp. 144–203.

43. For an example of this position, see Shimada Kenji, "Chūgoku no Rousseau" [China's Rousseau], pp. 66–85.

44. See, for example, Kojima Sukema, *Chūgoku no kakumei shisō* [Revolutionary Thought in China], pp. 45–50. Cf. Shimizu Morimitsu, *Shina shakai no kenkyū: shakaigaku-teki kōsatsu* [Studies in Chinese Society: A Sociological Inquiry], pp. 97 ff.

45. *Meng-tzu*, 5.A.5 (de Bary translation).

46. Ibid., 7.B.14 (my translation).

47. Ibid., 1.B.7 (Legge translation).

48. The most authoritative discussion of Mencius' political thought is still that in Hsiao, *Chung-kuo cheng-chih ssu-hsiang shih*, chap. 3.

49. Huang Tsung-hsi, "Hsüeh-hsiao" [Academies], in *Ming-i tai-fang lu* [A Plan for a Prince], pp. 9–13.

50. Ibid.

51. NP, p. 24. Liang Ch'i-ch'ao, "San-shih tzu-shu" [Autobiography at Thirty] YPSWC 11:17, gives the figure 3,000 instead of 1,200.

52. NP, pp. 25–27.

53. For a detailed discussion of the founding of this journal and the well-known disputes and misunderstandings between Liang and Wang K'ang-nien, see Chang P'eng-yüan, *Liang Ch'i-ch'ao yü Ch'ing-chi ke-ming* [Liang Ch'i-ch'ao and the Revolution of 1911], pp. 257–73.

54. "San-shih tzu-shu" YPSWC 11:17–18.

55. Hummel, *Eminent Chinese of the Ch'ing Period*, p. 351.

56. NP, pp. 31–33. Cf. "San-shih tzu-shu" YPSWC 11:18.

57. NP, pp. 38–39.

58. Ibid., pp. 22, 28–29.

59. Ibid.

60. Ibid., pp. 33, 47.

61. Ibid., p. 33.

62. Hummel, *Eminent Chinese of the Ch'ing Period*, pp. 703, 351; cf. NP, p. 42.

63. Ibid., pp. 42–43.

64. Ibid., pp. 57–60, 64–66.

65. Ibid., p. 61.

66. YPSCC 1:133.

67. "Hsi-hsüeh shu-mu piao hou-hsü" YPSWC 1:128.

68. "Lun chün-cheng min-cheng hsiang-shan chih li" [On the

Principle that Rule by the Monarch Will Be Succeeded by Rule by the People] YPSWC 2:7.

69. "Yü Yen Yu-ling hsien-sheng shu" [Letter to Mr. Yen] YPSWC 1:110. The YPSWC dates this letter as 1896. Ting Wen-chiang, however, dates the letter as 1897 (NP, pp. 41–42). The correct date is 1897, probably around the middle of the year. The content of the letter shows that it was written substantially later than the first two issues of the *Shih-wu pao*, which appeared in August, 1896. Liang spoke of Yen's letter to him in the second month of 1897 and of having waited several months before he replied (YPSWC 1:106–7).

70. "Pien-fa t'ung-i" YPSWC 1:10.

71. Ichiko Chūzō has pointed out that Liang's emphasis on education distinguished his reform program from that of K'ang Yu-wei, "Ryō Kei-chō no hempō undō" [Liang Ch'i-ch'ao's Reform Movement], pp. 71–83. For a Marxist study of Liang's thought on education in this period, see Abe Yō, "Ryō Kei-chō no kyōiku shisō to sono katsudō: bojutsu hempōki o chūshin to shite" [Liang Ch'i-ch'ao's Educational Thought and Activities: Focusing on the Period of the 1898 Reforms], pp. 301–23. Cf. Fung Yu-lan, "Liang Ch'i-ch'ao ti ssu-hsiang" [Liang Ch'i-ch'ao's Thought], pp. 128–41. Abe and Fung argue that Liang's stress on developing gentry education reflects his "landlord class views." Liang, it must be pointed out, saw the development of gentry education as only a preliminary step to his aim of spreading education among the people. "Pien-fa t'ung-i" YPSWC 1:88; cf. "Meng-hsüeh pao Yen-i pao ho-hsü" [Joint Preface to the *Meng-hsüeh pao* and the *Yen-i pao*] YPSWC 2:56–57.

72. "Pien-fa t'ung-i," p. 20.

73. On schools in general, see ibid., pp. 14–21. On teachers' colleges, academic societies, and education of women and children, see ibid., pp. 30–61.

74. Ibid., pp. 21–31.

75. Ibid., p. 54.

76. "Hsi-hsüeh shu-mu piao hsü-li" [Preface to *A Catalogue of Books on Western Learning*] YPSWC 1:124, 128.

77. "Ku i-yüan k'ao" [Inquiry into Ancient Parliaments] YPSWC 1:96.

78. "Yü Yen Yu-ling hsien-sheng shu" YPSWC 1:109.

79. "Hsü i Lieh-kuo sui-chi cheng-yao hsü" [Preface to the Continuation of the Translation of the International Yearbook] YPSWC 2:61.

80. "Tu Jih-pen shu-mu chih shu hou" [*After Reading the Catalogue of Japanese Books* (of K'ang Yu-wei)] YPSWC 2:53.

81. "Pien-fa t'ung-i" YPSWC 1:69.

82. Liang, "San-shih tzu-shu" YPSWC 11: 17.

83. NP, pp. 25–28.

84. Liang, "Hsi-hsüeh shu-mu piao hsü-li" YPSWC 1: 122.

85. Liang, *Hsi-hsüeh shu-mu piao.*

86. Liang, "Hsi-hsüeh shu-mu piao hsü-li" YPSWC 1: 124.

87. The contents of the "Hsi-cheng ts'ung-shu" are summarized in NP, p. 38; cf. "Hsi-cheng ts'ung-shu hsü" (Preface to *A Catalogue of Books on Western Government*) YPSWC 2:62–64.

88. In his *Hsi-hsüeh shu-mu piao*, Liang picked out this book and the missionary publication *Wan-kuo kung-pao* as the most important items.

89. Wang Shu-huai, *Wai-jen yü wu-hsü pien-fa* [Foreigners and the 1898 Reforms], pp. 1–70.

90. Richard, *Forty-five Years in China*, p. 225. NP, however, makes no mention of Liang's serving as Richard's secretary. The "Pien-fa t'ung-i" was published in the *Shih-wu pao* from the first issue (Aug. 9, 1896) to the 43rd issue (Oct. 26, 1897). Richard left Peking on February 25, 1896 (Richard, *Forty-five Years in China*, p. 258).

91. "Pien-fa t'ung-i" YPSWC 1:12–13.

92. "Ku i-yüan k'ao" YPSWC 1: 94–95.

93. "Ch'ing-tai hsüeh-shu kai-lun" YPSCC 34: 61–62.

94. Levenson, *Liang Ch'i-ch'ao and the Mind of Modern China*, pp. 1–2, 34–51.

CHAPTER 3

1. This graph is based on the one in Sanetō Keishū, *Chūgokujin Nihon ryūgaku shi* [A History of Chinese Students in Japan], p. 545.

2. Computed from Sanetō's "Hōsho Kayaku no gaikan" [A General Picture of Chinese Translations of Japanese Books], pp. 160–280, which contains a list of 2205 books spanning the period from 1895 to 1939. Sanetō began collecting materials for this list in 1929 and combed the catalogue of the Peiping Library in the course of his researches.

3. Computed from ibid.

4. Computed from ibid.

5. Ibid., pp. 211–26.

6. Satō Saburō, "Meiji ishin igo Nisshin sensō izen ni okeru Shinajin no Nihon kenkyū" [Chinese Studies of Japan after the Meiji Restoration and before the Sino-Japanese War (of 1894–95)],

pp. 1147–87, points out that even on the eve of the war, there was an increasingly receptive attitude toward Japan on the part of those Chinese who wrote about Japan. But the attitudes of the majority of the scholar officials no doubt changed only after the shock of defeat.

7. See, for example, K'ang's "Chin-ch'eng Jih-pen Ming-chih pien-cheng k'ao hsü" [Preface to an Account of the Political Reforms of Meiji Japan, Presented (to the Emperor) (1898)], in Chien Po-tsan et al., eds. *Wu-hsü pien-fa* [The 1898 Reforms] 3: 3.

8. Chang Chih-tung, "Ch'üan hsüeh p'ien" [Exhortation to Learn], *chüan* 203.

9. Huang was among the first to advocate learning from Japan. He was Councilor of the Chinese Delegation in Tokyo from 1877 to 1885, and wrote a history of Japan—*Jih-pen kuo-chih* (Hummel, *Eminent Chinese of the Ch'ing Period*, p. 351).

10. For an account of this early period (1872–1895) in the history of Chinese students abroad, see Wang, *Chinese Intellectuals and the West, 1872–1949*, pp. 41–50.

11. 8,000 is Sanetō's estimate. Other estimates range as high as 10,000 plus; see Kuo Mo-jo, "Chung-Jih wen-hua chih chiao-liu" [Cross Currents between Chinese and Japanese Cultures], in *Mo-jo wen-chi* [Works] 2:72; cf. Shu Hsin-ch'eng, *Chin-tai Chung-kuo liu-hsüeh shih* [A History of Overseas Study in Modern China], p. 46. Hackett, "Chinese Students in Japan, 1900–1910," *Papers on China* 3 (May 1949): 142, estimates 13,000. These higher estimates, as Sanetō points out, reflect the upward biases in contemporary reporting that stemmed from the tendency of many Chinese students of the time to enroll in several schools simultaneously in order to receive several diplomas (Sanetō, *Chūgokujin Nihon ryūgaku shi*, pp. 58–60).

12. Wang, *Chinese Intellectuals*, table 10, p. 510.

13. Ibid., p. 517, gives 2,387 for Japan, 207 for the U.S., and 375 for Europe. Sanetō, however, estimates that there were 4,000 Chinese students in Japan in 1909 (see fig. 1).

14. There were 1124 Chinese students in the U.S. in 1918, and 1637 in 1924 (Wang, *Chinese Intellectuals*, p. 510). The number going to Japan, on the other hand, declined sharply after 1914, as shown in fig. 1.

15. Ibid., pp. 105–11. Estimates of the number of students in France in 1920 range as high as 6000.

16. In Chang, "Ch'üan hsüeh p'ien," *chüan* 203:2.

17. 49.5% in 1916, and 52.5% in 1923 (Wang, *Chinese Intellectuals*, p. 177).

18. 68%, according to Wang's figures (ibid.).

19. Ibid.

20. By 1932 and 1939, the American-trained accounted for 45.5% and 51%, respectively, of the returned students who appeared in the *Who's Who*, while the Japanese-trained represented only 29.5% in 1932 and 21.7% in 1939 (computed from ibid.).

21. "Ch'ing-tai hsüeh-shu kai lun" [Intellectual Trends in the Ch'ing Period] YPSCC 34:71.

22. Yang Shou-ch'un, *Chung-kuo chin-tai ch'u-pan shih-liao* [Materials on the History of Publishing in Modern China], pp. 99–101, cited in Sanetō, *Chūgokujin Nihon ryūgaku shi*, pp. 282–83.

23. Kao Ming-k'ai and Lui Cheng-t'an, *Hsien-tai Han-yü wai-lai-tz'u yen-chiu* [A Study of Loan-words in Modern China], pp. 82–83. Cf. Zdenka Novotna, "Contributions to the Study of Loan-words and Hybrid Words in Modern Chinese," pp. 616–17.

24. Kao and Liu list 67 such examples in *Hsien-tai Han-yü . . .*, pp. 83–88.

25. Ibid., pp. 88–98. This is the most numerous of the three categories, accounting for 310 of the 468 loan-words from Japanese in Kao and Liu's set.

26. Novotna shows, for example, that in the fields of politics, economics, and philosophy, the majority of the terms borrowed from English, French, German, and Russian were in time superseded either by new creations or by the graphic loans from Japanese ("Contributions to the Study of Loan-words . . .," pp. 631–33, 638).

27. Kao and Liu worked with a set of 1285 loan-words, of which 468 were from Japanese. The preponderance of loans from Japanese is especially conspicuous in the areas mentioned—39/39 in law (*Hsien-tai Han-yü . . .*, p. 131); 47/73 in economics (pp. 121–22); 61/75 in philosophy (pp. 119–21). Cf. pp. 114–16 for politics, and pp. 125–26 for vocabulary related to education and society.

28. "Chung-kuo chin san-pai nien hsüeh-shu shih" [A History of Chinese Thought in the Recent Three Hundred Years] YPSCC 75:30.

29. NP, pp. 86, 99, 174. In 1911, Liang took a short trip to Taiwan, staying only two weeks (ibid., p. 331).

30. See chaps. 2 and 3 of my unpublished dissertation, "A Confucian Liberal: Liang Ch'i-ch'ao in Action and Thought."

31. NP.

32. YPSCC 2. These notes were published between 1899 and 1905, first in Liang's *Ch'ing-i pao*, then in his *Hsin-min ts'ung-pao*.

33. KMTKK. Containing some 3000 pages of contemporary Japanese police reports on Liang, this publication is the major un-

tapped source on Liang. I an indebted to Professor Ichiko Chūzō for first setting me on the trail that led to the discovery of these documents.

34. See, for example, "Tu *Jin-pen shu-mu chih* shu hou" [After Reading the *Catalogue of Japanese Books* (of K'ang Yu-wei)] YPSWC 2:53.

35. The fact that Liang took the Yoshida portion of his Japanese name from Yoshida Shōin is well-known (NP, p. 87). But Liang also named himself after Yoshida's student, Takasugi, as he pointed out in a conversation with the Japanese police (KMTKK 1:440086).

36. NP, p. 93.

37. On Liang's escape to Japan, see Nihon Gaimushō, *Nihon gaikō bunsho* [Documents on the Foreign Relations of Japan] 31(1): 658–742, and 32:537–57. Liang's friendship with the Okuma government was strengthened by the fact that the latter also intervened on behalf of Huang Tsun-hsien. Nihon Gaimushō, "Kō-sho nijūyonnen seihen" [The Coup d'État of 1898] KMTKK 1:491035, 491038, 491041, 491043. Some new materials on Liang's escape to Japan are discussed in Masuda Wataru, "Ryō Kei-chō no Nihon bōmei ni tsuite" [On Liang Ch'i-ch'ao's Refuge to Japan], *Tokyo Shinagaku hō* 13 (June 1967): 9–32.

38. KMTKK 1:440099.

39. Ibid.

40. Tōa Dōbun Kai, *Zoku Tai Shi kaikoroku* [Sequel to Records on China] 1: 647 ff.

41. See Liang's letter to Kashiwabara, dated March, 1900, in ibid., 2:648. Cf. NP, p. 83.

42. KMTKK 1:440129, 440016.

43. Tōa Dōbun Kai, *Zoku Tai Shi kaikoroku* 2:648.

44. KMTKK 1:440016, 440024.

45. "Pien-fa t'ung-i" YPSWC 1:83.

46. "Lun hsüeh Jih-pen-wen chih i" [On the Merits of Learning Japanese] YPSWC 4:82; cf. "Lun shang-yeh hui-i-suo chih i" [On the Merits of Commercial Associations] YPSWC 4:7–11.

47. "Ch'ing-i pao hsü-li" [Introductory Comments to the *Ch'ing-i pao*] YPSWC 3:31.

48. "Lun Chung-kuo chih chiang ch'iang" [China Will Be Strong] YPSWC 2:12.

49. "Pien-fa t'ung-i" YPSWC 1:83.

50. In *Gendai Nihon bungaku zenshū* 1 (Tokyo, 1931): 139–326.

51. The other two being Yano Fumio's *Keikoku bidan* [A Noble Tale of Statesmanship] and Suehiro Tetchō's *Setchūbai* [Plum Blossoms in the Snow]. Shiba's novel was said to have "raised the price

of paper in the metropolis" (Sansom, *The Western World and Japan*, p. 412).

52. "Chia-jen ch'i yü" [Strange Encounters of Elegant Females] YPSCC 88: 1–220.

53. NP, pp. 80–81.

54. Successive portions of the translation were published in the *Ch'ing-i pao*, beginning with the first issue on December 23, 1898, a short two months after Liang arrived in Tokyo.

55. This fact is evidenced by Liang's inconsistent deletions and additions, discussed below.

56. Shiba, *Kajin no kigu*, p. 153, translated and quoted in Sansom, *The Western World and Japan*, p. 414.

57. Ishida Takeshi, *Meiji seiji shisōshi kenkyū* [Studies of the History of Meiji Political Thought], p. 328.

58. Compare Shiba, *Kajin no kigu*, p. 153, with Liang, "Chia-jen ch'i-yü" YPSCC 88:15.

59. "Chia-jen ch'i-yü" YPSCC 88:25; in the original, Han Kei is introduced much earlier (Shiba, *Kajin no kigu*, p. 151), and appears several times before the end of the second chapter (pp. 153, 154, 159).

60. For example, in the fourth chapter, Liang left intact the identification of Han Kei as the servant of Yūran and Kōren ("Chia-jen ch'i-yü" YPSCC 88:43).

61. Shiba, *Kajin no kigu*, pp. 318 ff.

62. "Chia-jen ch'i-yü" YPSCC 88:220.

63. Only eleven of the sixteen chapters were published in the *Ch'ing-i pao*. Publication ceased with no. 35 of the *Ch'ing-i pao* (Feb. 10, 1900).

64. *Ch'ing-i pao*, no. 64 (Nov. 22, 1900). Cf. YPSCC 88:220.

65. "Ch'ing-i pao i-pai tz'e chu-tz'u" [A Congratulatory Message on the Occasion of the Hundredth Issue of the *Ch'ing-i pao*] YPSWC 6:54.

66. See Jansen, "Japanese Views of China during the Meiji Period," pp. 163–89.

67. "Tu Jih-pen Ta-wei Po-chüeh *K'ai-kuo wu-shih nien shih* shu hou" [After Reading Japan's Count Okuma's *A History of the Fifty Years Since the Founding of the Nation*] YPSWC 23:113–15.

68. For Liang's highly emotional reactions to the Demands, see "Chung-Jih tsui-chin chiao-she p'ing-i" [A Critique of the Recent Negotiations between China and Japan] YPSWC 32:91 ff. Cf. "Chiao-she hu ming-ling hu" [Negotiations or Commands?] YPSWC 32:104; and "T'ung-ting tsui-yen" [After the Pain, a Confession] YPSWC 33:1–9.

69. Okuma, of course, was the founder of the school (1882), known as the Tokyo Senmon Gakkō until 1902 (*Nihon rekishi jiten* [Tokyo, 1956–1960] 19:253–54).

70. "Tzu-yu shu" [Notes on Freedom] YPSCC 2:41–42.

71. Ibid., p. 1.

72. "Ta mou-chün wen Jih-pen chin-chih chiao-k'e-shu shih" [In Answer to Someone's Query about Japan's Banning of Text-books] YPSWC 14:30.

73. "*Ch'ing-i pao* i-pai ts'e chu-tz'u" YPSWC 6:57.

74. Huang, "A Confucian Liberal," chap. 3.

75. "Tzu-yu shu" YPSCC 2:8–9.

76. "Hsin-min shuo" [The New Citizen] YPSCC 4:10.

77. Ibid., p. 24.

78. Schwartz, in his *In Search of Wealth and Power: Yen Fu and the West*, pp. 3, 70, 82–83, and Onogawa Hidemi, in "Shinmatsu no shisō to shinkaron" [The Theory of Evolution and Late Ch'ing Political Thought], in *Shinmatsu seiji shisō kenkyū* [Studies in Late Ch'ing Political Thought], pp. 343–97, both suggested that Liang was profoundly influenced by Yen Fu's interpretations of social Darwinism. The principal evidence in favor of their suggestion consists of: 1. Liang knew Yen and corresponded with him, and he read a draft of Yen's *T'ien-yen lun* (A translation of Thomas H. Huxley's *Evolution and Ethics*) as early as 1896 (NP, p. 33); 2. Liang's ideas after 1898 bear some resemblances to Yen's thought. Neither Schwartz nor Onogawa mentioned Katō Hiroyuki. I would suggest, however, that the burden of the evidence points to the conclusion that Katō's influence was decisive in shaping Liang's reinterpretations of social Darwinism.

1. As Onogawa acknowledged, ideas derived from social Darwinism did not become decisive in Liang's thinking until after 1898. As the earlier quotation from Liang shows, Liang himself pointed out that the change in his thinking came as a result of reading Japanese books. 2. In the period when social Darwinian ideas pervaded Liang's thinking, i.e., 1898–1903, Liang referred not to Yen but to Katō as his authority. 3. Liang's vocabulary, such as *yu-sheng lieh-pai* (literally, the victory of the superior and the defeat of the inferior) and *ch'iang-ch'üan* (rights of the strong), was that of Japanese social Darwinism and Katō rather than of Yen; compare with Yen Fu, *Yen i ming-chu ts'ung-k'an* [A Collection of Yen (Fu's) Translations of Well-known Works]. *Ch'iang-ch'üan*, or *kyōken*, especially, was at the heart of both Katō's and Liang's interpretations of social Darwinism (see the discussion in the text that follows). 4. Although Liang's response to social Darwinism resembles Yen's in some re-

spects, his basic idea of a "new citizen" is clearly traceable to the joint influence of Katō, Fukuzawa, and Nakamura. Moreover, Liang's theory of imperialism can properly be understood only in the framework of Katō's formulation of *kyōken* (see the discussion below).

79. Katō, *Tensoku hyaku wa.*
80. Katō, *Kyōsha no kenri no kyōsō.*
81. Katō, *Tensoku hyaku wa,* p. 33.
82. Katō, *Kyōsha no kenri no kyōsō,* p. 27.
83. Katō, *Tensoku hyaku wa,* p. 29.
84. See Tabata, *Katō Hiroyuki,* pp. 53–54, 58, 138.
85. Spencer, *The Principles of Sociology* 2:596–97.
86. Ibid., p. 241.
87. Ibid., p. 640.
88. Ibid., p. 665.
89. Quoted in Carneiro, ed., *The Evolution of Society: Selections from Herbert Spencer's Principles of Sociology,* p. xlvi.
90. Spencer, *Principles of Sociology* 2:601.
91. "Tzu-yu shu" YPSCC 2:29–33, 91–98.
92. "Lun chin shih kuo-min ching-cheng chih ta-shih chi Chung-kuo ch'ien-t'u" [On the Trends in the Struggle among Citizenries in the Modern World and the Future of China] YPSWC 4:56–57.
93. "Hsin-min shuo" YPSCC 4:4.
94. Ibid., pp. 16–23.
95. "Ai-kuo lun" [On Patriotism] YPSWC 3:73.
96. See Huang, "A Confucian Liberal," chaps. 2 and 3.
97. "Tzu-yu shu" YPSCC 2:40–41.
98. Ibid., p. 31.
99. "Li-chi yü ai-t'a" [Egotism and Altruism] YPSWC 5:49.
100. "Tzu-yu shu" YPSCC 2:31.
101. Tabata, *Katō Hiroyuki,* pp. 37–40, 44–45.
102. On the content and reasons for this change, see Huang, "A Confucian Liberal," pp. 124–29.
103. Katō's translation was published in 1872. On the influence of Bluntschli's idea of the state as comparable to a human organism on Katō's thought, see Tabata, *Katō Hiroyuki,* pp. 84–85, 58–59.
104. *The Autobiography of Fukuzawa Yukichi,* trans. Kiyooka Ei-kichi, p. 337.
105. Smiles, *Self-Help,* p. 1.
106. Nakamura Masanao, *Saikoku risshi hen,* p. 5.
107. "Kuo-min shih ta yüan-ch'i lun" [The Ten Essential Spontaneous Attitudes of a Citizen] YPSWC 3:61–62.
108. "Tu-li lun" [On Independence], ibid., pp. 62–65.

109. "Lun tzu-tsun" [On Self-Respect], in "Hsin-min shuo" YPSCC 4:68–76.

110. "Hsin-min shuo" YPSCC 4:48.

111. "Tzu-yu shu" YPSCC 2:16.

112. See, for example, Blacker, *The Japanese Enlightenment: A Study of the Writings of Fukuzawa Yukichi*, p. 32.

113. Chaps. 1 to 17 of the "Hsin-min shuo" were written before Liang went to the U.S. in 1903. They appeared in no. 1 (Feb. 8, 1902) to no. 29 (April 11, 1903) of the *Hsin-min ts'ung-pao*. But the last three chapters were written after Liang's return from the U.S. The last chapter was not published until no. 72 (Jan. 9, 1906) of the journal. There is a sharp difference in tone and emphasis between the earlier and later portions. My reference here is to the first seventeen chapters. For a discussion of the last three chapters, see Huang, "A Confucian Liberal," pp. 127–28.

114. Liang, in the tradition of the Sung Confucianists, read *ch'in-min* as *hsin-min*. The translation used here is from de Bary et al., eds., *Sources of Chinese Tradition*, p. 129.

115. *Ta Hsüeh* 2:1. The translation used here is Legge's *The Chinese Classics* 1:361.

116. Ibid., 2:2.

117. *Meng-tzu*, 6.B.2.

118. *Ta Hsüeh* 1:6; cf. de Bary et al., eds., *Sources of Chinese Tradition*, p. 129.

119. "Hsin-min shuo" YPSCC 4:3.

120. "Tzu-yu shu" YPSCC 2:75.

121. "Hsin-min shuo" YPSCC 4:47–50.

122. Ibid., pp. 39–40.

123. Ibid., pp. 41–44.

124. Ibid., pp. 16–23.

125. Ibid., pp. 23–31.

126. Ibid., p. 96.

127. Ibid., pp. 104–8.

128. Ibid., pp. 71–74.

129. Ibid., pp. 80–96.

130. Ibid., pp. 50–54.

131. Ibid., pp. 76–80.

132. Ibid., pp. 7–11.

CHAPTER 4

1. *Dai Kan-Wa jiten* [The Great Chinese-Japanese Dictionary] 9:404.

2. *The Shorter Oxford English Dictionary*, 3rd ed., p. 1135.

3. "Tzu-yu shu" [Notes on Freedom] YPSCC, vol. 2. Successive portions appeared first in the *Ch'ing-i pao* in 1899; the final sections were published in the *Hsin-min ts'ung-pao* in 1905.

4. "Hsin-min shuo" [The New Citizen] YPSCC, vol. 4. Chaps. 1 to 17 were written before Liang went to the United States in 1903. They appeared in no. 1 (Feb. 8, 1902) to no. 29 (April 11, 1903) of the *Hsin-min ts'ung-pao*. The last three chapters were written after Liang's return from the United States. The last chapter was not published until no. 72 (Jan. 9, 1906) of the *Hsin-min ts'ung-pao*.

5. Ibid., pp. 40–44.

6. Ibid., pp. 45–50.

7. "Lo-li chu-i t'ai-tou Pien-hsin chih hsüeh-shuo" [The Thought of Bentham, the Authority of Utilitarianism] YPSWC 13:31.

8. Ibid., p. 39; cf. pp. 35–38.

9. Ibid., pp. 45–46.

10. Ibid., pp. 38–39.

11. "Lu-so hsüeh-an" [Rousseau's Thought] YPSWC 6:105.

12. "Cheng-chih-hsüeh hsüeh-li chih-yen" [A Systematic Discussion of the Principles of Politics] YPSWC 10:67.

13. Ibid., p. 69.

14. "Tzu-yu shu" YPSCC 2:1. Liang had no doubt learned about Mill from Japanese thinkers such as Fukuzawa Yukichi and Nakamura Masanao and had probably read some of Mill's work in Japanese translation. It seems unlikely that he had by this time read Yen Fu's translation of *Liberty* [Ch'ün chi ch'üan-chieh lun], the manuscript of which was not yet completed. Yen lost his manuscript during the Boxer disturbances in 1900 and did not recover it until 1903, when it was finally published. See Schwartz, *In Search of Wealth and Power: Yen Fu and the West*, pp. 130, 142.

15. "Lun cheng-fu yü jen-min chih ch'üan-hsien" YPSWC 10:1–6. Pp. 3–4 paraphrase portions of the first few pages of Mill's *Liberty*. Cf. Mill, *On Liberty*, pp. 1–5.

16. "Lun cheng-fu yü jen-min chih ch'üan-hsien" YPSWC 10:1.

17. Ibid., p. 2.

18. Mill, *Autobiography*, p. 253. Cf. *On Liberty*, pp. 5–6.

19. Ibid., pp. 76–103.

20. "Cheng-chih-hsüeh hsüeh-li chih-yen" YPSWC 10:69.

21. "Lun cheng-fu yü jen-min chih ch'üan-hsien," YPSWC 10:1–6. Cf. "Hsin-min shuo" YPSCC 4:40–44.

22. Mill, *Autobiography*, p. 242.

23. Stephen, *The English Utilitarians* 3:252.

24. Ibid., p. 74.

25. Ibid., p. 69.

26. "Ch'ing-tai hsüeh-shu kai-lun" [Intellectual Trends of the Ch'ing Period] YPSCC 34:63.

27. Ibid., p. 65.

28. Ibid., p. 56.

29. "Yü Yen Yu-ling hsien-sheng shu" [Letter to Mr. Yen Fu] YPSWC 1:110.

30. "Pao-chiao fei suo-i tsun K'ung-tzu lun" [Preserving the Faith Is Not the Way to Honor Confucius] YPSWC 9:59.

31. See, for example, "Chin-shih wen-ming ch'u-tsu erh ta-chia chih hsüeh-shuo" [The Thought of the Two Great Forefathers (Bacon and Descartes) of Modern Thought] YPSWC 13:11–12.

32. Mill, *Autobiography*, p. 254.

33. Ibid., p. 242.

34. "Ch'ing-tai hsüeh-shu kai-lun," p. 65.

35. Mill, *On Liberty*, pp. 79–80.

36. NP, pp. 174–91, provides a detailed record of Liang's itinerary, in addition to much of his correspondence during the year.

37. "Hsin ta-lu yu-chi chieh-lu" [A Condensed Record of (My) Travels in the New World] YPSCC 22:87.

38. Ibid., p. 39.

39. Ibid., p. 53.

40. Ibid., p. 91.

41. See Liang's report to K'ang in NP, pp. 188–90.

42. "Hsin ta-lu yu-chi chieh-lu" YPSCC 22:122–26.

43. See supra, note 4.

44. "Hsin-min shuo" YPSCC 4:130.

45. Ibid., pp. 149–51.

46. Ibid., pp. 135, 143–49.

47. The publication of this translation is said to have established Katō as the authority of political theory—*kokkagaku*—in Japan. Tabata, *Katō Hiroyuki*, p. 85.

48. Bluntschli, *The Theory of the State*, pp. 22, 15–23. Cf. "Cheng-chih-hsüeh ta-chia Po-lun-chih-li chih hsüeh-shuo" [The Thought of the Authority of Political Science, Bluntschli] YPSWC 13:70–71.

49. Ibid., p. 67.

50. Ibid., p. 89.

51. Ibid., p. 69.

52. Ibid., p. 89.

53. "K'ai-ming chuan-chih lun" YPSWC 17:13–83.

54. Ibid., pp. 14–15.

55. Ibid., p. 34.

56. Ibid., p. 21.

57. Ibid., pp. 21–22.
58. Ibid., p. 67.

CHAPTER 5

1. "Hsin Chung-kuo wei-lai chi" YPSCC 89:1–57.
2. *Hsin hsiao-shuo* (Yokohama, Nov., 1902 to Oct., 1905, 10 issues). The University of California Berkeley Library has vol. 1, no. 3, dated Jan. 13, 1903. Chap. 4 of the "Hsin Chung-kuo wei-lai chi," the last chapter, was published in this issue.
3. See the preface to the "Hsin Chung-kuo wei-lai chi" YPSCC 89:1.
4. Liang Ch'i-ch'ao, "Lun hsiao-shuo yü ch'ün-chih chih kuan-hsi" [On the Relationship between Fiction and Popular Government] YPSWC 10:6.
5. NP, pp. 165–66.
6. "Hsin Chung-kuo wei-lai chi" YPSCC 89:1–17.
7. Ibid., pp. 17–32.
8. Ibid., pp. 33–39.
9. Ibid., pp. 41–57.
10. "I-ta-li chien-kuo san chieh chuan" [Biographies of the Three Heroes Who Founded the Italian Nation] YPSCC 11:49.
11. Ibid., pp. 45–46, 51.
12. Ibid., p. 57.
13. *Ch'ing-i pao* (Yokohama, Dec. 23, 1898 to Dec. 31, 1901, 100 issues).
14. *Hsin-min ts'ung-pao* (Yokohama, Feb. 8, 1902 to Nov. 20, 1907, 96 issues).
15. Computed from YPSWC and YPSCC.
16. NP, pp. 42–43.
17. NP, pp. 42, 44; Wu Chuang [Hsien-tzu], *Chung-kuo min-chu hsien-cheng tang tang-shih* [A History of the Chinese Constitutional Democratic Party], p. 10. Cf. Feng Tzu-yu, *Ke-ming i-shih* [Anecdotal History of the Revolution] 2:32.
18. KMTKK 1:440067.
19. NP, p. 88; Feng, *Ke-ming i-shih* 2:32–34.
20. Ibid., p. 32. According to Feng, they were known as the "thirteen rebels" in K'ang's camp. The signatories to the letter included all those at the Enoshima meeting except Liang Ch'i-t'ien and Mai Chung-hua. The added members were T'ang Ts'ai-ch'ang, Lo P'u, another fellow student of Liang's from the Wan-mu ts'ao-t'ang, and Lin Kuei, one of the outstanding students from the Academy of Current Affairs in Hunan.

21. Feng, *Ke-ming i-shih* 1:72.

22. Schiffrin, *Sun Yat-sen and the Origins of the Chinese Revolution*, pp. 148–67, and 183–96, contains a comprehensive account of the early contacts between Liang and Sun. Cf. Chang P'eng-yüan, *Liang Ch'i-ch'ao yü Ch'ing-chi ke-ming* [Liang Ch'i-ch'ao and the Revolution of 1911], pp. 119–39.

23. Feng Tzu-yu, *Chung-hua min-kuo k'ai-kuo ch'ien ke-ming shih* [A History of the Revolutionary Movement before the Founding of the Republic] 1:44.

24. Ibid. Cf. Feng, *Ke-ming i-shih* 2:32, and NP, p. 89.

25. On January 24, after her plot to depose the emperor had been foiled by widespread protest, Tz'u-hsi appointed as heir apparent P'u-chün, the eldest son of her confidant Tsai-i. See Hummel, ed., *Eminent Chinese of the Ch'ing Period*, pp. 394, 732.

26. NP, pp. 140–41.

27. NP, pp. 109, 124.

28. Schiffrin, *Sun Yat-sen and the Origins of the Chinese Revolution*, p. 185.

29. NP, p. 130.

30. KMTKK 1:440043–49.

31. NP, p. 110.

32. The best account of this episode is Nagai Kazumi's "Tō Sai-jō to jiritsugun kigi" [T'ang Ts'ai-ch'ang and the Uprising of the Army for National Independence], *Nihon rekishi*, no. 85 (June 1955), pp. 16–21, and no. 88 (Oct. 1955), pp. 36–45. Cf. Kikuchi Takaharu, "Tō Sai-jō no jiritsugun kigi" [The Uprising of T'ang Ts'ai-ch'ang's Army for National Independence], pp. 13–23. Other accounts of this episode may be found in Schiffrin, *Sun Yat-sen and the Origins of the Chinese Revolution*, pp. 218–24, and Chang, *Liang Ch'i-ch'ao yü Ch'ing-chi ke-ming*, pp. 139–57, which goes into Liang's role in the plot.

33. NP, pp. 113–14.

34. On the Waichow uprising, see Schiffrin, *Sun Yat-sen and the Origins . . .*, pp. 214–55.

35. See the text of Liang's letter to Kashiwabara Buntarō, n.d. (summer 1900?), in Tōa Dōbun Kai, *Zoku Tai Shi kaikoroku* [Sequel to *Records on China*] 2:658.

36. Feng, *Ke-ming i-shih* 1:72; cf. Wu, *Chung-kuo min-chu . . .*, p. 35.

37. NP, p. 101; Wu, *Chung-kuo min-chu . . .*, p. 32; Chang, *Liang Ch'i-ch'ao yü . . .*, p. 142.

38. Liang complained, for example, of not being able to get any reply to his repeated letters to Wang Ching-ju and Ho Sui-t'ien, two of the key men at the society's headquarters. At one point Liang

urged Hsü Ch'in to return to Macao to take charge (NP, pp. 128–29, 102, 109, 122).

39. Ibid., p. 130.
40. Wu, *Chung-kuo min-chu* . . ., pp. 35–36.
41. NP, p. 130. Cf. Chang, *Liang Ch'i-ch'ao yü* . . ., p. 147.
42. NP, p. 112.
43. Chang, *Liang Ch'i-ch'ao yü* . . ., pp. 147–48.
44. Feng, *Ke-ming i-shih* 1:87–88; 2:34.
45. See, for example, Liang's letter to Chiang Kuan-yün in 1903 in which he writes, ". . . I swear that I will from now on leave the realm of empty talk (*k'ung-yen*) and enter into the realm of concrete endeavors. . . ." (NP, p. 175).
46. Ibid., p. 181.
47. Ibid., pp. 186–87.
48. Ibid., pp. 176–81.
49. See chap. 4.
50. Computed from YPSCC and YPSWC.
51. *Hsin-min ts'ung-pao.*
52. See chap. 4.
53. "Chung-kuo huo-pi wen-t'i" YPSWC 16:98–123.
54. "Pi-chih t'iao-i" YPSWC 22:1–28.
55. "Wai-chai p'ing-i" YPSWC 22:41–93.
56. "Hsien-cheng ch'ien-shuo" YPSWC 23:29–46.
57. "Chung-kuo kuo-hui chih-tu ssu-i" YPSWC 24:1–139.
58. "Lo-lan fu-jen chuan" YPSCC 11:1–61.
59. "Hsiung-chia-li ai-kuo-che Ko-su-shih chuan" YPSCC 10:1–27.
60. "Kuan-tzu chuan" YPSCC 28:1–81.
61. "Wang Ching-kung" YPSCC 27:1–217.
62. NP, p. 303.
63. The following account of the strike is based on Nagai Kazumi, "Iwayuru Shinkoku ryūgakusei torishimari kisoku jiken no seikaku" [The Nature of the Incident Arising from the So-called "Regulations Governing Chinese Students in Japan"], pp. 11–34, and Sanetō Keishū, *Chūgokujin Nihon ryūgaku shi* [A History of Chinese Students in Japan] pp. 461–94.
64. The full text of the regulations is given in Nagai's article, pp. 12–13.
65. "Chi Tung-ching hsüeh-chieh kung-fen shih" [On the Indignation and Protest of the Chinese Student Community in Tokyo], *Hsin-min ts'ung-pao*, no. 71 (Dec. 26, 1905), pp. 1–44. This article is not in the YPSWC or YPSCC.
66. Ibid., p. 30.

67. NP, p. 205.

68. "K'ai-ming chuan-chih lun" YPSWC 17:82.

69. "Cheng-chih yü jen-min" [Government and the People] YPSWC 20:7–19.

70. "Cheng-wen She hsüan-yen shu" [Declaration of the Political Information Club] YPSWC 20:22–24, 28.

71. NP, pp. 217, 241.

72. Ibid., p. 245–51.

73. Ibid., p. 217.

74. Ibid., pp. 214–16, 236–38, 240.

75. Ibid., pp. 250–51.

76. Ibid., pp. 216, 251–53.

77. "Cheng-wen She hsüan-yen shu " YPSWC 20:19–29.

78. NP, p. 218.

79. Ibid., pp. 258–59, 262–63.

80. Ibid., p. 267.

81. Ibid., pp. 273–74.

82. Chang, *Liang Ch'i-ch'ao yü* . . ., p. 187; cf. Li Chien-nung, *Chung-kuo chin pai-nien cheng-chih-shih* [A Political History of China in the Last Hundred Years], p. 265.

83. NP, p. 274.

84. The name of the Society to Protect the Emperor was changed to Constitutional Party (Hsien-cheng Tang) in 1906, after the royal decree on September 1. Wu, *Chung-kuo min-chu* . . ., pp. 47–48.

85. NP, p. 287.

86. Ibid., pp. 307, 313–15.

87. For the fullest available account of the petition movement in 1910, see Chang P'eng-yüan, *Li-hsien p'ai yü hsin-hai ke-ming* [Constitutionalists and the Revolution of 1911], pp. 63–77. Cf. Li, *Chung-kuo chin pai-nien* . . ., pp. 282–83.

88. For a fuller discussion of this society, see Chang, *Li-hsien p'ai yü hsin-hai ke-ming*, pp. 115–27. Cf. NP, pp. 314–15, 336.

89. Ibid., pp. 289–94.

90. Liang's maneuverings and plots during the final months of the dynasty have been told in some detail by Young, "The Reformer as Conspirator: Liang Ch'i-ch'ao and the 1911 Revolution," in Feuerwerker et al., eds., *Approaches to Modern Chinese History*, pp. 239–67. Unless otherwise noted, the details given in the following account are based on Young's article.

91. Feng, *Ke-ming i-shih* 1:73.

92. NP, pp. 339–42. This is the principal source upon which Young bases his account.

93. Li, *Chung-kuo chin pai-nien* . . ., pp. 310–12; cf. Powell, *The Rise of Chinese Military Power*, pp. 311–12.

94. Li, *Chung-kuo chin pai-nien* . . ., p. 315.

CHAPTER 6

1. The conventional interpretation of this event has been that Yüan staged the mutiny to convince the southern leaders that he could not leave Peking. See, for example, Li Chien-nung, *Chung-kuo chin pai-nien cheng-chih-shih* [A Political History of China in the Last Hundred Years], pp. 351–52. Wu Hsiang-hsiang, however, shows convincingly that such an interpretation would mean that Yüan was dangerously and unnecessarily playing with fire (*Sung Chiao-jen*, pp. 124–26).

2. I am indebted to Edward Friedman for pointing out to me the pivotal position that Li and his Wuhan power base occupied in the power configuration of the time. The idea can be found in Wu, *Sung Chiao-jen*, p. 205. The conventional interpretation of Li has been that he was an innocuous figurehead. See Li, *Chung-kuo chin pai-nien* . . ., pp. 304–5.

3. On T'ang and Sun's roles in the revolution, see Chang P'eng-yüan, *Li-hsien p'ai yü hsin-hai ke-ming* [Constitutionalists and the Revolution of 1911], pp. 143–50, 68–77, 197–200.

4. Chang Chien's financial influence was apparently critical to the very survival of the Nanking Provisional Government. See ibid., p. 131. On Chang Chien's activities in support of Yüan, see ibid., pp. 214–36.

5. Li Shou-k'ung, *Min-ch'u chih kuo-hui* [The Early Republican Legislature], p. 19. Li gives the name list of the Nanking Provisional Assembly on pp. 147–48. The provinces that had not declared independence were represented by delegates sent by the old provincial assemblies (Tzu-i chü) established in October, 1909.

6. The Nanking Provisional Assembly decided in March that its membership should be elected by the temporary provincial assemblies that had been established after the revolution. The provinces that had not established such assemblies were to be represented by the delegates sent by the military governors (ibid., p. 23). The membership of the Peking Provisional Assembly was in some cases substantially different from the Nanking Provisional Assembly. In the cases of Hunan, Hupei, Shantung, and Yunnan, the membership had merely expanded. But in the cases of Kwangtung, Kweichow, Chekiang, Kiangsi, Kiangsu, for example, there were radical changes. Compare the name lists in ibid., pp. 149–51, with pp. 147–

48. The full implications of these changes can only be understood through a detailed investigation of the developments in each of the provinces.

7. Each provincial assembly was to elect 10 representatives to the upper house. Membership in the lower house was apportioned according to the formula of one representative for every 800,000 people (ibid., pp. 81–82). The elections, of course, have yet to be studied in detail.

8. Yang Yu-ch'iung, *Chung-kuo cheng-tang shih* [A History of Political Parties in China], pp. 57–61.

9. Ibid., pp. 56, 61.

10. NP, p. 303.

11. On the relations between Liang and this group, see ibid., pp. 379, 396–98, 398–401.

12. Ibid., pp. 398–401.

13. Ibid., pp. 369–70, 372–73.

14. Wu, *Sung Chiao-jen*, pp. 122–23.

15. For some examples of the feuds between Liang's group and the T'ung-meng Hui in 1911–12, see NP, pp. 362–63, 400–401.

16. Ibid., pp. 380–83.

17. Ibid.

18. Ibid., pp. 411–12.

19. Ibid., p. 371.

20. Ibid., pp. 396–403.

21. Ibid., p. 405. Cf. Yang, *Chung-kuo cheng-tang shih*, p. 46, and Li Shou-k'ung, *Min-ch'u chih kuo-hui*, pp. 71–72.

22. NP, pp. 405–8.

23. Ibid., pp. 408–10.

24. Yang, *Chung-kuo cheng-tang shih*, p. 61.

25. NP, p. 418.

26. Ibid., pp. 414, 419. Cf. Yang, *Chung-kuo cheng-tang shih*, pp. 66–68.

27. NP, pp. 417–18.

28. On the general political atmosphere in early 1913, see Wu, *Sung Chiao-jen*, pp. 216–19.

29. Ibid., pp. 219–22, 224–26.

30. Li Shou-k'ung, *Min-ch'u chih kuo-hui*, pp. 94–95, 104–5, 107–8.

31. Ibid., pp. 105–9.

32. Ibid., pp. 111–14.

33. NP, pp. 422–23.

34. Ibid., p. 431. Cf. "Cheng-fu ta-cheng fang-chen hsüan-yen shu" [Declaration of the Guiding Principles of the Government] YPSWC 29:121. This declaration of the Hsiung Hsi-ling cabinet

was written by Liang (NP, p. 420). Cf. "Tz'u ssu-fa tsung-chang chih ch'eng-wen" [Letter Submitted in Resignation from the Post of Minister of Justice] YPSWC 31:32 and NP, pp. 433–34.

35. Ibid., pp. 429, 432. Cf. supra, note 34.

36. Li Shou-k'ung, *Min-ch'u chih kuo-hui*, pp. 119–20, 127–32.

37. Ibid., p. 135.

38. See Liang's own assessment in "Tz'u ssu-fa tsung-chang chih ch'eng-wen" YPSWC 31:33 and NP, p. 433.

39. Ibid., p. 415.

40. Ibid., pp. 421–22.

41. Ibid., p. 429.

42. See, for example, his essay written in 1913 on "Kuo-hui chih tzu-sha" [The Suicide of the Legislature] YPSWC 30:11–15.

43. NP, p. 434.

44. See, for example, "Chung-kuo huo-pi wen-t'i" [The Currency Problem in China] YPSWC 16:98–123, and "Pi-chih t'iao-i" [Discussions on Currency Regulations] YPSWC 22:1–28.

45. "Min-kuo ch'u-nien chih pi-chih kai-ke" [Currency Reform in the Early Years of the Republic] YPSWC 43:11.

46. "Yü chih pi-chih chin-yung cheng-ts'e" [My Monetary Policies] YPSWC 32:38; "Pi-chih t'iao-li li-yu shu" [Reasons for the Currency Regulations] YPSWC 32:2–3; "Cheng-li lan-fa chih-pi yü li-yung kung-chai" [Regulating the Abusive Issuance of Paper Currencies and Making Use of the National Debt] YPSWC 32:12–26; "Ni fa-hsing kuo-pi hui-tui-ch'üan shuo-t'ieh" [A Proposal for the Issuance of National Exchange Notes] YPSWC 32:26–31.

47. "Yü chih pi-chih chin-yung cheng-ts'e" YPSWC 32:41.

48. Yang Ju-mei, *Min-kuo ts'ai-cheng* [Finance in Republican China], pp. 9–23, and 42–50 of the appendices.

49. "Yü chih pi-chih chin-yung cheng-ts'e" YPSWC 32:50–51, 63, and "Min-kuo ch'u-nien chih pi-chih kai-ke" YPSWC 43:11–12.

50. NP, pp. 440–41.

51. "Yü chih pi-chih chin-yung cheng-ts'e" YPSWC 32:38.

52. NP, p. 460. Cf. "Kuo-t'i chan-cheng kung-li t'an" [On My Personal Experiences in the War over the Form of the National Polity] YPSCC 33:143.

53. NP, pp. 453–54.

54. Ibid., pp. 456, 446, 449.

55. "I tsai suo-wei kuo-t'i wen-t'i che" [How Strange Is the So-called Problem of the Form of the National Polity] YPSCC 33:85–91.

56. NP, p. 457.

57. "Kuo-t'i chan-cheng kung-li t'an" YPSCC 33:144.

58. "Chih Chi Liang-chi, Ch'en Yu-su, Hsiung T'ieh-yai, Liu

Hsi-t'ao shu" [Letter to Chi Liang-chi, Ch'en Yu-su, Hsiung T'ieh-yai and Liu Hsi-t'ao] YPSCC 33:27–28.

59. NP, pp. 462, 468–71.

60. Ibid., pp. 473–74.

61. Wu Kuan-yin, "Ping-ch'en ts'ung-chün jih-chi" [Diary of My Service in the Army in 1916], *Ta Chung-hua* 2, no. 10 (Oct. 20, 1916): 2 (entry dated March 4, 1916).

62. For a vivid account of Liang's trip to Kwangsi, see Liang's "Ts'ung-chün jih-chi" [Diary of My Service in the Army] YPSCC 33:121–27. Cf. NP, p. 482.

63. For the text of the telegram, see "Kuang-shi chih ke-sheng t'ung-tien" [Circular Telegram from Kwangsi to All Provinces] YPSCC 33:6–7. The telegram was taken to Lu by T'ang Chüeh-tun (NP, p. 482).

64. Ibid., pp. 483–84. Cf. Li Chien-nung, *Chung-kuo chin pai-nien* . . ., pp. 455–56.

65. For a more detailed outline of these political groups, see Yang, *Chung-kuo cheng-tang shih*, pp. 89–93, and Li Chien-nung, *Chung-kuo chin pai-nien* . . ., pp. 481–83.

66. "Chih Chi Liang-chi, Ch'en Yu-su, Hsiung T'ieh-yai, Liu Hsi-t'ao shu" YPSCC 33:28.

67. For an account of this event, called the Hai-chu affair, see Wu Kuan-yin, "Ping-ch'en ts'ung-chün jih-chi," p. 7. According to Wu, T'ang's murder was engineered by Yüan's henchman Liang Shih-i, in connivance with Lung. For Liang's reactions to this affair, see NP, pp. 485–86.

68. Ibid., p. 494.

69. See Liang's telegram to Lo P'ei-chin in YPSCC 33:81–82. Ts'ai died on November 8, 1916, at the Fukuoka Hospital in Japan (NP, p. 503).

70. See Liang's telegram to Li Yüan-hung in YPSCC 33:78. Cf. NP, p. 500, and "Yü pao-kuan chi-che t'an-hua" [Conversation with a Reporter] YPSCC 33:132–33.

71. NP, pp. 496–97.

72. Ibid., pp. 505–7.

73. Ibid., pp. 501–3.

74. Ibid., pp. 512, 514–15.

75. Li Chien-nung, *Chung-kuo chin pai-nien* . . ., pp. 489–90.

76. NP, pp. 510–12, 514–15. Cf. "Min-kuo ch'u-nien chih pi-chih kai-ke," pp. 16–17, and "Wai-chiao fang-chen chih yen" [The Guiding Principles of Our Foreign Policy] YPSWC 35:4–7.

77. Li Chien-nung, *Chung-kuo chin pai-nien* . . ., pp. 490–93, 514–15.

78. NP, pp. 518–20. Cf. "P'i fu-p'i lun" [Cracking Open the Restoration Argument] YPSCC 33:117–19.

79. NP, p. 520.

80. Ibid., p. 523.

81. Ibid., pp. 531–32.

82. Ibid., pp. 532–37.

83. See, for example, Li Chien-nung, *Chung-kuo chin pai-nien . . .*, pp. 512, 516.

84. For a list of these loans, see *Ajia rekishi jiten* [Encyclopedia of Asian History] 7:335–36.

85. Langdon, "Japan's Failure to Establish Friendly Relations with China," p. 250.

86. Hatano Yoshihiro, "Nishihara shakkan no kihonteki kōsō" [The Basic Conception of the Nishihara Loans], pp. 396–98, 409.

87. Wang Yün-sheng, *Liu-shih-nien lai chih Chung-kuo yü Jih-pen* [China and Japan in the Last Sixty Years], p. 127. Langdon, "Japan's Failure to Establish Friendly Relations," p. 256, concurs with Wang on this point.

88. NP, pp. 535–37.

89. Ibid., pp. 524, 526.

CHAPTER 7

1. NP, pp. 551–70, 599. For a full account, see Liang's "Ou yu hsin-ying lu" [Impressions from My European Journey] YPSCC 23:1–162.

2. NP, p. 554.

3. Ibid., p. 565.

4. Ibid., p. 559.

5. Chang, Chiang, Liu, and Yang accompanied Liang to Europe (NP, pp. 551, 565). Ting and Hsü joined the group there (NP, p. 552). On Chang, see *Ajia rekishi jiten* [Encyclopedia of Asian History] 6:279; Perleberg, *Who's Who in China*, and *Gendai Chūgoku jinmei jiten* [Biographical Dictionary of Contemporary China], p. 393. On Chiang, see *Ajia rekishi jiten* 4:414; Chia I-chün, ed., *Chung-hua min-kuo ming-jen chuan* [Biographies of Famous Personalities of Republican China], p. 125, and Liang's preface to his "Ch'ing-tai hsüeh-shu kai-lun" [Intellectual Trends in the Ch'ing Period] YPSCC, p. 34. On Liu, see NP, p. 316. On Ting, see Ting Wen-yüan's account of his brother in NP, pp. 5–9; cf. Charlotte Furth, *Ting Wen-chiang*, *Ajia rekishi jiten* 6:419, Yang Chia-lo, ed., *Min-kuo ming-jen t'u-chien* [A Biographical Dictionary of Republican Per-

sonalities, with Photographs] 1:4, and China Weekly Review, *Who's Who in China*, p. 230. On Hsü, see NP, pp. 558–59, 566.

6. NP, p. 559.

7. Ibid., p. 558.

8. Supra, note 1.

9. Schwartz, *In Search of Wealth and Power: Yen Fu and the West.*

10. Hughes, *Consciousness and Society*, p. 377.

11. Ibid., pp. 33–66.

12. Hofstadter, *Social Darwinism in American Thought*, p. 123.

13. "Ou yu hsin-ying lu" YPSCC 23:17.

14. Hughes, *Consciousness and Society*, pp. 37–38.

15. "Ou yu hsin-ying lu" YPSCC 23:9–14.

16. Ibid., pp. 15, 10–12.

17. Kwok, *Scientism in Chinese Thought, 1900–1950.*

18. Hughes, *Consciousness and Society*, p. 376.

19. "Ou yu hsin-ying lu" YPSCC 23:15.

20. Ibid., pp. 35–36.

21. "Chung-kuo jen chih tzu-chüeh," in "Ou yu hsin-ying lu" YPSCC 23:20–38.

22. Ibid., pp. 22–23.

23. Ibid., p. 24.

24. Ibid., p. 28.

25. Ibid., pp. 20–21, 35–38.

26. Ibid., p. 37.

27. "T'ao-hua shan chu" [Commentaries on the *Peach Blossom Fan*] YPSCC, vol. 95. "Chung-kuo chih mei-wen chi ch'i li-shih" [China's Verse Writing and Its History] YPSCC, vol. 74. "T'ao Yüan-ming" YPSCC, vol. 96. "Chu Shun-shui hsien-sheng nien-p'u" [A Chronological Biography of Chu Shun-shui] YPSCC, vol. 97. "Tai Tung-yüan hsien-sheng chuan" [A Biography of Tai Chen] YPSWC 40:40–52.

28. "Hsien-Ch'in cheng-chih ssu-hsiang shih" YPSCC, vol. 50. (Translated by L. T. Chen as *History of Chinese Political Thought during the Early Tsin Period*, London, 1930.) "Ch'ing-tai hsüeh-shu kai lun." "Chung-kuo chin san-pai-nien hsüeh-shu shih" YPSCC, vol. 75.

29. See list of fragmentary drafts in YPSCC, vol. 1. For the draft outline of the "A Cultural History of China," see YPSCC, vol. 43.

30. "Lao-tzu che-hsüeh" YPSCC, vol. 35. "Ju-chia che-hsüeh" YPSCC, vol. 103. "K'ung-tzu" YPSCC, vol. 36. "Mo Ching chiao-shih" YPSCC, vol. 38.

31. "Chung-kuo li-shih yen-chiu-fa pu-pien" [Supplement to "How to Study Chinese History"] YPSCC 99:9. Cf. "Ju-chia che-hsüeh," p. 7.

32. "Chung-kuo li-shih yen-chiu-fa pu-pien" YPSCC 99:144.
33. Ibid., p. 145.
34. Ibid., p. 150.
35. Ibid., p. 149.
36. "K'ung-tzu" YPSCC 36:43–44, 7–8, 51. Cf. "Hsien-Ch'in cheng-chih ssu-hsiang shih" YPSCC 50:78, 154.
37. "Ju-chia che-hsüeh" YPSCC 103:70.
38. "Hsien-Ch'in cheng-chih ssu-hsiang shih" YPSCC 103:64, 68–69.
39. Ibid., pp. 83, 163–64, 72. Cf. "K'ung-tzu" YPSCC 36:72.
40. "Hsien-Ch'in cheng-chih ssu-hsiang shih" YPSCC 103:183–84.
41. "K'ung-tzu" YPSCC 36: 54–55.
42. "Hsien-Ch'in cheng-chih ssu-hsiang shih" YPSCC 103:88.
43. Ibid., pp. 155–57.
44. "K'ung-tzu" YPSCC 36:54.
45. Ibid., pp. 56–57.
46. "Chuang-tzu t'ien-hsia p'ien shih-i" [Commentaries on the "T'ien-hsia" chapter of the *Book of Chuang-tzu*] YPSCC 77:2–4.
47. "K'ung-tzu" YPSCC 36:56.
48. "Hsien-Ch'in cheng-chih ssu-hsiang shih" YPSCC, pp. 64–65, 151, 217.
49. Ibid., pp. 4, 151.
50. "K'ung-tzu" YPSCC 36:58, 54.
51. For a general discussion of the polemics, see Chow Ts'e-tsung, *The May Fourth Movement: Intellectual Revolution in Modern China*, pp. 333–37. For a fuller discussion, see Kwok, *Scientism in Chinese Thought, 1900–1950*, pp. 135–60.
52. Chang Chün-mai, "Jen-sheng kuan" [View of Life], in Ya-tung t'u-shu kuan, *K'e-hsüeh yü jen-sheng kuan* [Science and Metaphysics] (Shanghai, 1927), pp. 9–10.
53. "Jen-sheng kuan yü k'e-hsüeh: tui yü Chang Ting lun-chan te p'i-p'ing" [Science and Metaphysics: a Critique of the Polemics between Chang and Ting] YPSWC 40:23–25.
54. "Fei wei" [Against Isms] YPSWC 41:82–84.
55. Wu Chih-hui, *Wu Chih-hui wen-chi* [Works of Wu Chih-hui], p. 111.
56. "Hsien-Ch'in cheng-chih ssu-hsiang shih" YPSCC 103:71; cf. pp. 73, 183.
57. Ibid.

Glossary

"Ai-kuo lun" 愛國論
Asahi shinbun 朝日新聞
baai 場合
bungaku 文學
bunka 文化
bunmei 文明
Ch'a-k'eng 茶坑
Chang Chi 張繼
Chang (Carsun) Chia-sen (Chün-mai) 張嘉森 (君勱)
Chang Chien 張謇
Chang Chih-tung 張之洞
Chang Hsüeh-ching 張學璟
Chang Hsün 張勳
Chang P'eng-yüan 張朋園
Chang Ping-lin 章炳麟
Chang Shao-tseng 張紹曾
Chang Tsung-hsiang 章宗祥
ch'ang-ho 場合
Chen kao-huang 鍼膏肓
Ch'en Kuo-yung 陳國鏞
Ch'en Meng 陳猛
Ch'en Pao-chen 陳寶箴
Ch'en San-li 陳三立
Ch'en T'ien-hua 陳天華
Ch'en Tu-hsiu 陳獨秀
Ch'en T'ung-fu 陳通甫
Cheng Chen-to 鄭振鐸
"Cheng-chih-hsüeh hsüeh-li chih-yen" 政治學學理撫言
"Cheng-chih-hsüeh ta-chia Po-lun-chih-li chih hsüeh-shuo" 政治學大家伯倫知理之學説
cheng-fu 政府
"Cheng-fu ta-cheng fang-chen hsüan-yen shu" 政府大政方針宣言書
Cheng Hsiao-hsü 鄭孝胥
Cheng Hsüan 鄭玄
"Cheng-li lan-fa chih-pi yü li-yung kung-chai" 整理濫發紙幣與利用公債
Cheng-lun 政論
Cheng-wen She 政聞社
chi-chiu 祭酒
Chi Chung-yin 籍忠寅
"Chi Tung-ching hsüeh-chieh kung-fen shih" 記東京學界公憤事
Ch'i fei-chi 起癈疾
chia-chih 價值
"Chia-jen ch'i-yü" 佳人奇遇
Chiang Fang-chen 蔣方震
Chiang Kuan-yün 蔣觀雲
ch'iang-ch'üan 強權
Ch'iang-hsüeh Hui 強學會
"Chiao-she hu ming-ling hu" 交涉乎命令乎

195

"Chih Chi Liang-chi, Ch'en Yu-su, Hsiung T'ieh-yai, Liu Hsi-t'ao shu" 致籍亮疇, 陳幼蘇, 熊鐵厓, 劉希陶書
chih-p'ei 支配
chin-ch'ü mao-hsien 進取冒險
Chin-pu Tang 進步黨
Chinrinshi 沈倫士
"Chin-shih wen-ming ch'u-tsu erh ta-chia chih hsüeh-shuo" 近世文明初祖二大家之學説
Ch'in Li-shan 秦力山
ch'in min 親民
ching-shen 精神
Ching Ti 景帝
"*Ch'ing-i pao* hsü li" 清議報叙例
"*Ch'ing-i pao* i-pai ts'e chu-tz'u" 清議報一百冊祝辭
"Ch'ing-tai hsüeh-shu kai lun" 清代學術概論
Chōsen Gumi 朝鮮組
Chou Hung-yeh 周宏業
Ch'ou-an Hui 籌安會
ch'ou-hsiang 抽象
Chu Hsi 朱熹
chu-hsi 主系
chu-i 主義
Chu-ke Liang 諸葛亮
Chu Shun-shui 朱舜水
"Chu Shun-shui hsien-sheng nien-p'u" 朱舜水先生年譜
chü-jen 舉人
chü-lo-pu 俱樂部
ch'uan-wen chih shih 傳聞之世
"Ch'üan hsüeh p'ien" 勸學篇
Chuang-tzu 莊子
"Chuang-tzu t'ien-hsia p'ien shih i" 莊子天下篇釋義
Chuang Ts'un-yü 莊存與
Ch'un-ch'iu cheng-tz'u 春秋正辭
chün-ch'üan 君權
Ch'ün chi ch'üan-chieh lun 羣己權界論

Chung-hua Ke-ming Tang 中華革命黨
Chung-hua Min-kuo Lien-ho Hui 中華民國聯合會
Chung-i Yüan 衆議院
"Chung-Jih tsui-chin chiao-she p'ing-i" 中日最近交涉平議
"Chung-Jih wen-hua chih chiao-liu" 中日文化之交流
"Chung-kuo chih mei-wen chi ch'i li-shih" 中國之美文及其歷史
"Chung-kuo chin san-pai nien hsüeh-shu shih" 中國近三百年學術史
"Chung-kuo huo-pi wen-t'i" 中國貨幣問題
"Chung-kuo-jen chih tzu-chüeh" 中國人之自覺
"Chung-kuo kuo-hui chih-tu ssu-i" 中國國會制度私議
"*Chung-kuo li-shih yen-chiu-fa* pu-pien" 中國歷史研究法補編
chung-yung 中庸
chūshō 抽象
dōbun 同文
dokuritsu jison 獨立自尊
dōshu 同種
Enoshima 江の島
Fa mo-shou 發墨守
fan-tung 反動
"Fei wei" 非唯
Feng Kuo-chang 馮國璋
Feng Tzu-yu 馮自由
fu-ch'iang 富強
Fukuzawa Yukuchi 福澤諭吉
Hai-chu affair (shih-pien) 海珠事變
handō 反動
Han-shüeh 漢學
Han Kei 范卿
Han Wen-chü 韓文舉
Hirayama Shū 平山周
ho-ch'ün 合羣

Ho Hsiu 何休
hōjū hiretsu 放縱卑劣
Ho Sui-t'ien 何穗田
hsi 系
Hsi-cheng ts'ung-shu 西政叢書
"*Hsi-cheng ts'ung-shu* hsü" 西政叢書叙
"*Hsi-hsüeh shu-mu piao* hou hsü" 西學書目表後序
"*Hsi-hsüeh shu-mu piao* hsü li" 西學書目表序例
Hsia Tseng-yu 夏曾佑
Hsiang-hsüeh hsin-pao 湘學新報
hsiao-k'ang 小康
"Hsien-cheng ch'ien shuo" 憲政淺説
Hsien-cheng Shang-chüeh Hui 憲政商榷會
Hsien-cheng Tang 憲政黨
"Hsien Ch'in cheng-chih ssu-hsiang shih" 先秦政治思想史
Hsien-yu Hui 憲友會
Hsin ch'ing-nien 新青年
"Hsin Chung-kuo wei-lai chi" 新中國未來記
Hsin-hsüeh wei-ching k'ao 新學偽經考
Hsin-hui 新會
hsin-min 新民
"Hsin-min shuo" 新民説
"Hsin shih-hsüeh" 新史學
"Hsin ta-lu yu-chi chieh-lu" 新大陸遊記節錄
hsin-wang 新王
hsing-chih 形質
Hsing Chung Hui 興中會
hsing-shih 行事
"Hsiung-chia-li ai-kuo-che Ko-su-shih chuan" 匈加利愛國者噶蘇士傳
Hsiung Hsi-ling 熊希齡
Hsü Chi-yü 徐繼畬
Hsü Ch'in 徐勤

Hsü Fo-su 徐佛蘇
Hsü Hsin-liu 徐新六
"Hsü i *Lieh-kuo sui-chi cheng-yao* hsü" 續譯列國歳計政要敍
Hsüeh-hai T'ang 學海堂
hsüeh-hsiao 學校
hsün-ku 訓詁
Hsün-tzu 荀子
Hu Han-min 胡漢民
Hu Shih 胡適
Huang Hsing 黃興
Huang K'e-ch'iang 黃克強
Huang Su-ch'u 黃溯初
Huang Tsun-hsien 黃遵憲
Huang Tsung-hsi 黃宗羲
Huang Wei-chih 黃為之
hui 會
Hui-chou (Waichow) 惠州
I-k'uang 奕劻
Ichiko Chūzō 市古宙三
Inugai Tsuyoshi 犬養毅
Ishida Takeshi 石田雄
i-shih 議事
i-shih chih jen 議事之人
"I-ta-li chien-kuo san chieh chuan" 意大利建國三傑傳
"I tsai suo-wei kuo-t'i wen-t'i che" 異哉所謂國體問題者
i-wu ssu-hsiang 義務思想
i-yüan 議院
jen 仁
jen-cheng 仁政
jen-hsi 閩系
Jen-kung 任公
jen-min 人民
"Jen-sheng kuan" 人生觀
"Jen-sheng kuan yü k'e-hsüeh: tui yü Chang Ting lun-chan te p'i-p'ing" 人生觀與科學：對於張丁論戰的批評
Jih-pen kuo chih 日本國志
jichi 自治
jiyū 自由

"Ju-chia che hsüeh" 儒家哲學
kagaku 科學
k'ai-ming 開明
k'ai-ming chuan-chih 開明專制
"K'ai-ming chuan-chih lun" 開
　明專制論
Kajin no kigu 佳人の奇遇
kakkan 客觀
kakumei 革命
K'ang Yu-wei 康有為
k'ao-cheng 考證
Kashiwabara Buntarō 栢原文太郎
Katō Hiroyuki 加藤弘之
Kawakami Hajime 河上肇
ke-ming 革命
k'e-fu 克服
k'e-hsüeh 科學
k'e-kuan 客觀
K'e-lu Faction (P'ai) 客廬派
Keikoku bidan 經國美談
kokkagaku 國家學
kokufuku 克服
Konoe Atsumaro 近衛篤麿
Kōren 紅蓮
Ku Chieh-kang 顧頡剛
Ku Hung-ming 辜鴻銘
"Ku i-yüan k'ao" 古議院考
ku-jen chih ch'üan 古人之全
Ku-liang Commentary (chuan) 穀
　梁傳
Ku-liang fei-chi 穀梁癈疾
Ku-shih pien 古史辨
Kuan Chung 管仲
"Kuan-tzu chuan" 管子傳
"Kuang-hsi chih ke-sheng t'ung-
　tien" 廣西致各省通電
Kuang-wu Ti 光武帝
Kung-ho Chien-she T'ao-lun
　Hui 共和建設討論會
Kung-ho Tang 共和黨
kung-te 公德
Kung Tzu-chen 龔自珍
Kung-yang 公羊

K'ung Hung-tao 孔弘道
K'ung Shang-jen 孔尚任
"K'ung-tzu" 孔子
K'ung-tzu kai-chih k'ao 孔子改制考
k'ung-yen 空言
kuo-chia 國家
Kuo-hui 國會
"Kuo-hui chih tzu-sha" 國會之
　自殺
Kuo-min Hsieh-chin Hui 國民協
　進會
"Kuo-min shih ta yüan-ch'i lun"
　國民十大元氣論
Kuomintang 國民黨
"Kuo-t'i chan-cheng kung-li
　t'an" 國體戰爭躬歷談
kyōken 強權
Lan T'ien-wei 藍天蔚
"Lao-tzu che-hsüeh" 老子哲學
li 隸
"Li-chi yü ai-t'a" 利己與愛他
Li Ching-t'ung 李敬通
Li Ch'ü-ping 李去病
Li Ch'ün 李羣
Li Hung-chang 李鴻章
Li Lieh-chün 李烈鈞
Li Ping-huan 李炳寰
Li Tuan-fen 李端棻
Li Yüan-hung 黎元洪
"Li yün" 禮運
Liang Ch'i-ch'ao 梁啓超
Liang Ch'i-t'ien 梁啓田
Liang Pao-ying 梁寶瑛
Liang Ping-kuang 梁炳光
Liang Shih-i 梁士詒
Liang Wei-ch'ing 梁維清
Lin Ch'ang-min 林長民
Lin Kuei 林圭
Lin Tse-hsü 林則徐
Liu Ch'ung-chieh 劉崇傑
Liu Feng-lu 劉逢禄
Liu Hsin 劉歆
Liu Shih-p'ei 劉師培

Lo Jun-nan 羅潤楠
"Lo-lan fu-jen chuan" 羅蘭夫人傳
"Lo-li chu-i t'ai-tou Pien-hsin
    chih hsüeh-shuo" 樂利主義泰斗
    邊沁之學説
Lo P'ei-chin 羅佩金
Lo P'u 羅普
Lo Tsai-t'ien 羅在田
Lu Jung-t'ing 陸榮廷
"Lu-so hsüeh-an" 盧梭學案
Luan-chou 灤州
"Lun cheng-fu yü jen-min chih
    ch'üan-hsien" 論政府與人民之
    權限
"Lun chin-shih kuo-min ching-
    cheng chih ta-shih chi Chung-
    kuo ch'ien-t'u" 論近世國民競爭
    之大勢及中國前途
"Lun chün-cheng min-cheng
    hsiang-shan chih li" 論君政民
    政相嬗之理
"Lun Chung-kuo chih chiang
    ch'iang" 論中國之將強
"Lun Chung-kuo hsüeh-shu
    pien-ch'ien chih ta-shih" 論中
    國學術變遷之大勢
"Lun hsiao-shuo yü ch'ün-chih
    chih kuan-hsi" 論小説與羣治之
    関係
"Lun hsüeh Jih-pen-wen chih i"
    論學日本文之益
"Lun shang-yeh hui-i-suo chih
    i" 論商業會議所之益
"Lun tzu-tsun" 論自尊
Lung Chi-kuang 龍濟光
Ma Liang 馬良
Mai Chung-hua 麥仲華
Mai Meng-hua 麥孟華
Mao Tse-tung 毛澤東
Meirokusha 明六社
"*Meng-hsüeh pao Yen-i pao ho-
    hsü*" 蒙學報演義報合敍
mibun 身分

min-ch'i 民氣
min-chu 民主
Min-chu Tang 民主黨
min-ch'üan 民權
"Min-kuo ch'u-nien chih pi-chih
    kai-ke" 民國初年之幣制改革
Min-pao 民報
min-pen 民本
Min She 民社
min-tsu ti-kuo chu-i 民族帝國主義
"Ming-i tai-fang lu" 明夷待訪録
Miyazaki Torazō (Tōten) 宮崎寅
    藏 (滔天)
"*Mo-ching* chiao-shih" 墨經校釋
Mo-tzu 墨子
Nakamura Masanao 中村正直
Nan-hsüeh Hui 南學會
Neng-tzu 能子
nien-p'u 年譜
"Ni fa-hsing kuo-pi hui-tui-
    ch'üan shuo-t'ieh" 擬發行國幣
    匯兑券説帖
Nishihara Kamezō 西原亀三
Okuma Shigenobu 大隈重信
Oshima 大島
Ou Chü-chia 歐榘甲
"Ou yu hsin-ying lu" 歐遊心影録
pai-hua 白話
p'ai 派
p'ang-hsi 旁系
pao-chiao 保教
"Pao-chiao fei suo-i tsun K'ung-
    tzu lun" 保教非所以尊孔子論
Pao-huang Hui 保皇會
Peiyang 北洋
"Pi-chih t'iao-i" 幣制條議
"Pi-chih t'iao-li li-yu shu" 幣制
    條例理由書
"P'i fu-p'i lun" 闢復辟論
"Pien-fa t'ung-i" 變法通議
Ping-ch'en Chü-lo-pu 丙辰倶樂部
"P'ing-chün p'ien" 平均篇
Po Hu T'ung 白虎通

"Po K'ang Yu-wei chih tsung-t'ung tsung-li shu" 駁康有為致總統總理書
Po Wen-wei 柏文蔚
p'o-huai 破壞
pu-tang chu-i 不黨主義
P'u-chün 溥儁
P'u-i 溥儀
P'u Tien-chün 蒲殿俊
san-shih 三世
"San-shih tzu-shu" 三十自述
san-t'ung 三統
Setchūbai 雪中梅
shakai 社會
Shan-ch'i (Prince Su) 善耆 (肅親王)
Shanhaikwan 山海關
she 社
she-hui 社會
shen-fen 身分
Shen pao 申報
Shen Ping-k'un 沈秉堃
sheng-p'ing 升平
sheng-yüan 生員
Shiba Shirō 柴四郎
shihai 支配
shih-chieh chu-i te kuo-chia 世界主義的國家
shih-chung 時中
Shih-wu Hsüeh-t'ang 時務學堂
Shōda Kazue 勝田主計
shou-hsü 手續
shu 恕
shuai-luan 衰亂
shugi 主義
su-wang 素王
Suehiro Tetchō 末廣鐵腸
Sun Hung-i 孫洪伊
Sun Mei 孫眉
Sun Yat-sen (Wen) 孫逸仙 (文)
Sung Chiao-jen 宋教仁
suo-chien chih shih 所見之世
suo-wen chih shih 所聞之世

ta-chuan 大篆
"Ta mou-chün wen Jih-pen chin-chih chiao-k'e-shu shih" 答某君問日本禁止教科書事
Ta-t'ung shu 大同書
Tai Chen 戴震
Tai K'an 戴戡
"Tai Tung-yüan hsien-sheng chuan" 戴東原先生傳
t'ai-hsüeh 太學
t'ai-p'ing 太平
Takasugi Shinsaku 高杉晋作
T'an Hsi-yung 譚錫鏞
T'an Ssu-t'ung 譚嗣同
T'an Yen-k'ai 譚延闓
T'ang Chi-yao 唐繼堯
T'ang Chüeh-tun 湯覺頓
T'ang Hua-lung 湯化龍
T'ang Shou-ch'ien 湯壽潛
T'ang Ts'ai-ch'ang 唐才常
T'ao Ch'ien (Yüan-ming) 陶潛 (淵明)
"T'ao-hua shan chu" 桃花扇註
T'ao-yüan Faction (P'ai) 韜園派
"T'ao Yüan-ming" 陶淵明
tenpu jinken 天賦人權
tenshoku 天職
Terauchi Masatake 寺內正毅
tetsuzuki 手続
t'ieh-k'uo 帖括
T'ieh-liang 鐵良
t'ien-hsia 天下
T'ien Pang-hsüan 田邦璿
T'ien-yen lun 天演論
ting-chang 定章
Ting Wen-chiang 丁文江
Tōa Dōbun Kai 東亞同文會
Tōa Kai 東亞會
Tōkai Sanshi 東海散士
Tōkyō Senmon Gakkō 東京專門學校
Tsai-feng 載澧
Tsai-i 載漪

tsai-i 災異
Tsai-t'ao 載濤
Tsai-tse 載澤
Ts'ai Chung-hao 蔡鐘浩
Ts'ai O 蔡鍔
Ts'an-i Yüan 參議院
Ts'ao Chü-jen 曹聚仁
Tseng Kuo-fan 曾國藩
tso hsin-min 作新民
Tso-shih ch'un-ch'iu 左氏春秋
Tso-shih kao-huang 左氏膏肓
"Ts'ung-chün jih-chi" 從軍日記
"Tu *Jih-pen shu-mu chih* shu hou"
  讀日本書目志書後
"Tu Jih-pen Ta-wei Po-chüeh
  K'ai-kuo wu-shih nien shih shu
  hou" 讀日本大隈伯爵開國五十年
  史書後
"Tu-li lun" 獨立論
Tuan Ch'i-jui 段祺瑞
Tuan-fang 端方
Tung Chung-shu 董仲舒
t'ung-ching chih-yung 通經致用
t'ung-ch'ing hsin 同情心
T'ung-i Kung-ho Tang 統一共和
  黨
T'ung-i Tang 統一黨
"T'ung ting tsui-yen" 痛定罪言
Tzu-cheng Yüan 資政院
tzu-chih 自治
tzu-hsin 自新
Tzu-i Chü 諮議局
Tzu-jen 子任
Tzu-li Hui 自立會
tzu-tsun 自尊
tzu-yu 自由
Tzu-yu shu 自由書
"Tz'u ssu-fa tsung-chang chih
  ch'eng-wen" 辭司法總長職呈文
"Wai-chai p'ing-i" 外債平議
"Wai-chiao fang-chen chih-yen"
  外交方針質言
Wan-kuo kung-pao 萬國公報

Wan-mu Ts'ao-t'ang 萬木草堂
Wang An-shih 王安石
Wang Ching-ju 王鏡如
"Wang Ching-kung" 王荊公
Wang Ching-wei 汪精衛
Wang Fu-chih 王夫之
Wang K'ang-nien 汪康年
Wang Mang 王莽
Wang Ta-hsieh 汪大燮
wei-hsin 維新
wei-yen ta-i 微言大義
Wei Yüan 魏源
wen-hsüeh 文學
wen-hua 文化
wen-ming 文明
wen-yen 文言
Wu Chih-hui 吳稚暉
Wu Hsiang-hsiang 吳相湘
Wu Lu-chen 吳禄貞
Wu Ti 武帝
Wu T'ing-fang 伍廷芳
Yamada Ryōsei 山田良政
Yang-chou shih-jih chi 揚州十日記
Yang Chu 楊朱
Yang Tu 楊度
Yang Wei-hsin 楊維新
Yano Fumio (Ryūkei) 矢野文雄
  (龍溪)
Yen-chiu Hsi 研究系
Yen Fu 嚴復
Yen Hsi-shan 閻錫山
Yin-ping shih chuan-chi 飲冰室專集
Yin-ping shih wen-chi 飲冰室文集
yin-yang 陰陽
Ying-huan chih lüeh 瀛環志略
Yoshida Shin 吉田晋
Yoshida Shōin 吉田松陰
yu-sheng lieh-pai 優勝劣敗
yu-ssu 有司
"Yü chih pi-chih chin-yung
  cheng-ts'e" 余之幣制金融政策
Yü-chün 毓鋆

"Yü pao-kuan chi-che t'an-hua"
　　與報館記者談話
"Yü Yen Yu-ling hsien-sheng
　　shu" 與嚴幼陵先生書

yüan-ch'i 元氣
Yüan K'e-ting 袁克定
Yüan Shih-k'ai 袁世凱
Yüran 幽蘭

Bibliography

A COMMENT ON THE LITERATURE

Few figures in modern China have received as much scholarly attention as has Liang Ch'i-ch'ao. The bibliography that follows, though by no means comprehensive, contains twenty-eight scholarly titles on different aspects of Liang's life and thought. These studies span the decades from the late 1920s to the present.

One useful way to categorize the existing scholarship on Liang is to divide them by Ting Wen-chiang's *nien-p'u* of Liang, a three-volume collection of biographical materials, first published in 1958. Ting's *nien-p'u* is a biographer's dream—it contains thousands of Liang's letters, drawn, according to the introduction by Hu Shih, from a collection of "nearly 10,000" of Liang's letters. The materials are chronologically arranged and are headed by Ting's perceptive comments. These letters enable us to get much closer to the person of Liang—his sentiments, private thoughts, personal relations, the intrigues in which he was involved, and so on. They also render obsolete much of the pre-1958 scholarship on Liang.

The late Professor Joseph R. Levenson's pioneering *Liang Ch'i-ch'ao and the Mind of Modern China* was first published in 1953. Its chief contribution lies not in its scholarship but in the provocative and controversial hypothesis it presents about "the mind of modern China." The study raised an old cliché—"emotionally committed to the East and intellectually committed to the West"—to a high level of intellectual sophistication and eloquence. Liang emerged in this study as a man who was continually trying to salvage his pride in being Chinese by apologizing for his heritage, by frantically asserting the equivalence or superiority of Chinese civilization over Western civilization—he was trying, in the words of that book, "to smother the conflict between history and value." I recall that, as a graduate student, I was dazzled by the neatness of the idea and by the sparkling brilliance of the book.

It was only when I was challenged to reach beneath the sparkles for the concrete evidence, for precise information and precise ideas, that I began to question its value as a study of Liang. Was not the hypothesis too neat and simple? Why was it that when I myself read Liang's writings, I could detect no such continual conflict between his emotions and his intellect? Instead, a completely different picture emerged. Although Levenson depicted Liang's mind before 1898 as "already intellectually alienated from his tradition but still emotionally tied to it," Liang's writings of that period show unmistakably that he was still very much tied to K'ang Yu-wei's Kung-yang Confucianism. Levenson depicted Liang after 1898 as a man who was racked by inconsistencies of thought stemming from the same conflicting intellectual and emotional allegiances, but the evidence he cited actually suggest tensions of different sorts: between Liang's desire for a strong state and his liberal-democratic aspirations, and between the paths of reform and revolution. Levenson completely overlooked the profound changes in Liang's thought on these questions during the years of 1902 and 1903. Again, while Levenson argued that Liang in his final period adopted the simplistic apologist formula of a "spiritual East" and a "materialistic West," even a cursory examination of Liang's writings of that period will show that Liang clearly had no use for such a formula and that he remained committed to liberal ideals. I have since come to disagree completely with Levenson's interpretations, but I remain indebted to his book for its stimulating challenge.

It would be pointless to engage here in a dispute of footnotes, to list and demonstrate the many errors of fact and of reading in that book. The discussion that follows will bring out some of the other approaches that have been employed and indicate the main areas in which Levenson's study has been superseded.

In sharp contrast to *Liang Ch'i-ch'ao and the Mind of Modern China* is the forty-seven-page chapter on Liang in Professor K. C. Hsiao's *Chung-kuo cheng-chih ssu-hsiang shih* (A History of Chinese Political Thought), first published in 1946–48. One might be led by the panoramic scope of the entire work to expect cursory treatments of individual thinkers, but the chapters actually amount to individual monographs in themselves. The chapter on Liang is based on so thorough a reading of Liang's writings, such careful documentation and judicious interpretation that it must still be considered the most authoritative short treatment of Liang's political thought. Although much new evidence has been accumulated on Liang during the past two decades, I for one can still find no substantial disagreement with the analysis presented. Professor Hsiao was the first to stress the decisive importance of liberal ideas in Liang's thought.

Another valuable essay is that by Cheng Chen-to, written almost immediately after Liang's death. Cheng had the advantage of personal acquaintance with Liang and of being almost his contemporary. His essay remains the best short account of Liang the person, his life, and his thought. Cheng was among the first to employ a periodization of Liang's life that has since become standard, even though he, as did Levenson, overlooked the profound changes in Liang's thinking during 1902–1903. Cheng was the first to emphasize the central importance of the idea of *hsin-min* in Liang's thought.

No discussion of the pre-1958 scholarship on Liang can be complete without mention of the outstanding contributions by two Japanese scholars, Nakamura Tadayuki and Onogawa Hidemi. Writing in the 1940s, Professor Nakamura examined in detail Japanese influence on Liang's literary writings, and opened up the entire subject of Japanese influence on modern Chinese literature. Professor Onogawa focused on the decisive influence that social Darwinism had on Liang's thought during the period from 1896 to 1903. The essay was a path breaker, even though the analysis was wanting in precision and Onogawa overlooked the role that Meiji Japanese thinkers played in shaping Liang's thinking on evolution.

Among the studies that have drawn upon the materials in Ting's *nien-p'u,* the most extensive is Chang P'eng-yüan's *Liang Ch'i-ch'ao yü Ch'ing-chi ke-ming* (Liang Ch'i-ch'ao and the Revolution of 1911). Chang's book shows the extent to which Liang's thinking had already departed from K'ang Yu-wei's in the years before 1898, and treats in greater detail than previous works Liang's actions and thought before 1911. It attempts a quantitative assessment of Liang's influence in helping to bring about the revolution. Chang's other contribution, *Li-hsien p'ai yü hsin-hai ke-ming* (Constitutionalists and the Revolution of 1911), draws extensively upon the "county histories" (*hsien-chih*) to show convincingly that the constitutionalists who staffed the provincial assemblies came overwhelmingly from the old ruling class of examination-degree holders. This important book also breaks the ground for detailed studies of the power configurations and events in each of the individual provinces before and during the revolution. Harold Schiffrin's *Sun Yat-sen and the Origins of the Chinese Revolution* details the early relations between the revolutionaries and Liang. Ernest Young's "The Reformer as Conspirator: Liang Ch'i-ch'ao and the 1911 Revolution" draws chiefly upon the *nien-p'u* to give the most detailed available account of Liang's political maneuverings in late 1911. Chang Hao's short essay, "Liang Ch'i-ch'ao and Intellectual Changes in the late Nineteenth Century," points suggestively to the complexities of the Confucian options open to Liang in the 1890s.

A word must be said about the contribution of Benjamin Schwartz's *In Search of Wealth and Power: Yen Fu and the West*, even though it does not deal directly with Liang. Earlier American scholarship on modern Chinese thought often suffered from a Westerncentric attitude—if a Chinese thinker's new ideas differed from their Western sources of inspiration, scholars often simply presupposed inadequate understanding. And some could not refrain from poking fun at the supposed naïveté of their subjects. This weakness is especially apparent in Levenson's study of Liang, for example. Schwartz's study was in 1964 a refreshing new departure. The first question he posed about Yen Fu was: what are the differences between Yen's ideas and those of his mentors? Then, "what do these differences tell us about Yen's concerns?" He goes on, "does not Yen have something fresh and incisive to tell us about the West?" De Tocqueville's example long ago taught American and European historians to respect the observations of a perceptive traveler. Schwartz's study of Yen suggested the need for a similar attitude before one could really understand and appreciate Liang. The study was the first to point out that the appeal of liberalism and social Darwinism in modern China was, in the first instance, due to their supposed relevance to the urgent concerns for a strong state.

My own dissertation, completed in 1966, and now this expanded and revised study, begins with the question: what is the precise content of Liang's political thought? I have tried to trace in some detail the Kung-yang, Meiji Japanese and Western origins of Liang's ideas. In so doing, I hope I have succeeded in showing the inadequacy of the glib categories of "Confucian heritage" and "Western impact" to which our field has grown so accustomed. China and the West did not represent mutually exclusive wholes to Liang, as Levenson's analysis might have led us to believe, but each a tremendously complex range of intellectual alternatives. Liang's liberal ideas were neither simply "Western" or "Chinese," nor simply "intellectual" or "emotional," but a mixture of diverse elements.

I have also tried to examine the relations and tensions between the different components of Liang's liberal ideas—not between his "Chinese" and "emotional" commitments on the one hand and his "Western" and "intellectual" commitments on the other, but between specific nationalistic and liberal concerns, and between specific Confucian and liberal ones.

Another aspect that distinguishes this study from earlier studies is the attempt here to pose the question of the relation between Liang's ideas and his actions, between his aspirations and the realities of modern China. I have tried to tell the story of the agonizing experiences of a modern Chinese liberal in action; I attempt to show the manner in which the ever widening gap between aspirations and realities shaped Liang's thinking.

I have not attempted to write a comprehensive biography. Many aspects of Liang's career remain nearly totally unexplored. The essays of Kamiya Masao and Ueda Nakao have opened the subject of Liang's role in the development of modern Chinese historiography. Masuda Hajime showed that Liang's influence on the literary revolution should receive detailed treatment. Liang's contributions to the history of modern Chinese journalism, economic thought, and Buddhism have yet to be studied; and much more needs to be done on Liang's life and thought after 1912.

The most important source materials on Liang are now more readily available than before. In addition to Ting's *nien-p'u* and the comprehensive collection of Liang's writings in the *Yin-ping shih ho-chi*, the more important journals that Liang edited, such as the *Hsin-min ts'ung-pao* and the *Ch'ing-i pao*, have now been reprinted. I recall that in 1964, the complete original *Ch'ing-i pao* could be found only at the Waseda University Library and the Ueno branch of the Diet Library in Tokyo.

The Japanese materials on Liang that I have used had not hitherto been examined. Most of them are readily available: the collections of the Tōa Dōbun Kai, the Japanese books that Liang read or translated, and Sanetō Keishū's publications on the Chinese students in Japan can all be obtained at most major libraries. The Japanese police reports on Liang can be perused in the original at the Gaimushō in Tokyo or borrowed in microfilm from the Oriental library at the University of California at Los Angeles. These reports contain a wealth of information on Liang's activities in Japan, his contacts with Japanese and with the overseas Chinese in Japan, and his involvement in a variety of political intrigues within China. They have yet to be explored fully in a study of the activities of Liang and his followers during the period from 1898 to 1912.

The fact is that a full-length biography of Liang, one which will bring him to life and do full justice to the wide-ranging scope of his mind, has yet to be done.

WESTERN

Abegg, Lily. *The Mind of East Asia*. Translated from German by
A. J. Crick and E. E. Thomas. London and New York: Thames
& Hudson, 1952.
Baker, Herschel. *The Dignity of Man: Studies in the Persistence of an
Idea*. Cambridge, Mass.: Harvard University Press, 1947.
Barker, Ernest. *Social Contact: Essays by Locke, Hume, and Rousseau*.
London: Oxford University Press, 1947.
Becker, Carl. *Modern Democracy*. New Haven, Conn.: Yale University
Press, 1941.
Blacker, Carmen. *The Japanese Enlightenment: A Study of the Writings
of Fukuzawa Yukichi*. Cambridge: At the University Press, 1964.
Bluntschli, J. K. *The Theory of the State*. Translated from the 6th
German ed. Oxford: The Clarendon Press, 1898.
Bodde, Derk. "Harmony and Conflict in Chinese Philosophy." In
Studies in Chinese Thought, edited by Arthur Wright, pp. 19–80.
Chicago: University of Chicago Press, 1953.
Brinton, Crane. *English Political Thought in the Nineteenth Century*.
London: E. Benn, 1933.
Carneiro, Robert L., ed. *The Evolution of Society: Selections from Her-
bert Spencer's Principles of Sociology*. Chicago: University of Chicago
Press, 1967.
Chang Hao. "Liang Ch'i-ch'ao and Intellectual Changes in the
Late Nineteenth Century." *Journal of Asian Studies* 29, no. 1
(November 1969): 23–33.
China Weekly Review. *Who's Who in China*. 5th ed. Shanghai: 1932.
Chow Ts'e-tsung. *The May Fourth Movement: Intellectual Revolution in
Modern China*. Cambridge, Mass.: Harvard University Press,
1960. Vol. 2: *Research Guide to the May Fourth Movement: Intellectual
Revolution in Modern China*. Cambridge, Mass.: Harvard Univer-
sity Press, 1960.
d'Elia, Pascal M. "Un Maitre de la Jeune Chine: Liang K'i
Tch'ao." *T'oung Pao* 18 (1917): 249–94.
DeBary, William Theodore; Wing-tsit Chan; and Burton Watson,
eds. *Sources of Chinese Tradition*. New York: Columbia University
Press, 1960.
De Ruggiero, Guido. *The History of European Liberalism*. Translated
from Italian by R. G. Collingwood. 1927. Boston: Beacon Press,
1964.
Fairbank, John King and Banno Masataka. *Japanese Studies of Modern China*. Tokyo: Charles E. Tuttle Co., 1955.

Fairbank, John King and Liu Kwang-ching. *Modern China: A Bibliographical Guide to Chinese Works 1898–1937*. 1950. Cambridge, Mass.: Harvard University Press, 1961.

Fukuzawa Yukichi. *The Autobiography of Fukuzawa Yukichi*. Translated by Kiyooka Eikichi. Tokyo: The Hokuseido Press, 1934.

Fung Yu-lan. *A History of Chinese Philosophy*. Translated by Derk Bodde. 2 vols. Princeton, N. J.: Princeton University Press, 1953.

Furth, Charlotte. *Ting Wen-chiang*. Cambridge, Mass.: Harvard University Press, 1970.

Gray, F. "Historical Writing in Twentieth-Century China: Notes on Its Background and Development." In *Historians of China and Japan*, edited by Wm. G. Beasley and E. G. Pulleyblank, pp. 186–212. London: Oxford University Press, 1961.

Hayes, Carlton J. H. *A Generation of Materialism 1871–1900*. 1941. New York: Harper, 1963.

——. *The Historical Evolution of Modern Nationalism*. New York: R. R. Smith, Inc., 1931.

Hofstadter, Richard. *Social Darwinism in American Thought*. 1944. Rev. ed., Boston: Beacon Press, 1965.

Hsiao, K. C. "K'ang Yu-wei and Confucianism." *Monumenta Serica* 18 (1959): 96–212.

——. "Problem of Modernization: Evaluation of Civilizations," draft of pt. 2 of chap. 3, sec. C of Professor Hsiao's study of K'ang Yu-wei. Presented before the Modern Chinese History Colloquium, University of Washington, 1964.

——. "Liang Ch'i-ch'ao." In *Biographical Dictionary of Republican China*, edited by Howard Boorman. 4 vols. New York: Columbia University Press, 1967–71. This is the best short summary of Liang's life and thought.

——. "Road to Utopia: the Book of the Great Community," part of Professor Hsiao's study of K'ang Yu-wei. Presented before the Modern Chinese History Colloquium, University of Washington, 1963.

Huang, Philip C. "A Confucian Liberal: Liang Ch'i-ch'ao in Action and Thought." Ph. D. dissertation, University of Washington, 1966.

Hughes, Stuart. *Consciousness and Society*. 1958. New York: Vintage Books, Inc., 1961.

Hummel, Arthur W., ed. *Eminent Chinese of the Ch'ing Period*. 1943–44. Reprint, Taipei: Literature House, 1964.

Jansen, Marius. *The Japanese and Sun Yat-sen*. Cambridge, Mass.: Harvard University Press, 1954.

——. "Japanese Views of China during the Meiji Period." In *Ap-*

proaches to Modern Chinese History, edited by Albert Feuerwerker et al. Berkeley and Los Angeles: University of California Press, 1967.

Kōsaka Masaaki. *Japanese Thought in the Meiji Era*. Translated by David Abosch. Tokyo: Tōyō Bunko, 1958.

Kwok, D. W. Y. *Scientism in Chinese Thought, 1900–1950*. New Haven and London: Yale University Press, 1965.

Langdon, Frank C. "Japan's Failure to Establish Friendly Relations with China." *Pacific Historical Review* 26, no. 3 (August 1957): 245–58.

Laski, Harold. *The Rise of European Liberalism: an Essay in Interpretation*. London: G. Allen & Unwin, 1948.

Legge, James, trans. *The Chinese Classics*. 2d rev. ed. Vols. 1 and 2. Oxford: Clarendon Press, 1893–95.

Levenson, Joseph R. *Confucian China and Its Modern Fate*. 3 vols. Berkeley: University of California Press, 1958–65.

——. *Liang Ch'i-ch'ao and the Mind of Modern China*. 1953. Cambridge, Mass.: Harvard University Press, 1959.

Liang Ch'i-ch'ao. *History of Chinese Political Thought in the Early Tsin Period*. Translated by L. T. Chen. London: Kegan Paul & Co., 1930.

Li Chien-nung. *The Political History of China 1840–1928*. Edited and translated by Teng Ssu-yü and Jeremy Ingalls. Princeton, N.J.: D. Van Nostrand Co., 1956.

Mill, J. S. *"On Liberty" and "Considerations on Representative Government."* Introduction by R. B. McCallum. Oxford: B. Blackwell, 1948.

——. *Autobiography*. New York: Holt, 1873.

——. *On Liberty*. Boston: Atlantic Monthly Press, 1921.

Moore, C. A., ed. *Essays in East West Philosophy*. Honolulu: University of Hawaii Press, 1951.

Nagai Nichio. "Herbert Spencer in Early Meiji Japan." *The Far Eastern Quarterly* 14, no. 1 (November 1954): 55–65.

Novotna, Zdenka. "Contributions to the Study of Loan-Words and Hybrid Words in Modern Chinese." *Archiv Orientalni*, no. 35 (1967).

Perleberg, Max. *Who's Who in China*. Hong Kong: 1954.

Powell, Ralph. *The Rise of Chinese Military Power, 1895–1912*. Princeton, N.J.: Princeton University Press, 1955.

Richard, Timothy. *Forty-five Years in China*. London: T. Fisher Unwin, 1916.

Sansom, G. B. *The Western World and Japan*. 1949. New York: Knopf, 1962.

Scalapino, Robert A., and Harold Schiffrin. "Early Socialist Currents in the Chinese Revolutionary Movement: Sun Yat-sen versus Liang Ch'i-ch'ao." *The Journal of Asian Studies* 18, no. 3 (May 1959): 321–42.

Schiffrin, Harold Z. *Sun Yat-sen and the Origins of the Chinese Revolution.* Berkeley and Los Angeles: University of California Press, 1968.

Schwartz, Benjamin. *In Search of Wealth and Power: Yen Fu and the West.* Cambridge, Mass.: Harvard University Press, 1964.

Smiles, Samuel. *Self Help.* London: John Murray, 1905.

Snow, Edgar. *Red Star over China.* 1938. New York: Grove Press, 1961.

Spencer, Herbert. *Principles of Sociology.* 3 vols. New York: D. Appleton and Co., 1904.

Spengler, Oswald. *The Decline of the West.* 2 vols. New York: Knopf, 1945.

Stephen, Leslie. *John Stuart Mill. The English Utilitarians,* vol. 3. London: Duckworth and Co., 1900.

Thompson, Laurence G. *Ta T'ung Shu: the One World Philosophy of K'ang Yu-wei.* London: George Allen & Unwin, 1958.

Tjan Tjoe-som. *Po Hu T'ung: the Comprehensive Discussions in the White Tiger Hall.* Leiden: E. J. Brill, 1949.

Tsurumi, Yusuke. *The Liberal Movement in Japan.* New Haven, Conn.: Yale University Press, 1925.

Wang, Y. C. *Chinese Intellectuals and the West, 1872–1949.* Chapel Hill, N. C.: University of North Carolina Press, 1966.

Wilhelm, Hellmut. "Ch'en San-li." In *Biographical Dictionary of Republican China,* edited by Howard Boorman. 4 vols. New York: Columbia University Press, 1967–71.

Wilhelm, Richard. *The Soul of China.* Translated by John Holroyd Reece; poems translated by Arthur Waley. New York: Harcourt, Brace & Co., 1928.

Woo Kang. *Les Trois Théories Politiques du Tch'ouen Ts'ieou.* Paris: E. Leroux, 1932.

Young, Ernest P. "The Reformer as Conspirator: Liang Ch'i-ch'ao and the 1911 Revolution." In *Approaches to Modern Chinese History,* edited by Albert Feuerwerker et al. Berkeley and Los Angeles: University of California Press, 1967.

Yu, George T. *Party Politics in Republican China: The Kuomintang, 1912–1924.* Berkeley and Los Angeles: University of California Press, 1966.

JAPANESE

Abe Yō 安部洋. "Ryō Kei-chō no kyōiku shisō to sono katsudō:
bojutsu hempōki o chūshin to shite" 梁啓超の教育思想とその活動:
戊戌變法期を中心として [Liang Ch'-ch'ao's Educational Thought
and Activities: Focusing on the Period of the 1898 Reforms],
Kyūshū daigaku kyōikubu kiyō 九州大學教育學部紀要 [Bulletin of the
Department of Education of Kyūshū University] 6 (Fukuoka,
1959): 301-23.

Ajia rekishi jiten アジア歴史辭典 [Encyclopedia of Asian History]. 10
vols. Tokyo: Heibonsha, 1959–62.

Chūgoku kankei no kiji mokuroku—Nihon oyobi Nihonjin, Taiyō 中國関係の
記事目録—日本及び日本人, 太陽 [A List of Entries Pertaining to China
in the *Japan and the Japanese* and *The Sun*]. Manuscript, Tōyō
Bunko.

Gaimushō Ajiakyoku 外務省アジア局 [Asian Department of the
Foreign Ministry]. *Gendai Chūgoku jinmei jiten* 現代中國人名辭典 [A
Biographical Dictionary of Contemporary China]. Tokyo: Gaikō
Jigō-sha, 1962.

Hatano Yoshihiro 波多野善大. "Nishihara shakkan no kihonteki kōsō"
西原借款の基本的構想 [Basic Concept of the Nishihara Loans]. In
Nagoya daigaku bungakubu jisshūnen kinen ronshū 名古屋大學文學部十週
年記念論集 [Essays Commemorating the Tenth Anniversary of the
Department of Literature of Nagoya University], pp. 393–416.
Nagoya, 1958.

Honda Shigeyuki 本田成之. *Shina keigakushi ron* 支那經學史論 [A
History of Classical Learning in China]. Tokyo: Kōbundō, 1927.

Ichiko Chūzō 市古宙三. "Ryō Kei-chō no hempō undō" 梁啓超の変法
運動 [Liang Ch'i-ch'ao's Reform Movement]. *Kokushigaku* 国史学
[Journal of Japanese History] 54 (February 1951): 71–83.

Ichiko Chūzō. "Hokyō to hempō" 保教と変法 [Preserving the Faith
and Reforming the Institutions]. In *Kindai Chūgoku no shakai to
keizai* 近代中国の社会と經濟 [Society and Economy of Modern
China], edited by Niida Noboru 仁井田陞, pp. 113–38. Tokyo:
Tōhō Shoin, 1951.

Ishida Takeshi 石田雄. *Meiji seiji shisōshi kenkyū* 明治政治思想史研究
[Studies in the History of Meiji Political Thought]. Tokyo, 1954.

Itano Chōhachi 板野長八. "Kō Yū-i no daidō shisō" 康有為の大同思想
[K'ang Yu-wei's Concept of *ta-t'ung*]. In *Kindai Chūgoku kenkyū*
近代中国研究 [Researches in Modern China]. Tokyo, 1948.

——. "Ryō Kei-chō no daidō shisō" 梁啓超の大同思想 [Liang Ch'i-
ch'ao's Concept of *ta-t'ung*]. In *Wada hakushi kanreki kinen Tōyō-shi*

ronsō 和田博士還暦記念東洋史論叢 [Collection of Essays on Chinese History in Celebration of Dr. Wada's Sixtieth Birthday], pp. 69–84. Tokyo: Dai Nippon Yūbenkai Kōdansha, 1951.

Kamiya Masao 神谷正男. "Ryō Kei-chō no rekishigaku" 梁啓超の歴史学 [Liang Ch'i-ch'ao's Historical Scholarship]. *Rekishigaku kenkyū* 歴史学研究 105 (December 1942): 1069–96.

Katō Hiroyuki 加藤弘之. *Tensoku hyaku wa* 天則百話 [Hundred Essays on the Law of Evolution]. Tokyo, 1899.

——. *Kyōsha no kenri no kyōsō* 強者の権利の競争 [Competition and the Right of the Strongest]. Tokyo, 1893.

Kikuchi Takaharu 菊池貴晴. "Tō Sai-jō no jiritsugun kigi" 唐才常の自立軍起義 [The Uprising of T'ang Ts'ai-ch'ang's Army for National Independence]. *Rekishigaku kenkyū* 170 (April 1954): 13–23.

Kindai Chūgoku Kenkyū Iinkai 近代中國研究委員会. "Chūgokubun zasshi ronsetsu kiji mokuroku" 中國文雜誌論説記事目録 [Tables of Contents of Chinese Journals and Gazetteers], vol. 2. Reprinted from *Kindai Chūgoku kenkyū* 3: 273–336; n. d.

Kojima Sukema 小島祐馬. *Chūgoku no kakumei shisō* 中國の革命思想 [Revolutionary Thought of China]. Tokyo: Kōbundō, 1950.

Kokuryūkai 黑龍会. [Black Dragon Society] *Tōa senkaku shishi kiden* 東亞先覺志士記傳 [Memoirs of Early East Asian Patriots]. 3 vols. Tokyo: Kokuryūkai, 1933–36.

Masuda Hajime 増田渉. "Ryō Kei-chō ni tsuite—bungakushi-teki ni mite" 梁啓超について—文學史的にみて [On Liang Ch'i-ch'ao—from the Standpoint of Literary History]. *Jimbun kenkyū* 人文研究 [Studies in the Humanities] 6, no. 6 (July 1955): 49–66.

Miyazaki Torazō 宮崎寅藏. *Sanjūsan nen no yume* 三十三年の夢 [Thirty-three Years' Dream). Reprinted in *Ajia shugi* アジア主義 [Pan-Asianism], vol. 9 of *Gendai Nihon shisō taikei* 現代日本思想大系 [Outline of Contemporary Japanese Thought], pp. 133–63. Tokyo: Chikuma Shobō, 1963.

Nagai Kazumi 永井算己. "Iwayuru Shinkoku ryūgakusei torishimari kisoku jiken no seikaku" 所謂清國留學生取締規則事件の性格 [The Nature of the Incident Arising from the So-called "Regulations Governing Chinese Students in Japan"]. *Shinshū Daigaku kiyō* 信州大學紀要 2 (July 1952): 11–34.

——. "Tō Sai-jō to jiritsugun kigi" 唐才常と自立軍起義 [T'ang Ts'ai-ch'ang and the Uprising of the Army for National Independence]. *Nihon rekishi* 日本歴史 85 (June 1955): 16–21; 88 (October 1955): 36–45.

Nakamura Masanao 中村正直. *Saikoku risshi hen* 西國立志篇 (The Success of the Western Nations). Tokyo, 1876.

Nakamura Tadayuki 中村忠行. "Tokutomi Roka to gendai Chūgoku

bungaku" 德富蘆花と現代中國文學 [Tokutomi Roka and Modern Chinese Literature]. *Tenri daigaku gakuhō* 天理大學學報, 1, nos. 2–3 (October 1949): 1–28; 2, nos. 1–2 (November 1950): 55–84.

Nakamura Tadayuki. "*Shin Chūgoku mirai ki* kōsetsu: Chūgoku bungei ni oyoboseru Nihon bungei no eikyō no ichi rei"「新中國未來記」攷説——中國文藝に及ぼせる日本文藝の影響の一例 [A Study of "The Future of the New China" (by Liang Ch'i-ch'ao): One Example of the Influence of Japanese Literature on Chinese Literature]. *Tenri daigaku gakuhō* 1, no. 1 (May 1949): 63–95.

——."Chūgoku bungei ni oyoboseru Nihon bungei no eikyō" 中國文藝に及ぼせる日本文藝の影響 [The Influence of Japanese Literature on Chinese Literature]. *Taidai bungaku* 臺大文學 7, no. 4 (December 1942): 214–43; 7, no. 6 (April 1943): 362–84; 8, no. 2 (August 1943): 86–152; 8, no. 4 (June 1944), 27–85; 8, no. 5 (November 1944), 42–111.

Nihon Gaimushō 日本外務省. "Kō-sho nijūyonnen seihen" 光緒二十四年政變 [The Coup d'État of 1898]. In *Kakkoku naisei kankei zasshū: Shina no bu* 各國内政関係雑集: 支那の部 [Miscellaneous Collection Pertaining to Domestic Affairs of Foreign Countries: China]. Vol. 1, unpublished documents.

——. *Nihon gaikō bunsho* 日本外交文書 [Documents on the Foreign Relations of Japan], nos. 31 and 32. No. 31, 2 vols., Tokyo: Nihon Kokusairengō Kyōkai, 1954; no. 32, Tokyo, 1955.

——. "Kakumeitō kankei" 革命黨関係 [Pertaining to the Revolutionary Party]. In *Kakkoku naisei kankei zasshū: Shina no bu*. Vols. 1–4, unpublished documents. Contemporary Japanese police reports on Liang and the revolutionaries—a major, unexplored, Japanese source.

Nohara Shirō 野原四郎." Anākisuto to go-shi undō" アナーキストと五四運動 [Anarchists and the May Fourth Movement]. In *Kindai Ajia shisō-shi: Chūgoku hen* 近代アジア思想史: 中國篇 [History of Modern Asian Thought: Volume on China] 1: 145–78. Tokyo: Kōbundō, 1960.

Nomura Kōichi 野村浩一. "'Kakumeiha' to 'kairyōha' no shisō" 革命派と改良派の思想 [The Thought of the "Revolutionary Faction" and the "Reformist Faction"] in *Kindai Ajia shisō-shi: Chūgoku hen* 1:95–144. Tokyo: Kōbundō, 1960.

——. "Shinmatsu Kōyōgaku no keisei to Kō Yū-i no rekishiteki igi" 清末公羊學の形成と康有為の歴史的意義 [The Development of Kungyang Thought in Late Ch'ing and the Historical Meaning of K'ang Yu-wei]. *Kokka gakkai zasshi* 國家學会雑誌 [Journal of Association of Political and Social Science] 71, no. 7 (July 1957): 706–

65; 72, no. 1 (January 1958): 32–64; 72, no. 3 (March 1958): 256–320.

Onogawa Hidemi 小野川秀美. *Shinmatsu seiji shisō kenkyū* 清末政治思想研究 [Studies in Late Ch'ing Political Thought]. Kyoto, 1960. The chapter entitled "Shinmatsu no shisō to shinkaron" 清末の思想と進化論 [The Doctrine of Evolution and Late Ch'ing Thought] was first published in *Tōhō gakuhō* 東方學報 [Journal of Oriental Studies] 21 (March 1952): 1–36.

Sanetō Keishū 實藤惠秀. *Chūgokujin Nihon ryūgaku shi* 中國人日本留學史 [A History of Chinese Students in Japan]. Tokyo, 1960.

———. "Hōsho Kayaku no gaikan" 邦書華譯の概観 [A General Picture of Chinese Translations of Japanese Books]. *Tōa kaihō* 東亞解放 2, no. 2 (February 1940): 160–280.

———. *Nihon bunka no Shina e no eikyō* 日本文化の支那への影響 [The Influence of Japanese Culture on China]. Tokyo: Keisetsu Shoin, 1940.

Sanetō bunko 實藤文庫 [Special Collection of Sanetō (Keishū)], at the Hibiya Library, Tokyo. Contains a portion of Sanetō's personal library gathered over decades of research on Sino-Japanese cultural relations. Includes many diaries of Chinese students in Japan.

Satō Shinji 佐藤震二. "Shinchō makki ni okeru Ryō Kei-chō no seiji shisō—sono keisei katei o chūshin to shite" 清朝末期に於ける梁啓超の政治思想—その形成過程を中心として [The Political Thought of Liang Ch'i-ch'ao in the Last Period of the Ch'ing Dynasty: Focusing on Its Process of Development]. *Akademia* アカデミア 3 (1952): 90–103.

Satō Saburō 佐藤三郎. "Meiji ishin igo Nisshin sensō izen ni okeru Shinajin no Nihon kenkyū" 明治維新以後日清戰爭以前に於ける支那人の日本研究 [Chinese Studies of Japan after the Meiji Restoration and before the Sino-Japanese War]. *Rekishigaku kenkyū*, no. 83 (November 1940): 1147–87.

Shiba Shirō 柴四郎. *Kajin no kigu* 佳人の奇遇 [Strange Encounters of Elegant Females]. Reprinted in *Gendai Nihon bungaku zenshū* 現代日本文學全集 [Complete Collection of Contemporary Japanese Literature] 1: 139–326. Tokyo: Kaizō-sha, 1931.

Shimada Kenji 島田虔次. "Chūgoku no Ruso—" 中國のルソー [China's Rousseau]. *Shisō* 思想 [Ideology], 435 (September 1960): 66–85.

Shimizu Morimitsu 清水盛光. *Shina shakai no kenkyū: shakaigakuteki kōsatsu* 支那社会の研究—社会學的考察 [Studies in Chinese Society: a Sociological Inquiry]. Tokyo: Iwanami Shoten, 1939.

Tabata Shinobu 畑田忍. *Katō Hiroyuki* 加藤弘之. Tokyo: Yoshikawa Kōbunkan, 1959.

Takahashi Yūji 高橋勇治. "San-min shugi ni taisuru Ryōkei-chō no hanbaku" 三民主義に対する梁啓超の反駁 [Liang Ch'i-ch'ao's Refutations of the Three People's Principles]. *Tōa mondai* 東亞問題 [Problems of East Asia] 4, no. 10 (1942).

Takeuchi Yoshimi 竹内好 et al. *Chūgoku kakumei no shisō* 中國革命の思想 [Chinese Revolutionary Thought]. Tokyo: Iwanami Shoten, 1953.

Tōa Dōbun Kai 東亞同文会. *Zoku Tai-Shi kaikoroku* 続対支回顧録 [Sequel to *Records on China*]. 2 vols. Tokyo: Dai Nippon Kyōka Tosho, vol. 1, 1942; vol. 2, 1941. Contains several letters from K'ang Yu-wei and Liang Ch'i-ch'ao to Kashiwabara Buntarō not available elsewhere.

Ueda Nakao 上田仲雄. "Ryō Kei-chō no rekishikan" 梁啓超の歴史観 [Liang Ch'i-ch'ao's View of History] *Iwate shigaku kenkyū* 岩手史學研究 32 (December 1959): 1–14.

CHINESE

Chang Chih-tung 張之洞. "Ch'üan hsüeh p'ien" 勸學篇 [Exhortation to Learn]. In *Chang Wen-hsiang kung ch'üan-chi* 張文襄公全集 [Complete Works of Chang Chih-tung], *chüan* 203. Reprint, Taipei: Wen hai, 1963.

Chang Chün-mai 張君勱. "P'ing Liang Jen-kung hsien-sheng 'Ch'ing-tai hsüeh-shu kai lun' san ta wen-t'i" 評梁任公先生「清代學術概論」三大問題 [A Critique of Mr. Liang Ch'i-ch'ao's *Intellectual Trends in the Ch'ing Period*: Three Major Problems] *Chung-hua tsa-chih* 2 no. 1 (January 16, 1964): 9–11.

Chang Ch'i-yün 張其昀. "Tao Liang Jen-kung hsien-sheng" 悼梁任公先生 [Mourning Mr. Liang Ch'i-ch'ao]. *Shih-hsüeh tsa-chih* 史學雜誌 vol. 1, no. 5 (November 1929).

Chang P'eng-yüan 張朋園. *Li-hsien p'ai yü hsin-hai ke-ming* 立憲派與辛亥革命 [Constitutionalists and the Revolution of 1911]. Taipei: Institute of Modern History, The Academia Sinica, 1969.

——. *Liang Ch'i-ch'ao yü Ch'ing-chi ke-ming* 梁啓超與清季革命 [Liang Ch'i-ch'ao and the Revolution of 1911]. Taipei: Institute of Modern History, The Academia Sinica, 1964.

Chang Yin-lin 張蔭麟 (Su-ch'ih 素癡). "Chin-tai Chung-kuo hsüeh-shu-shih shang chih Liang Jen-kung hsien-sheng" 近代中國學術史上之梁任公先生 [Mr. Liang Ch'i-ch'ao in the History of Recent Chinese Scholarship and Thought]. *Lun-heng* 論衡, vol. 67 (January 1929).

Chao Feng-t'ien 趙豐田. "Wei-hsin jen-wu: Liang Ch'i-ch'ao" 維新人物:梁啓超 [A Reformist Personage: Liang Ch'i-ch'ao]. *Ta-kung pao shih-ti chou-k'an* 大公報史地週刊, vol. 108 (October 23, 1936).

Ch'en Ch'iao 陳鰲. "Wu-hsü cheng-pien shih fan pien-fa jen-wu chih cheng-chih ssu-hsiang" 戊戌政變時反變法人物之政治思想 [The Political Thought of Those Opposed to Reform at the Time of the Coup d'etat of 1898]. In *Chung-kuo chin-tai-shih lun-ts'ung* 中國近代史論叢 [Collection of Essays on Modern Chinese History], edited by Wu Hsiang-hsiang 吳相湘 et al., 1, no. 7: 148–70. Taipei: Cheng chung, 1959. Reprinted from *Yen-ching hsüeh-pao* 燕京學報, vol. 25 (June 1939).

Ch'en Tu-hsiu 陳獨秀. "Po K'ang Yu-wei chih tsung-t'ung tsung-li shu" 駁康有為致總統總理書 [Disputing K'ang Yu-wei's Letter to the President and the Premier]. *Hsin ch'ing-nien* 新青年 [New Youth], vol. 2, no. 2 (October 1, 1916).

Cheng Chen-to 鄭振鐸. "Liang Jen-kung hsien-sheng" 梁任公先生 [Mr. Liang Ch'i-ch'ao]. *Hsiao-shuo yüeh-pao* 小説月報, 20, no. 2 (February 10, 1929): 333–56.

Cheng Ho-sheng 鄭鶴聲. *Chin-shih Chung Hsi shih-jih tui-chao piao* 近世中西史日對照表 [Sino-Western Historical Calendar for the Modern Period]. 1936. Reprint, Taipei: Commercial Press, 1962.

Chi Chung-yin 籍忠寅. "Wan Liang Jen-kung hsien-sheng shih" 挽梁任公先生詩 [Elegy of Mr. Liang Ch'i-ch'ao]. *Hsüeh-heng* 學衡 [The Critical Review], vol. 67 (January 1929): cover page.

Chia I-chün 賈逸君, ed. *Chung-hua min-kuo ming-jen chuan* 中華民國名人傳 [Biographies of Famous Personalities of Republican China]. Peiping: Wen-hua Hsüeh-she, 1932–33.

Chien Po-tsan 翦伯贊 et al, eds. *Wu-hsü pien-fa* 戊戌變法 [The 1898 Reforms]. 4 vols. Shanghai: People's Press, 1957.

Ch'ien Mu 錢穆. *Chung-kuo chin san-pai-nien hsüeh-shu-shih* 中國近三百年學術史 [A History of Chinese Thought in the Last Three Hundred Years]. 1937. Reprint, Taipei: The Commercial Press, 1959.

Chou Shih-chao 周世釗. "Ti-i shih-fan shih-tai te Mao chu-hsi" 第一師範時代的毛主席 [Chairman Mao at the Time of the First Normal School]. *Hsin kuan-ch'a* 新觀察 2, no. 2 (January 25, 1951): 10–13.

Chou Wen-kao 周文膏, "Liang Ch'i-ch'ao ho pao-chang wen-hsüeh te kuan-hsi tsen-yang" 梁啓超和報章文學的關係怎樣 [What Is the Relationship between Liang Ch'i-ch'ao and Journalistic Writing?]. *Wen-hsüeh pai-t'i* 文學百題 1935: 7 (July 1935).

Chou Yü-t'ung 周予同. *Ching ku chin wen hsüeh* 經古今文學 [New and Old Text Classical Learning]. Shanghai: Commercial Press, 1926.

Chu Yung-chia 朱永嘉. "P'i-p'an Liang Ch'i-ch'ao te wei-hsin chu-i che-hsüeh" 批判梁啓超的唯心主義哲學 [A Critique of Liang Ch'i-ch'ao's Idealistic Philosophy]. *Fu-tan hsüeh-pao* 復旦學報 [The Fuh-tan University Journal] 1957: 1, 127–44.

Chung-yung 中庸 [The Doctrine of the Mean].

Fang Chao-ying 房兆楹. *Ch'ing-mo min-ch'u yang-hsüeh hsüeh-sheng t'i-ming lu ch'u chi* 清末民初洋學學生題名錄初輯 [An Initial Compilation of the Lists of Chinese Students Abroad in the End of Ch'ing and the Beginning of the Republic]. Taipei: Institute of Modern History, The Academia Sinica, 1962.

Feng Tzu-yu 馮自由. *Chung-hua Min-kuo k'ai-kuo ch'ien ke-ming shih* 中華民國開國前革命史 [A History of the Revolutionary Movement before the Founding of the Republic]. 1944. 2 vols. Taipei: Commercial Press, 1953.

——. *Ke-ming i-shih* 革命逸史 [Anecdotal History of the Revolution]. 1939. 2 vols. Taipei: Commercial Press, 1953.

Fung Yu-lan 馮友蘭. *Chung-kuo che-hsüeh-shih* 中國哲學史 [A History of Chinese Philosophy]. Reprinted by the Department of History of Taiwan University as *Chung-kuo ssu-hsiang-shih*, n. d. Translated by Derk Bodde. 2 vols. Princeton, N.J.: Princeton University Press, 1953.

——. "Liang Ch'i-Ch'i-ch'ao ti ssu-hsiang" 梁啓超底思想 [Liang Ch'i-ch'ao's Thought]. In *Chung-kuo che-hsüeh-shih lun-wen ch'u-chi* 中國哲學史論文初集 [Essays on the History of Chinese Philosophy, First Volume], pp. 218–31. 1958. Shanghai: People's Press, 1962.

Hou Shu-t'ung 侯樹彤. "Ch'ing-mo hsien-cheng yün-tung kang-yao" 清末憲政運動綱要 [An Outline of the Constitutional Movement in Late Ch'ing]. In *Keng-wu lun-wen chi* 庚午論文集 (no. 5 of *Yen-ta cheng-chih-hsüeh ts'ung-k'an* 燕大政治學叢刊) [Yenching Political Science Series] 1: 1–52. B. A. thesis, Yenching University, 1930.

Hou Wai-lu 侯外盧. *Chung-kuo tsao-ch'i ch'i-meng ssu-hsiang-shih* 中國早期啓蒙思想史 [A History of Enlightened Thought in "Early Modern" China]. Peking: People's Press, 1956.

Hsiao Kung-ch'üan 蕭公權. *Chung-kuo cheng-chih ssu-hsiang-shih* 中國政治思想史 [A History of Chinese Political Thought]. 1946–48. Taipei: Commercial Press, 1961.

Hsieh Pin 謝彬. *Min-kuo cheng-tang shih* 民國政黨史 [A History of Political Parties in Republican China]. 1926. Taipei: Wen-hsing Bookstore, 1961.

"Hsin-hai Luan-chou ping-pien chi" 辛亥灤州兵變記 [The Luan-chou Revolt in 1911]. In *Hsin-hai ke-ming* 辛亥革命 [The Revolution of 1911] 6: 331–33. Shanghai: Peoples' Press, 1957.

Hsiung Shih-li 熊十力. *Tu-ching shih-yao* 讀經示要 [Guide to Study of the Classics]. 1945. Reprint, Taipei: Kuang-wen Bookstore, 1960.

Hsü Shih-ch'ang 徐世昌. *Ch'ing-ju hsüeh-an* 清儒學案 [Ch'ing Scholars]. 1939. Reprint, 8 vols., Taipei: Shih-chieh Book Co., 1962.

Hu Peng 胡浜. "Wu-hsü pien-fa shih-ch'i Liang Ch'i-ch'ao te ssu-hsiang" 戊戌變法時期梁啓超的思想 [Liang Ch'i-ch'ao's Thought in the Period of the 1898 Reforms]. *Kuang-ming jih-pao shih-hsüeh chou-k'an* 光明日報史學週刊, vol. 77 (March 1, 1956).

Hu Shih 胡適. *Ssu-shih tzu-shu* 四十自述 [Autobiography at Forty]. Reprint, Taipei: Yüan-tung T'u-shu Kung-ssu, 1964.

Huang Tsung-hsi 黃宗羲. *Ming-i tai-fang lu* 明夷待訪録 [A Plan for a Prince]. In *Li-chou Ch'uan-shan wu shu* 梨州船山五書 [Five Essays of Huang Tsung-hsi and Wang Fu-chih], edited by Yang Chia-lo 楊家駱. Taipei: Shih-chieh Bookstore, 1962.

K'ang Yu-wei 康有為. "Chung-kuo chin-hou ch'ou-an ting ts'e" 中國今後籌安定策 [Setting the Plan for Establishing Peace and Order in China from Now On]. In *Yüan-shih tao-kuo chi* 袁氏盜國記 (Records of Yüan [Shih-k'ai]'s Robbery of the Nation) edited by Huang I 黃毅. 1916. Taipei: Wen-hsing Book Co., 1962.

K'ang Yu-wei and Liang Ch'i-ch'ao. *K'ang Liang shou-cha ts'e* 康梁手札冊 [Letters of K'ang and Liang]. Photo reprint, Tōyō Bunko, n. d. Contains several letters of Liang not available elsewhere.

Kao Ming-k'ai 高名凱 and Liu Cheng-t'an 劉正埮. *Hsien-tai Han-yü wai-lai-tz'u yen-chiu* 現代漢語外來詞研究 [A Study of Loan-words in Modern Chinese]. Peking Wen-tzu Kai-ke Ch'u-pan-she, 1968.

Ko Kung-chen 戈公振. *Chung-kuo pao-hsüeh shih* 中國報學史 [A History of Chinese Journalism]. 1927. Reprint, Taipei: Hsüeh-sheng Bookstore, n. d.

Ku Chieh-kang 顧頡剛, ed. *Ku-shih pien* 古史辨 [A Symposium on Ancient History], vol. 1. Reprinted from the 1926 edition of P'o She (Publisher), Hong Kong, 1962.

Kuan Yü-heng 關玉衡. "Chi-nien Liang Jen-kung hsien-sheng" 記念梁任公先生 [In Memory of Liang Ch'i-ch'ao]. *Pei-p'ing ch'en-pao hsüeh-yüan* 北平晨報學苑, vol. 231 (January 20, 1932).

Kung Tzu-chen 龔自珍. *Kung Tzu-chen ch'üan-chi* 龔自珍全集 [Complete Works and Essays of Kung Tzu-chen]. Reprint, Shanghai: Chung-hua Bookstore 1959.

Kuo Mo-jo 郭沫若. *Mo-jo wen-chi* 沫若文集 [Collected Works and Essays of Kuo Mo-jo], vol. 2. Peking: People's Literature Press, 1959.

Li Chien-nung 李劍農. *Chung-kuo chin pai-nien cheng-chih-shih* 中國近百年政治史 [A Political History of China in the Last Hundred Years]. 1947. 2 vols. Taipei: Commercial Press, 1962. Some very useful information was deleted in the translation by Teng Ssu-yü and Jeremy Ingalls.

Li Shou-k'ung 李守孔. "Kuang-hsü wu-hsü ch'ien-hou ke-ming pao-huang liang p'ai chih kuan-hsi" 光緒戊戌前後革命保皇兩派之関係 [The Relationship between the Revolutionary Faction and the Emperor Protection Faction before and after 1898]. *Ta-lu tsa-chih* 大陸雜誌 [La Terre], vol. 25, no. 1 (July 15, 1962), and vol. 25, no. 2 (July 31, 1962).

——. *Min-ch'u chih kuo-hui* 民初之國會 [The Early Republican Legislature]. Taipei, 1964.

Liang Ch'i-ch'ao 梁啓超, ed. *Ch'ing-i pao* 清議報 [Upright Discussions] [original English title: *The China Discussion*]. Thrice monthly, Yokohama, 1898–1901.

——, ed. *Ch'ing-i pao ch'üan-pien* 清議報全編 [Complete Edition of the *Upright Discussions*]. Yokohama, n. d. (1902). Substantially different from the original *Ch'ing-i pao*.

——, ed. *Chung-wai kung-pao (chung-wai Chi-wen)* 中外公報 (中外紀聞) [Chinese and Foreign News]. Daily, Shanghai, 1895–96.

——, ed. *Hsi-hsüeh shu-mu piao* 西學書目表 [A Catalogue of Books on Western Learning], 3 *chüan; Tu hsi-hsüeh shu fa* 讀西學書法 [How to Study Western Books], appended. Shanghai: Shih-wu pao kuan, 1896.

——, ed. *Hsin hsiao-shuo* 新小説 [New Fiction]. Irregular, Yokohama, 1902–5. The University of California Berkeley library has vol. 1, no. 3, dated January 13, 1903.

——, ed. *Hsin-min ts'ung-pao* 新民叢報 [The New Citizen]. Twice monthly, Yokohama, 1902–7.

——. *Liang Jen-kung hsien-sheng chiang-yen chi* 梁任公先生講演集 [Collected Lectures and Speeches of Mr. Liang Ch'i-ch'ao]. 3 vols. Hong Kong: San-ta ch'u-pan-she, n. d. Supplements the *Yin-ping shih ho-chi*.

——, ed. *Kuo-feng pao* 國風報 [The National Spirit]. Thrice monthly, Shanghai, 1910–11.

—— and Wang K'ang-nien 汪康年, eds. *Shih-wu pao* 時務報 [Current Affairs] [original English title: *The China Progress*]. Thrice monthly, Shanghai, 1896–1898.

——, ed. *Ta Chung-hua* 大中華 [The Great Chung-hua Journal]. Monthly, Shanghai, 1915–16.

——. Two letters to Tokutomi Sohō, kept at the Sohō Bunko of Dōshisha Daigaku in Kyoto. n. d. (1902?) I am indebted to Professor Shimada Kenji for calling my attention to these letters.

——. *Yin-ping shih ho-chi* 飲冰室合集 [Collected Works and Essays of Liang Ch'i-ch'ao]. 148 vols. in 40 books. Shanghai: Chung-hua Bookstore, 1932.

——, ed. *Yung-yen* 庸言 [Justice]. Twice monthly, Tientsin, 1912–14.

Mao I-heng 毛以亨. *Liang Ch'i-ch'ao*. Hong Kong: Ya-chou Publishing House, 1957.

Meng-tzu 孟子 [The Mencius].

Miou Feng-lin 繆鳳林. "Tao Liang Cho-ju hsien-sheng" 悼梁卓如先生 [Mourning Mr. Liang Ch'i-ch'ao]. *Hsüeh-heng* 學衡 [The Critical Review] 67 (January 1929): 1–6.

P'i Hsi-jui 皮錫瑞. *Ching-hsüeh li-shih* 經學歷史 [A History of Classical Learning]. Introduction and notes by Chou Yü-t'ung. Hong Kong: Chung-hua Bookstore, 1961.

Shu Hsin-ch'eng 舒新城. *Chin-tai Chung-kuo liu-hsüeh shih* 近代中國留學史 [A History of Education Abroad in Modern China]. 1927. Shanghai: Chung-hua Bookstore, 1933.

Ta-hsüeh 大學 [The Great Learning].

Ting Min 丁民, ed. *Tang-tai Chung-kuo jen-wu chih* 當代中國人物誌 [Important Personalities of Contemporary China]. Shanghai, 1939.

Ting Wen-chiang 丁文江, ed. *Liang Jen-kung hsien-sheng nien-p'u ch'ang-pien ch'u-kao* 梁任公先生年譜長編初稿 [First Draft of a Chronological Biography of Liang Ch'i-ch'ao]. 3 vols. Taipei: Shih-chieh Book Co., 1958.

Ts'ao Chü-jen 曹聚仁. *Wen-t'an wu-shih nien* 文壇五十年 [Fifty Years of the Literary World]. Hong Kong: Hsin Wen-hua Ch'u-pan-she, 1956.

Tuan-fang 端方. *Tuan Chung-min kung tsou-kao* 端忠敏公奏稿 [Memorials of Tuan-fang]. 16 *chüan*. Many of these were drafted by Liang Ch'i-ch'ao.

Uno Tetsujin 宇野哲人. *Chung-kuo chin-shih ju-hsüeh shih* 中國近世儒學史 [A History of Confucianism in Recent China]. Translated by Ma Fu-ch'en 馬福辰. Taipei: Chung-hua Wen-hua Ch'u-pan Shih-yeh Wei-yüan-hui, 1957.

Wang Chieh-p'ing 王介平 and Li Jun-ts'ang 李潤蒼. "P'i-p'an Liang Ch'i-ch'ao te fan-tung shih-hsüeh kuan-tien ho fang-fa" 批判梁啟超的反動史學觀點和方法 [A Critique of Liang Ch'i-ch'ao's Reactionary View and Method of History]. *Ssu-ch'uan ta-hsüeh hsüeh-pao* 四川大學學報 [The Szechuan University Journal] 1959: no. 4 (April 1959).

Wang Shu-huai 王樹槐. *Wai-jen yü wu-hsü pien-fa* 外人與戊戌變法 [Foreigners and the 1898 Reforms]. Taipei: Institute of Modern History, The Academia Sinica, 1965.

Wang Yün-sheng 王芸生. *Liu-shih nien lai chih Chung-kuo yü Jih-pen* 六十年來之中國與日本 [China and Japan in the Last Sixty Years]. 6 vols. Tientsin: Ta-kung Pao She, 1934.

Wu Chih-hui 吳稚暉. *Wu Chih-hui wen-chi* 吳稚暉文集 [Collected Works and Essays of Wu Chih-hui]. Shanghai, 1936.

Wu Hsiang-hsiang 吳相湘. *Sung Chiao-jen* 宋教仁. Taipei: Wen-hsing Book Co., 1964.

Wu Chuang [Hsien-tzu] 吳莊 (憲子). *Chung-kuo Min-chu Hsien-cheng*

Tang tang-shih 中國民主憲政黨黨史 [A History of the Constitutional Democratic Party of China]. San Francisco: World Daily News, 1952.

Wu Kuan-yin 吳貫因. "Ping-ch'en ts'ung-chün jih-chi" 丙辰從軍日記 [Diary of Service in the (Protect the Nation) Army in 1916]. *Ta Chung-hua* 大中華 [The Great Chung-hua Magazine], vol. 2, no. 10 (October 20, 1916).

Wu Tse 吳澤. *K'ang Yu-wei yü Liang Ch'i-ch'ao* 康有為與梁啓超 [K'ang Yu-wei and Liang Ch'i-ch'ao]. Shanghai: Hua-hsia Bookstore, 1948.

Ya-tung t'u-shu kuan 亞東圖書館. *K'e-hsüeh yü jen-sheng kuan* 科學與人生觀 [Science and Metaphysics]. Shanghai, 1927.

Yang Chia-lo 楊家駱, ed. *Min-kuo ming-jen t'u-chien* 民國名人圖鑑 [A Biographical Dictionary of Republican Personalities, with Photographs]. N. p., 1936.

Yang Fu-li 楊復禮. *K'ang Liang nien-p'u kao* 康梁年譜稿 [Draft of a Chronological Biography of K'ang and Liang]. 3 vols., mimeographed, 1938. Available at the Far Eastern Library, University of Washington.

Yang Ju-mei 楊汝梅. *Min-kuo ts'ai-cheng lun* 民國財政論 [Finance in Republican China]. Shanghai: Commercial Press, 1927.

Yang Yu-chiung 楊幼烱. *Chung-kuo cheng-tang shih* 中國政黨史 [A History of Political Parties in China]. Shanghai: Commercial Press, 1937.

Yen Fu 嚴復. *Yen i ming-chu ts'ung-k'an* 嚴譯名著叢刊 [A Collection of Yen's Translations of Well-known Works]. 8 vols. Shanghai: Commercial Press, 1931.

Yü Ping-ch'üan 余秉權. *Chung-kuo shih-hsüeh lun-wen yin-te, 1902-1962* 中國史學論文引得 [Chinese History: Index to Learned Articles, 1902-1962]. Hong Kong: Hong Kong East Asia Institute, 1963.

Yü Shao-tseng 余紹曾, comp. *Liang-shih yin-ping shih ts'ang-shu mu-lu* 梁氏飲冰室藏書目錄 [Catalogue of Books in the Ice-Drinker's Studio of Liang]. 4 *ts'e*. Peiping: National Peiping Library, 1933.

——. "Liang Jen-kung yü Tseng Mu-han" 梁任公與曾慕韓 [Liang Ch'i-ch'ao and Tseng Ch'i]. *Min-chu ch'ao* 9, no. 11 (June 1, 1959): 15–18.

Index

Academy of Current Affairs (Shih-wu Hsüeh-t'ang), 26, 90; former students of, 91, 95–96, 117, 185n20
Agriculture and Commerce, Minister of, 125
Allen, Young J., 33
Allgemeines Staatsrecht, 61, 81. See also Bluntschli, Johann Kaspar
Anarchists: in Liang's thought, 155
Anglo-Saxons: Liang's views on, 66
Anti-Manchuism: of Liang, 26, 85–86, 90; of Sun Yat-sen, 93
Anti-monarchical movement, 130–32, 134
Asahi Shimbun, 101
Assemblies. See Consultative Assembly; I-yüan; Legislature, national; Nanking, Provisional Assembly; National Assembly; Peking Provisional Assembly
Association to Prepare for Constitutional Government, 106
Australia: Liang's visit to, 45
Austria-Hungary, 135
Authority (ch'üan): Liang's views on, 28–29, 72. See also Kyōken (rights of the strong); Min-ch'üan (people's authority or people's rights)

Bentham, Jeremy, 68, 70–72, 144
Bergson, Henri, 143
Bismarck, Otto Fürst von, 69
Bluntschli, Johann Kaspar, 61, 81, 99, 180n103
Book of Chuang-tzu, 155

Boutroux, Étienne, 147
Boxer War, 27
Bubonic plague scare, 96
Buddhism, 19, 152
Bunmei (wen-ming), 54–55. See also Modernity

Cavour, Camillo di, 87, 89
Chang, Carsun, 106, 118, 143, 157, 158, 192n5
Chang Chi, 133
Chang Chien, 104, 106–8, 114, 117, 121, 125, 188n4
Chang Chih-tung, 5, 25, 41–42, 94, 96, 104, 161
Chang Hsüeh-ching, 91–92, 95
Chang Hsün, 136–37, 164
Chang Ping-lin, 103, 161
Chang Shao-tseng, 109–10
Chang Tsung-hsiang, 135
Chien Kuo-yung, 91
Ch'en Pao-chen, 26, 28
Ch'en San-li, 26
Ch'en T'ien-hua, 101–3
Ch'en Tu-hsiu, 7, 158
Ch'en T'ung-fu, 12
Cheng Chen-to, 6, 205
Cheng Hsiao-hsü, 104, 106
Cheng Hsüan, 17
Cheng-wen She (Political Information Society), 104–5, 107
Ch'eng Hao and Ch'eng I, 152–53
Chi Chung-yin, 118, 120, 134
Chiang Fang-chen, 143, 192n5
Chiang Kuan-yün, 97, 104

Ch'iang-ch'üan (rights of the strong), 179–80n*78*. *See also* Kyōken (rights of the strong)

Ch'iang-hsüeh Hui (Society for the Propagation of Learning), 24, 32

Chin-pu Tang, 4, 121, 123–27, 133

Ch'in Li-shan, 91, 95–96

Ch'in-min (hsin-min), 64, 181n*114*. *See also* New citizen (*hsin-min*)

China Revolutionary Party. *See* Chung-hua Ke-ming Tang

Chinese Communist Party, 164. *See also* Communism

Ch'ing-i pao (Upright Discussions), 48, 51–52, 54, 90, 91, 178n*54*

Chōsen gumi (Korean Goup), 138

Chou (last emperor of Shang), 22

Chou Hung-yeh, 91

Ch'ou-an Hui, 130

Chu Hsi, 152–53

Chu Shun-shui, 151

Chuang Ts'un-yü, 16–17

Chuang-tzu, Book of, 155

Ch'üan. See authority (*ch'üan*)

Chün-ch'üan (authority of the ruler), 29

Chung-hua Ke-ming Tang. (China Revolutionary Party), 133

Chung-hua Min-kuo Lien-ho Hui, 116. *See also* T'ung-i Tang

Chung-kuo mi-shih (Secret History of China), 92

Chung-wai kung-pao (International Gazette), 24–25

Chung-yung (middle way), 154–58

Classic of History, 17

Classics: Liang's re-evaluation of, 151–55. *See also* Confucianism; Confucius

"Cliques" and "clubs," 133, 135, 137, 139

Colloquial language: writing of, advocated by Liang, 6, 30–31. *See also* Loan-words; Neologisms

Communism, 164; Liang's view of, 159

Competition and the Rights of the Strong, 56

Confucianism, 3; and Liang's thought, 8–9, 20–21, 63–64, 71, 153–56, 161–62, 164; and Tung Chung-shu, 14–16; and K'ang Yu-wei, 19–20; as a religion, 20, 75

Confucius: Tung Chung-shu's view of, 14; and Heaven, 15; K'ang Yu-wei's views of, 19–20; Liang's views on, 20,

151, 153

Confucius as a Reformer (K'ung-tzu kai-chih k'ao), 19

Constitution: Japan's, a model for China, 32, 36; for China, 110, 126–27, 130, 133

Constitutional Association, 106

Constitutional government: Liang's advocacy of, 4, 59, 103–4, 130, 148–49, 163; movement for, 106–8, 114, 126; and Yüan Shih-k'ai, 125, 133

"Constitutional monarchy": in K'ang Yu-wei's thought, 19, 24

Constitutional Party. *See* Hsien-cheng Tang

Consultative Assembly, 110

Corruption: criticized by Liang, 30

"Culture": in Pan-Asianism, 47, 49

Currency, Bureau of, 128

Currency problems: Liang's views on, 100, 128–29, 137–39

Current Affairs. See Shih-wu pao

Customs Office, 129

Darwinism. *See* Social Darwinism

The Decline of the West, 145

Deep Significance of the Spring and Autumn Annals, 153

Democracy: elements of, in Confucianism, 20–21; Liang's views on, 20–21, 28, 31–32, 34, 46, 59–60, 63, 71, 80, 98, 162–63; elements of, in Mencian thought, 22–24; idea of, and the revolution of 1911, 115; and the intellectual revolution, 160–61. *See also* Constitution; Constitutional government

Despotism: benevolent, of Mencius, 21; enlightened, Liang's concept of, 81–82, 99, 103,122, 150

Dōbun Kai, 47

Dokuritsu jison (independence and self-respect), 62

Education, 7,33, 69; Liang's views on, 4, 30, 154, 164, 173n*71*; school for girls, 25; school for training translators, 27; in Japan, 53–54; Japanese Ministry of, 53–54, 100; China's Minister of, 125

Eight-legged essay, 7; abolished, 27

Empirical scholarship, 16–17

Empress Dowager. *See* Tz'u-hsi
England: admired by Liang, 55, 64, 76–77; admired by Japanese, 62; liberal thinkers of, 68 (*see also* Bentham, Jeremy; Mill, John Stuart; Spencer, Herbert); and World War I, 134; Liang's visit to, 142
Enlightened despotism. *See* Despotism
Enoshima group, 91, 94–96, 184–85n20
Eunuchs, 106
Europe: Chinese students in, 42, 175n-13,15; Liang's trip to, 142–45, 192n5
Evolution and Ethics (translated by Yen Fu), 25, 179n78
Examination system, 7, 42; Liang's progress through, 11–12; Liang's views of, 30, 33
"Exhortation to Learn," 42

Feng Kuo-chang, 131–32, 134, 136, 139
Feng Tzu-yu, 91–92, 184–85n20
Finance, Minister of, 109,125; Liang as, 137. *See also* Currency problems
Finance in Republican China, 129
Five Power Banking Consortium, 124
Footbinding: society opposed to, 25
France: Chinese students in, 42, 175n-15; Liang's visit to, 142–43
Frederick II, 82
Fu-ch'iang (wealth and power), 54–55, 59
Fukuzawa Yukichi, 61–64, 180n78, 182-n14
"The Future of the New China." *See* Liang Ch'i-ch'ao, publications

Germany, 134–35; Liang's visit to, 142
Gladstone, William Ewart, 69
Gold reserves, China's, 137–39. *See also* Currency problems
Gradualism: of Liang, 80, 126, 142, 148, 156, 158
Great community (*ta-t'ung*), 19, 29, 153–54
The Great Community (*Ta-t'ung shu*), 13, 19, 20, 171n33
Great Learning, 64–65

Han Ching Ti, 14
Han Kuang-wu Ti, 14
Han learning (*Han-hsüeh* or *k'ao-cheng*), 16–18

Han Wen-chü, 90–92, 95
Han Wu Ti, 14
Hawaii: Liang's visit to, 45, 46, 92–93, 95–96
Heaven, 15–16, 22; *tenshoku* (heavenly calling), 52
Hidden and subtle meanings (*wei-yen ta-i*), 14–15, 17,153
Hirayama Shū, 47
History: Liang's influence on the writing of, 6; Liang's views on, 151–52
Ho Hsiu, 14, 16–17,153
Ho Sui-t'ien, 186n38
Hsia Tseng-yu, 25
Hsiang-hsüeh hsin-pao (*New Hunan Gazette*), 26
Hsiao Kung-ch'üan, 16, 204–5
Hsien-cheng Shang-chüeh Hui (Society to Confer on Constitutional Government), 133
Hsien-cheng Tang (Consitutional Party), 106, 114, 187n84
Hsien-yu Hui (Society of the Friends of Constitutional Government), 108,118
Hsin ch'ing-nien (*New Youth*),7
"Hsin Chung-kuo wei-lai chi." *See* Liang Ch'i-ch'ao, publications: "The Future of the New China"
Hsin hsiao-shuo (*The New Fiction*), 6, 84
Hsin-hsüeh wei-ching k'ao (*A Study of the Forged Classics of the Hsin Dynasty*), 13, 19
Hsin-min: read *ch'in-min*, 64, 181n114; (new citizen), concept of (*see* New citizen)
Hsin-min ts'ung-pao (*Journal of the New Citizen*), 5–7, 90, 97–99, 102, 181n113
Hsin-wang (new king), 14
Hsing Chung Hui (Society to Revive China), 103
Hsiung Hsi-ling cabinet, 125
Hsü Chi-yu, 12
Hsü Ch'in, 97, 109, 186
Hsü Fo-su, 104, 107–8, 118, 120
Hsü Hsin-liu, 143, 192n5
Hsüan-t'ung Emperor. *See* P'u-i
Hsüeh-hai T'ang, 12, 13
Hsün-ku (a mode of textual criticism), 12
Hsün-tzu, 15, 20–21
Hu Han-min, 103, 113, 116, 124
Hu Shih, 6, 7

Huang Hsing, 118, 124
Huang Su-ch'u, 131
Huang Tsun-hsien, 25–26, 41, 175n9, 177n37
Huang Tsung-hsi, 23, 26
Huang Wei-chih, 91, 95
Hughes, Stuart, 145
Humaneness. See *Jen*
Humboldt, Wilhelm von, 76
Hunan: reform program in, 25–26. See also Academy of Current Affairs
"Hundred days" reforms, 26–27. See also Reform
Hundred Essays on the Law of Evolution, 56
Huxley, Thomas H., 25, 179n78

I-k'uang, 106, 109–10
I-yüan (representative assemblies), 28–30, 34
An Illustrated Gazetteer of the Maritime Countries, 18
Imperial Guards, 109–10
Imperialism: Liang's views on, 4, 48, 52, 56–59, 61, 67, 158; Katō Hiroyuki's and Herbert Spencer's views on, 56–57
Individualism: Liang's views on, 73–74
Intellectuals, 5, 141–42, 158, 160, 164. See also May Fourth intellectual revolution
Interior, Minister of, 137
Introduction to the Principles of Morals and Legislation, 70
Inugai Tsuyoshi, 47, 52, 53
Ishida Takeshi, 50
Italy: Liang's visit to, 142

Jansen, Marius, 47
Japan: Chinese students in, 7, 36–37, 41–44, 100–103, 105, 175n11, 13, 14, 176n11, 13, 14, 20; Liang influenced by, 9, 31–32, 161–62; issue of democracy in, 21; exile of Liang in, 35, 121; influence of, on China, 36–45, 103; Chinese reformers and revolutionaries in, 44, 90–91 (see also Enoshima group); Chinese community in, 104; Army Officers' Academy, 109; Liang's return to, 110; and World War I, 134–35; loans from, 137–38
Japanese language: loan-words from, in

Chinese, 44, 176n26, 27
Jen (humaneness): Liang's views on, 153–54, 156; *jen-cheng* (humane government), 15
Journal of the New Citizen, See *Hsin-min ts'ung-pao*
Justice, Minister of, 137; Liang as, 125

K'ai-ming chuan-chih. See Despotism
Kajin no kigu (*Strange Encounters of Elegant Females*), 178n51; Liang's translation of, 48–52, 178n54, 55, 59, 60
K'ang Yu-wei, 7, 41, 103, 104, 114; and the constitutional movement, 4, 106, 109, 160; influence on Liang, 5, 8, 12–13, 32, 34; and the New Text school, 14, 16–17; and the Kung-yang doctrines, 15, 18–20, 171n36; Western influence in the thought of, 21, 24; and the "hundred days" reforms, 26–27; arbitrariness of, 74–75; and the plot against the Empress Dowager, 79; and the revolutionaries, 90–93; and the restoration plot, 95–96; Liang's relations with, 97–98, 105, 162; and the plot against Yüan Shih-k'ai, 106; alliance of, with Chang Hsün, 164. See also Pao-huang Hui
Kashiwabara Buntarō, 47, 52, 53
Katō Hiroyuki, 56–61, 63–64, 69, 76, 81, 179–80n78, 180n103, 183n47
Kawakami Hajime, 41
K'e-lu faction, 133
Konoe Atsumarō, 47
Korea: Liang's views on, 51
Korean Group (Chōsen gumi), 138
Kossuth, Louis, 100
Kropotkin, Peter, 145
Ku Chieh-kang, 6
Ku Hung-ming, 158
Ku-liang Commentary, 153
Kuan Chung, 100
Kuang-shü Emperor, 26–27; plot to restore, 92–96; death of, 108
Kung-ho Chien-she T'ao-lun Hui, 118, 120
Kung-ho Tang, 116–18, 120–22
Kung Tzu-chen, 14, 18, 170n27, 170–71 n28, 171n29
Kung-yang Commentary, 15, 17, 153; doctrines based on, 18–20, 34, 153, 161–62, 171n29, 36

INDEX   227

Kung-yang reformers, 15, 16. *See alos*
K'ang Yu-wei; Kung Tzu-chen; Wei
Yüan
K'ung Shang-jen, 151
K'ung-tzu kai-chih k'ao (*Confucius as a
Reformer*), 19
Kuo-hui. *See* Legislature, national
Kuo-min Hsieh-chin Hui, 118, 120
Kuomintang, 4, 117, 121–28, 131–33,
136, 137, 148, 164
Kyōken (rights of the strong), 56–57, 60–
61, 179–80n78

Lan T'ien-wei, 109–10
Language. *See* Colloquial language;
Loan-words; Neologisms
Lao Tzu, 151
Legalists, Liang's view of, 155
Legislature, national, 116–17, 124, 127–
28, 133–36, 139, 189n7
Levenson, Joseph, 34, 203–4, 206
Li Ching-t'ung, 91
Li Ch'ün, 91
Li Hung-chang, 5
Li Lieh-chün, 116, 124
Li Ping-huan, 91, 95–96
Li script, 14
Li Tuan-fen, 12
Li Yüan-hung, 112–13, 116–21, 123,
132, 134, 136, 188n2
"Li yün," 19, 20, 153, 171n36
Liang Ch'i-ch'ao: summary of career of,
3–4; influenced by stay in Japan, 3,
31–32, 43–67, 161–62, 179–80n78;
and revolution, 3–5, 79–80, 84–90,
97, 105, 107, 164, 184–85n20; influence of writings of, 4–6, 24–25, 27, 90,
97, 99; views of, on education, 4, 30,
154, 164, 173n71; and reform, 5, 24–
35, 84–89, 99–111 (*see also* Reform);
position of, in Chinese intellectual
history, 5–10, 75–76; names known
by, 7, 46, 177n35; family background
and early education, 11–12; marriage
of, 12; and New Text Confucianism,
13, 20–24, 34, 161–62; and the translation bureau, 25, 27; concept of
majority in the thought of, 71–73;
and individualism, 73–74; intellectual flexibility of, 74–75; political
ambitions of, 99–100, 110, 114, 117–
21, 133–34; in government office,

110–11, 125–29, 137–39; and national
politics after the revolution of 1911,
114–15, 117–40, 164; brother of,
117; return of, to China, 121; withdrawal of, from public life, 140; visit
of, to Europe, 142–45, 192n5; activities of, after World War I, 142–59;
syncretism of, 142, 146–47, 150–52,
155–57, 161–62; languages studied by,
143; thought of, influenced by World
War I, 145–46, 162; views of, on *jen*,
153–54, 156; "middle way" of, 154–
58. *See also* Liberalism; Liberty;
Nationalism; Power, national; Social
Darwinism
—publications: "Against Isms," 157;
*A Catalogue of Books on Western
Government*, 33; *A Catalogue of Books
on Western Learning*, 31–33; *Chronological Biography*, 45; "The Currency
Problem in China," 100; "Discussions on Currency Regulations,"
100; "Enlightened Despotism," 81,
103; "Foreign Loans," 100; "The
Future of the New China," 84–86, 92,
97, 110–11, 119, 163; "General
Trends in the Development and
Changes in Chinese Thought," 6;
*History of Chinese Political Thought in
the pre-Ch'in Period*, 151; *History of Chinese Thought in the Last Three Hundred
Years*, 151; "The Hungarian Patriot
Louis Kossuth," 100; "Impressions
from My European Journey," 144–
47, 150; *Intellectual Trends in the Ch'ing
Period*, 151; "Introduction to Consti-
tutional Government," 100; "The
New Citizen," 58, 64, 69, 77, 80, 99,
148–49, 181n113, 184n4; "Notes on
Freedom," 45, 53, 69; "On Inde-
pendence," 63; "On the Limits of
Authority Between the Government
and the People," 72–73; "On Reform," 30, 33; "On Self-Respect,"
62; "Personal Views on China's
Parliamentary System," 100; "Self-
help," 63, 69; *A Study of the Forged
Classics of the Hsin Dynasty* (with
K'ang Yu-wei), 13, 19
Liang Ch'i-t'ien, 91
Liang Pao-ying (father of Liang Ch'i-
ch'ao), 11

Liang Ping-kuang, 91–92, 95
Liang Shih-i, 191n67
Liang Wei-ch'ing (grandfather of Liang
  Ch'i-ch'ao), 11
Liberalism, 4; in Liang's thought, 9, 29,
  68–78,84, 144–50, 155–65; modern
  Chinese, 160–65
Liberty (*tzu-yu*): Liang's views on, 65,
  69–70, 74, 76–77, 80, 82–83, 90, 162,
  164
Lin Ch'ang-min, 137
Lin Kuei, 91, 95–96, 185n20
Lin Tse-hsü, 141, 170n27
"Literary inquisition" of the Ch'ien-
  lung period, 16
Literary revolution, 6. *See also* Collo-
  quial language
Literati, and the New Text revival, 16
Liu Ch'ung-chieh, 143, 192n5
Liu Feng-lu, 17–18, 170n26, 27
Liu Hsin, 13–14, 17,19
Liu Shih-p'ei, 158,161
Lo Jun-nan, 91
Lo P'u, 95, 185n20
Loan-words: in Chinese from Japanese,
  44, 176n26,27
Lu Jung-t'ing, 131, 132
Luan-chou revolt, 110
Lung Chi-kuang, 131, 132, 134

Ma Liang, 105
Mackenzie, Robert, 33
Mahāyāna Buddhism, 19. *See also* Bud-
  dhism
Mai Chung-hua, 91,95
Mai Meng-hua, 91
Majority: Liang's concept of, 71–73
Manchus. *See* Anti-Manchuism
Mao Tse-tung, 7, 140, 159, 164
Marxist works: translated into Chinese,
  41, 43
May Fourth intellectual revolution, 3,
  5–9, 44, 67, 141, 146, 158, 160, 162.
  See also Students, Chinese
Mazzini, Joseph, 87, 89, 100
Meirokusha, 64
Mencius/*Mencius*, 15, 20–24, 34, 65
Middle way (*chung-yung*), 154–58
Military power: in Chinese national
  politics, 4, 109–10, 112–17, 123–25,
  127, 131–32, 135–40, 148, 163–64,
  188n1. *See also* Yüan Shih-k'ai

Military science: translations on, 32–33
Mill, John Stuart, 68, 70, 72–76, 144,
  182n14
Min-chu (people's rule), 19, 28–31,34
Min-chu Tang, 120–21
Min-ch'üan (people's authority or peo-
  ple's rights), 28–30, 34, 54, 90
Min-pao, 99, 105
Min-pen. See Primacy of the people
Min She, 116–17, 120
Min-tsu ti-kuo-chu-i (national imperial-
  ism), 58
Missionaries, 33
Miyazaki Torazō, 47
Mo Ching, Liang's commentary on, 151
Mo-tzu, 154
Modernity: Liang's views on, 53–55, 59,
  63, 67
Modernization, 3, 36, 67, 103; Liang's
  views on, 4,77,162–64. *See also* Reform
Monarchy. *See* Anti-monarchical move-
  ment
Morality: Liang's views on, 63–65, 77,
  162

Nakamura Masanao, 61–64, 180n78,
  182n14
Nan-hsüeh Hui (Reform Association
  of South China), 26
Nanking, 112; Provisional Assembly,
  115, 118, 188n5, 6; Provisional
  Government, 188n4
Napoleon I, 82
National Assembly, 111
National imperialism (*min-tsu ti-kuo-chu-
  i*), 58
Nationalism, 36, 115; in Liang's
  thought, 4, 49, 56, 58–59, 63–65, 76,
  83, 84, 88, 90, 149; of Katō Hiro-
  yuki, 56–57. *See also* Power, national
Negroes, 78
Neo-Confucianism: Liang's views on,
  152
Neologisms, 69
New citizen (*hsin-min*): Liang's concept
  of, 61, 64–66, 70, 77, 80, 90, 142, 162–
  64 180n78; of Mao, 159
"The New Citizen" ("Hsin-min shuo")
  See Liang Ch'i-ch'ao, publications
The New Fiction. See Hsin hsiao-shuo
*New Hunan Gazette. See Hsiang-hsüeh hsin-
  pao*

New Text school: Ch'ing, 8, 13, 16–20, 34, 170–71n28; Han, 13–16

New Youth. See Hsin ch'ing-nien

Nietzsche, Friedrich Wilhelm, 145

1916 Club (Ping-ch'en Chü-lo-pu), 133, 135

The 19th Century: A History, 33

Nishihara Kamezō, 138

"Nishihara loans," 138

Okuma Shigenobu, 47, 52–53, 179n69; government of, 138, 177n37

Old Text school, 13–14

On Liberty, 72–73, 182n14

Onogawa Hidemi, 179–80n78, 205

Opium War, 18

Ou Chü-chia, 90–92, 95

Overseas Chinese, 79–80, 93–94, 98, 131. *See also* Japan; Students, Chinese

Overseas Chinese Association, 94

Pai-hua. See Colloquial language

Pan-Asianism, 47–54

Pao-huang Hui (Society to Protect the Emperor), 78–79, 85, 92–98, 186n38, 187n84

Peiyang Army, 112–13, 125, 127, 188n1

Peking Provisional Assembly, 115–16, 118, 188–89n6

People's rights: in Japan, 54. *See also Min-ch'üan*

People's rule. *See Min-chu*

A Plan for a Prince, 26

Po Wen-wei, 116, 124

P'o-huai, 6

Poetry: Liang's essay on, 151

Police: bureau, 26; records (Japanese), 45, 93, 177n35

Political Information Society. *See* Cheng-wen She

Portents *(tsai-i),* 15–16

Power, national: Liang's views on, 31–32, 58–61, 63–64, 70, 76–77, 149–50, 162–63; Nakamura Masanao's views on, 62–63; and ideology, 164. *See also Fu-ch'iang*

Press: freedom of, in Japan, 53–54; American and Chinese compared, 78; of San Francisco's Chinatown, 79

Primacy of the people *(min-pen),* 21–23, 34–35, 60, 155–56

P'u-chün, 185n25

P'u-i, 108-9, 136

P'u Tien-chün, 114

Race: Liang's views on, 47–50, 54, 66, 99. *See also* Anti-Manchuism; Pan-Asianism

Reciprocity *(shu),* 154

Reform: Liang's views on and actions toward, 5, 24–35, 84–98, 99–111; Confucian rationale for, 15; program in Hunan, 25–26; the "hundred days" of, 26–27; missionary writings on, 33; advocated, 35–36, 41, 44, 141, 160; and *fu-ch'iang,* 55

Reform Association of South China. *See* Nan-hsüeh Hui

Representative government. *See* Democracy

Research Clique (Yen-chiu Hsi), 133, 137, 139

Restoration plot, 92–96

Returned students, 42–43, 176n20. *See also* Students, Chinese

Revolution: and Liang, 3–5, 79–80, 84–90, 97, 105, 107, 164, 184–85n20 (*see also* Enoshima group); of 1911, 5, 112, 114–15; support for, 44, 108; the "second," 124–25. *See also* Literary revolution; May Fourth intellectual revolution

Roland, Madame, 100

Rousseau, Jean Jacques, 71, 72, 81

Russo-Japanese War, 42, 103

San Francisco, Chinatown of, 79

San-t'ung, 15, 19

Schwartz, Benjamin, 144–45, 179–80n 78, 206

Science: applied, 33; Liang's views on, 145–46; Carsun Chang's view of, 157–58

Secret History of China (Chung-kuo mi-shih), 92

Secret societies, 93

"Self confidence," 69

Self-discipline *(tzu-chih),* 66

Self-Government Association, 106

"Self-help": Liang's essay on, 63, 69. *See also* Smiles, Samuel

Self-strengthening movement, 5, 41, 141

Shan-ch'i (Prince Su), 104, 106, 109

Shang dynasty: last emperor of, 22

Shen pao, 129
Shen Ping-k'un, 114, 116
Shiba Shirō. *See Kajin no kigu*
Shih-chung, 156
Shih-wu Hsüeh-t'ang. *See* Academy of Current Affairs
Shih-wu pao (*Current Affairs*), 25, 91
Shimonoseki, Treaty of, 24
Shōda Kazue, 138
Shu (reciprocity), 154
Simonds, Frank Herbert, 147
Sino-Japanese War (1894–95), 3, 41, 51, 175n6
Smiles, Samuel: *Self-Help*, 62
Snow, Edgar, 7
Social Darwinism: in Liang's thought, 4, 56–61, 66, 76, 82, 145, 162, 179–80n78
Societies (*hui, she*), 133. *See also* Cheng-wen She; Ch'iang-hsüeh Hui; Ch'ou-an Hui; Chung-hua Min-kuo Lien-ho Hui; Hsien-cheng Shang-chüeh Hui; Hsien-yu Hui; Hsing Chung Hui; Kung-ho Chien-she T'ao-lun Hui; Kuo-min Hsieh-chin Hui; Min She; Nan-hsüeh Hui; Pao-huang Hui; T'ung-meng Hui; Tzu-li Hui
Spencer, Herbert, 56–57, 61, 68, 69, 144, 145
Spengler, Oswald, 145
Spring and Autumn Annals, 14–15, 17, 20, 153
State: as an organic entity, 81–82, 99, 180n103
Stephen, Leslie, 74
Strange Encounters of Elegant Females. *See Kajin no kigu*
Students, Chinese: in Japan, 7, 36–37, 41–44, 100–103, 105, 175n11, 13, 14, 176n20; abroad outside of Asia, 41–43, 175n11, 13, 14, 15, 176n20; "returned," 42–43, 176n20; pro-revolution, 107. *See also* May Fourth intellectual revolution
A Study of the Forged Classics of the Hsin Dynasty (*Hsin-hsüeh wei-ching k'ao*), 13, 19
Su, Prince (Shan-ch'i), 104, 106, 109
Su-wang ("uncrowned king"), 14, 19
The Success of the Western Nations, 62–63
Sun Hung-i, 107–8, 114, 118, 133
Sun Mei, 93

Sun Yat-sen, 4, 47, 103, 118, 121, 133, 137, 140, 160, 164; Liang's relations with, 79–80, 91–96
Sung Chiao-jen, 103, 115, 116, 118–19, 123–24, 128, 133
Syncretism: of Liang, 142, 146–47, 150–52, 155–57, 161–62

Ta-chuan script, 13–14
Ta-t'ung School: in Tokyo, 91, 95; in Yokohama, 93–94
Ta-t'ung shu (The Great Community), 13, 19, 20, 171n33. *See also* Great community
Tai Chen, 151
Tai K'an, 131
T'ai-p'ing Rebellion, 18
Taiwan: Liang's visit to, 176n29
Takasugi Shinsaku, 46, 177n35
T'an Hsi-yung, 91
T'an Ssu-t'ung, 25–27, 69
T'an Yen-k'ai, 114, 116
T'ang Chi-yao, 116, 132
T'ang Chüeh-tun, 133–34, 191n67
T'ang Hua-lung, 114, 118, 120, 137
T'ang Shou-ch'ien, 106
T'ang Ts'ai-ch'ang, 26, 90, 91, 94–96, 109, 185n20
T'ao Ch'ien, 151
T'ao-yüan faction, 133
Taoists: Liang's view of, 155
Ten Days' Sacking of Yang Chou (*Yang-chou shih-jih chi*), 26, 90
Tenpu jinken (natural rights), 56
Tenshoku (heavenly calling), 52. *See also* Heaven
Terauchi Masataka, 138
"Three ages" theory, 16, 19, 153
T'ieh-k'uo, 12
T'ieh-liang, 106
T'ien Pang-hsüan, 91, 95–96
T'ien-yen lun (by Yen Fu), 25, 179n78
Ting Wen-chiang, 128, 143, 157, 192n5
Tōa Dōbun Kai, 47
Tōa Kai, 47
Tokyo: Chinese students and exiles in, 44; Ta-t'ung School in, 91, 95 (*see also* Ta-t'ung School); Senmon Gakkō, 179n69. *See also* Japan
Translation: bureau, 25, 27; of works on medicine, 33; of Japanese books into Chinese, 36, 38–41, 43, 45. *See also*

PUBLICATIONS ON ASIA OF THE INSTITUTE FOR COMPARA-
TIVE AND FOREIGN AREA STUDIES
(Formerly Far Eastern and Russian Institute Publications on Asia)

1. Compton, Boyd (trans. and ed.). *Mao's China: Party Reform Documents, 1942–44*. 1952. Reissued 1966. Washington Paperback, 1966.
2. Chiang, Siang-tseh. *The Nien Rebellion*. 1954.
3. Chang, Chung-li. *The Chinese Gentry: Studies on Their Role in Nineteenth-Century Chinese Society*. Introduction by Franz Michael. 1955. Reissued 1967. Washington Paperback on Russia and Asia-4.
4. *Guide to the Memorials of Seven Leading Officials of Nineteenth-Century China*. Summaries and indexes of memorials to Hu Lin-i, Tseng Kuo-fan, Tso Tsung-tang, Kuo Sung-tao, Tseng Kuo-ch'üan, Li Hung-chang, Chang Chih-tung. 1955.
5. Raeff, Marc. *Siberia and the Reforms of 1822*. 1956.
6. Li Chi. *The Beginnings of Chinese Civilization: Three Lectures Illustrated with Finds at Anyang*. 1957. Reissued 1968. Washington Paperback on Russia and Asia-6.
7. Carrasco, Pedro. *Land and Polity in Tibet*. 1959.
8. Hsiao, Kung-chuan. *Rural China: Imperial Control in the Nineteenth Century*. 1960. Reissued 1967. Washington Paperback on Russia and Asia-3.
9. Hsiao, Tso-liang. *Power Relations within the Chinese Communist Movement, 1930–1934*. Vol. I: *A Study of Documents*. 1961. Vol. II: *The Chinese Documents*. 1967.
10. Chang, Chung-li. *The Income of the Chinese Gentry*. Introduction by Franz Michael. 1962.
11. Maki, John M. *Court and Constitution in Japan: Selected Supreme Court Decisions, 1948–60*. 1964.
12. Poppe, Nicholas, Leon Hurvitz, and Hidehiro Okada. *Catalogue of the Manchu-Mongol Section of the Toyo Bunko*. 1964.
13. Spector, Stanley. *Li Hung-chang and the Huai Army: A Study in Nineteenth-Century Chinese Regionalism*. Introduction by Franz Michael. 1964.

Loan-words; Neologisms
Tsai-feng, 108–10
Tsai-i, 105n25
Tsai-i (portents), 15–16
Tsai-t'ao, 109–10
Tsai-tse, 106, 109
Ts'ai Chung-hao, 91, 95
Ts'ai 0, 26, 91, 116, 117, 131, 132, 134, 191n69
Ts'an-i yüan. *See* Nanking
Tseng Kuo-fan, 5
Tso Commentary, 17
Tso-shih ch'un-ch'iu, 17
Tuan Ch'i-jui, 131, 134–40, 164
Tuan-fang, 103, 104, 106
Tung Chung-shu, 14, 17, 153
T'ung-i Kung-ho Tang, 116
T'ung-i Tang, 116–17
T'ung-meng Hui, 101, 103, 105, 107, 110, 112–14, 116, 119
Twenty-one Demands, 36, 53, 138
Tzu-li Hui (Society for National Independence), 94
Tzu-yu (liberty), the term, 69
Tz'u-hsi, 4, 26–27, 79, 92, 103, 106, 108⟨ 185n25

United States: Liang's views on, 31; Chinese students in, 41–42, 43, 175n-13, 14, 176n20; Liang's visit to, 45, 78–80, 97–98; Chinese communities in, 79; and World War I, 134
Upright Discussions. See Ch'ing-i pao

Waichow uprising, 94
Wan-mu ts'ao-t'ang, 12, 20, 32, 90–91
Wang An-shih, 100
Wang Ching-ju, 186n38
Wang Ching-wei, 103
Wang Mang, 13, 14
Wang Ta-hsieh, 125
Wang, Y. C., 42
Warlordism. *See* Military power
Waseda University, 53
Wealth and power (*fu-ch'iang*), 54–55, 59

Wei-yen ta-i. See Hidden and sub meanings
Wei Yüan, 14, 18, 141, 170n27, 170–71 28
Wen-ming (bunmei), 54–55. *See also* M dernity
Wen-yen, 6
Western impact, 9, 31–32, 141–42; te nological, 3, 41. *See also* West learning
Western learning: and K'ang Yu-v 19, 21, 24; and Liang, 21, 31– 152, 161–62. *See also* Democra Liberalism; Science; Social Darw ism; Syncretism; Translation
Wilson, Woodrow, 143
Work ethic, 62
World War I, 134, 145, 146, 162
Wu Chih-hui, 103, 157–58
Wu Hsiang-hsiang, 123, 188n1
Wu Lu-chen, 109, 110
Wu T'ing-fang, 25
Wuchang uprising, 109, 112
Wuhan: as a revolutionary base, *See also* Li Yüan-hung

Yamada Ryōsei, 47
Yang-chou shih-jih chi (Ten Days' Sa of Yang Chou), 26
Yang Chu, 154
Yang Ju-mei, 129
Yang Tu, 104
Yang Wei-hsin, 143, 192n5
Yen-chiu Hsi. *See* Research Clique
Yen Fu, 5, 25, 29, 75, 173n69, 179– 78, 182n14
Yen Hsi-shan, 113–14, 116
Yin-yang thought, 15–16
Ying-huan chih-lüeh (A Brief Descripti the World), 12
Yoshida Shin: name adopted by Li 46, 177n35
Yoshida Shōin, 46, 177n35
Yüan K'e-ting, 129-30
Yüan Shih-k'ai, 104, 106–14, 11 *passim*, 140, 164, 188n1

14. Michael, Franz, and Chung-li Chang. *The Taiping Rebellion: History and Documents*. Vol. I: *History*. 1966. Vols. II and III: *Documents and Comments*. 1971.
15. Shih, Vincent Y. C. *The Taiping Ideology: Its Sources, Interpretations, and Influences*. 1967.
16. Poppe, Nicholas. *The Twelve Deeds of Buddha: A Mongolian Version of the Lalitavistara; Mongolian Text, Notes, and English Translation*. 1967. Paper.
17. Hsia, Tsi-an. *The Gate of Darkness: Studies on the Leftist Literary Movement in China*. Preface by Franz Michael. Introduction by C. T. Hsia. 1968.
18. Hsiao, Tso-liang. *The Land Revolution in China, 1930–1934: A Study of Documents*. 1969.
19. Gasster, Michael. *Chinese Intellectuals and the Revolution of 1911: The Birth of Modern Chinese Radicalism*. 1969.
20. Thornton, Richard C. *The Comintern and the Chinese Communists, 1928–1931*. 1969.
21. Lin, Julia C. *Modern Chinese Poetry: An Introduction*. 1972.
22. Huang, Philip C. *Liang Ch'i-ch'ao and Modern Chinese Liberalism*. 1972.